The Road
to the
White House
2024

★ ★ ★ ★ ★ ★ ★ ★   ★ ★ ★ ★ ★ ★ ★

The Politics of Presidential Elections

The Road
to the
White House
2024

The Politics of Presidential Elections

Twelfth Edition

Stephen J. Wayne
Georgetown University

ROWMAN & LITTLEFIELD
Lanham • Boulder • New York • London

Acquisitions Editor: Jon Sisk
Acquisitions Assistant: Katherine Berlatsky
Sales and Marketing Inquiries: textbooks@rowman.com

Credits and acknowledgments for material borrowed from other sources, and
reproduced with permission, appear on the appropriate pages within the text.

Published by Rowman & Littlefield
An imprint of The Rowman & Littlefield Publishing Group, Inc.
4501 Forbes Boulevard, Suite 200, Lanham, Maryland 20706
www.rowman.com

86-90 Paul Street, London EC2A 4NE

Library of Congress Control Number: 2023934423

ISBN: 978-1-5381-8203-1 (cloth : alk. paper)
ISBN: 978-1-5381-8204-8 (pbk. : alk. paper)
ISBN: 978-1-5381-8205-5 (ebook)

∞™ The paper used in this publication meets the minimum requirements of American
National Standard for Information Sciences—Permanence of Paper for Printed Library
Materials, ANSI/NISO Z39.48-1992.

Dedication

*To the memory of my parents and grandparents, who
encouraged my interests in politics and my pursuit
of higher education; to my wife, Cheryl, who has
tolerated my passion for politics and keeps me pointed
in the right political direction; and to my students and
colleagues, whose questions, wisdom, and comments,
and, in some cases, their own political careers, have
strengthened my understanding of and appreciation for
a properly functioning democratic political system.*

The presidential vote in the Electoral College in 2020.

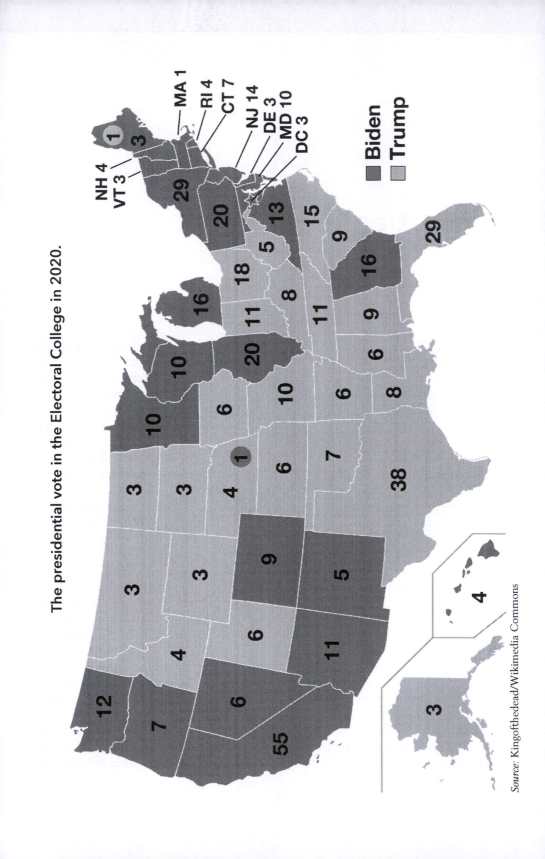

NH 4
VT 3
MA 1
RI 4
CT 7
NJ 14
DE 3
MD 10
DC 3

Biden
Trump

1
3
29
20
13
15
16
18
5
11
9
20
16
8
11
16
9
10
6
10
6
8
6
10
6
7
38
3
3
4
1
3
6
9
3
6
5
4
11
12
7
6
55
4
3

Source: Kingofthedead/Wikimedia Commons

Preface

We are in another presidential election cycle. It follows two of the most costly and contentious elections in US history. The new electoral cycle occurs within an inflated economic environment and the pandemic that began in 2020, both of which have generated discontent and accelerated wage gaps between men and women, skilled and unskilled workers, and minority racial groups and the white majority. The noneconomic issues include immigration reform and enforcement, the role of government in providing social services and regulating private activities, abortion, climate change, racial and ethnic discrimination as well as contentious international issues, especially relations with Russia and China and the domestic impact of US assistance to Ukraine.

The American electorate remains polarized. The proportion of Americans identifying themselves as Independents has increased. Add to these, the public's differing perceptions of the Trump and Biden presidencies. Debate in the 2024 campaign will be framed by these issues and perceptions.

The election cycle is two years, but the campaign began earlier, and the results will continue well after it. By the end of the 2024 election, the electorate will be weary to the point of numbness; the presidential candidates, their campaign staffs and volunteers exhausted, and one side disappointed, even bitter to the point of contesting the result. Moreover, billions of dollars will be raised and spent. Is it necessary to have such a vigorous, often nasty, public debate and contentious electoral process? Perhaps not, but free and frequent elections are critical for a democracy. They are a means by which the people can judge the candidates, keep the winners accountable, and hold them responsible for the decisions they make in office.

Elections tie citizens to their government. But for the voters to make an intelligent judgment, they need information about the qualifications of the candidates, the policies they propose, and the partisan labels they wear. Does the current presidential electoral system encourage the most qualified candidates to run? Does it force them to discuss the most important issues, present feasible policy solutions, and talk candidly about themselves and their policies? Does the electorate get the kind of information it needs to make an enlightened voting decision? Will the results of the election fairly and accurately reflect the beliefs, opinions, interests, and needs of the population as a whole? Is the system consistent with principles and practices of a democratic electoral process?

A primary goal of this book is to answer these questions. It does so by describing and evaluating the presidential election system from the perspectives of the candidates, the parties, and the American people. As with its previous editions, *The Road to the White House 2024* discusses the legal, political, and financial framework in which the election occurs; the process by which the major parties nominate their standard-bearers and position themselves for the general election; the strategies, tactics, and operations of the presidential campaigns themselves; print and online news coverage and advertising; and the use and abuse of social media for communicating with voters; the mood of the electorate and how that mood affects the results of the election; and finally, how the election is likely to shape governance in 2025 and thereafter.

This edition emphasizes the changes that have shaped electoral politics in recent years: the flood of money to candidates and the groups that support them; the communications revolution and the opportunities and challenges it presents for the candidates, their advisers, and the voters; and fake news and foreign interference in the election.

The continuities from past presidential elections will also be examined: the parties' nomination processes, the Electoral College system of campaigning and voting, traditional and social medias, the tone and amount of news coverage, television debates and political commercials, partisan appeals, voting patterns, and the transition to governing.

Outline

The book is organized into four parts. Part I discusses the arena in which presidential elections occur. Its three chapters examine the electoral system, campaign finance, and the political environment. Chapter 1 provides a historical overview of nominations as well as elections with a discussion of controversial and close Electoral College results as well as the attempt to change the results of the official Electoral College vote in 2020. Chapter 2 describes recent developments in campaign finance, the Supreme Court's decision on independent spending, the demise of public funding, the expansion of private donors and the amounts they contribute, the role of party and nonparty groups, and the cumulative impact of these factors on election outcomes. In the third chapter, continuities and changes in the political environment serve as the principal focus. How that environment shapes turnout, solidifies partisanship, and affects the composition of the parties' electoral coalitions will also be examined with an eye on the past and a glimpse into the foreseeable future.

Part II describes and analyzes the presidential nomination process. Chapter 4 discusses the reforms that the parties have made in the way they select their standard-bearers, the legal issues that have arisen from these reforms, and the effect these reforms have had on the candidate, the parties, and the electorate. Chapter 5 continues this discussion through the competitive stage of the caucuses and primaries. This chapter pays particular attention to the strategies of the candidates and the hurdles they must overcome, illustrating these strategies and hurdles with case studies from recent nomination campaigns. Chapter 6 describes the period after the nominees have been effectively determined through the parties' national nominating conventions that formally choose their standard-bearers and launch their general election campaigns. It indicates the methods by which the successful candidates try to unify partisans after a divisive caucus and primary process, appeal to Independents, improve their leadership image, which may have been damaged during the nomination quest, and begin to confront their partisan opponents and design themes for their election campaigns.

Part III examines the general election itself. Chapter 7 describes the strategies, tactics, and operations of the campaigns. It assesses the new communication technologies that have been used to identify voters, target appeals, and assesses their impact. This discussion is illustrated with case studies from 2004 to 2020. Chapter 8 turns to the news media: how the press covers the election and how the candidates try to affect that coverage with paid advertising, scripted public performances, and participation in the presidential debates. It then examines the impact of these efforts on turnout, voting behavior, and the criteria necessary for a democratic electoral process.

Part IV looks at and beyond the elections. Chapter 9 discusses and evaluates forecasts based on quantitative data by political scientists, pre-election polls and their accuracy, and finally the vote itself: who won and why and what difference the outcome of the election is likely to have for the country. It also examines the difficulties presidential candidates encounter in fulfilling the promises they made when running for office and the leadership imagery they projected during the campaign. Chapter 10 considers problems that have beset the electoral system and discusses proposed reforms to alleviate these problems. It addresses some of the major contemporary controversies from party rules to campaign finance to news media coverage to the Electoral College itself within the context of American democracy.

Purpose

Elections link the people with their public officials, a vital component of a functioning democracy. However, that link is far from perfect. Voting is individualized, yet governing is a collective undertaking. Not everyone participates in elections, but government makes rules for all the people, including those who do not or, are not, eligible to vote. Presidential candidates regularly overpromise and underdeliver. They create unrealistic expectations that are impossible to achieve by the president alone in a system of shared powers and frequently divided partisan control of government. Consequently, any hopefulness that a campaign generates among voters frequently fades into disillusionment, apathy, and even cynicism as the new or reelected administration progresses.

How can we improve elections? How can we encourage more of the citizenry to participate? How can we persuade the most qualified people to run? How can we level the playing field? How can we ensure that the mood of the voters will be reflected in the results of the election and that government officials will be responsive to the electorate, pursuing the public's interest? In other words, how can we make sure that elections achieve their principal goals: to select the most qualified people, to provide a blueprint for governing, and to hold elected officials individually and collectively accountable for their decisions and actions in office?

Without information on how the system works, whether it is functioning properly and meeting its objectives, we cannot answer these questions and assess the merits of our electoral democracy. We cannot cajole the citizenry to meet its civic responsibilities and turn out to vote; we cannot recruit the best and the brightest to give up their privacy, shift their family responsibilities to others, and, in many cases, sacrifice financially to run for office; we cannot improve the people–government–public policy connection for which elections are the critical link. In the case of presidential politics, ignorance is definitely not bliss, nor is the norm always or usually the ideal.

The road to the White House is long and arduous. In fact, it has now become more difficult to travel than in the past. Yet, surprisingly, given all the criticism, there continue to be many would-be travelers. Evaluating their journey is essential to rendering an intelligent judgment on election day. However, more is at stake than simply choosing the occupant of the Oval Office. The system itself is on trial in every election. That is why it is so important to understand and appreciate the intricacies of the process and to participate in it. Only an informed and active citizenry can determine whether the nation is being served well by the way we go about choosing our presidents and have some say in determining what they will do in office.

Acknowledgments

Few books are written alone. I would like to express my thanks to the many people who have reviewed and helped me with the twelve editions of this book: Adam McGlynn, East Stroudsburg University; Judithanne John Bruce, University of Mississippi; Richard Cole, University of Texas at Arlington, Lisa Langenbach, Middle Tennessee State University; Adam McGlynn, East Strausberg University; Judithanne McLauchlan, University of South Florida St. Petersburg; Jeff Dense, Eastern Oregon University; Anthony Corrado Jr., Colby College; Stephen C. Craig, University of Florida at Gainesville; James W. Davis, Washington University; Gordon Friedman, Southwest Missouri State University; Jay S. Goodman, Wheaton College; Anne Griffin, the Cooper Union; Marjorie Randon Hershey, Indiana University; Hugh L. LeBlanc, George Washington University; KuoWei lee, PanAmerican University; Robert T. Nakamura, State University of New York at Albany; Richard G. Niemi, University of Rochester; Diana Owen, Georgetown University; Charles Prysby, the University of North Carolina at Greensboro; Michael Robinson, Georgetown University; Lester Seligman, University of Illinois; Earl Shaw, Northern Arizona University; John W. Sloan, University of Houston; Priscilla Southwell, University of Oregon at Eugene; William H. Steward, University of Alabama; Edward J. Weissman, Washington College; and Clyde Wilcox, Georgetown University.

Finally, everyone makes personal sacrifices in writing a book. I want to thank my wife, Cheryl, for her patience and understanding for the more than forty years that this book has been part of my professional life. She has helped me greatly by assuming many of the obligations of family life as I worked on each new edition.

Stephen J. Wayne
Professor of Government Emeritus
Georgetown University

About the Author

Stephen J. Wayne (BA, University of Rochester; MA and PhD, Columbia University) is a professor emeritus of government at Georgetown University. He taught at Georgetown for twenty-nine years, and before that, at George Washington University for twenty years. He was also on the faculty of the US Naval Postgraduate School while serving on active duty in the US Navy and on the faculty of Ohio Wesleyan University.

A Washington-based expert on the American presidency, he has authored or edited thirteen books, published in thirty-one editions, and more than one hundred articles, chapters, and book reviews. In addition to *The Road to the White House*, he has written *The Legislative Presidency, Is This Any Way to Run a Democratic Election?, Personality and Politics: Obama For and Against Himself*, and *The Biden Presidency: Polarization, Politics, and Policy*.

A source for journalists covering the White House, Professor Wayne regularly appeared on television and radio news and discussion programs and has consulted for television documentaries on the presidency, testified before Congress on presidential elections, appeared before both Democratic and Republican advisory committees on the presidential nomination process, directed a presidential transition project for the National Academy of Public Administration, and participated in the White House Transition projects conducted by the Presidency Research Group.

He has lectured widely at colleges and universities in the US and abroad on the American presidency, national elections, and personality and politics. For more than forty years, he conducted seminars on the presidency for senior US federal executives for the Office of Personnel Management and met with international visitors and journalists visiting the US.

Contents

PART ONE ★ ★ ★ ★ ★
The Electoral Arena   1

PART THREE ★ ★ ★ ★ ★
The General Election Campaign   139

Figures, Tables, and Boxes

Boxes

The Electoral Arena

Presidential Selection

A Historical Overview

Introduction

The road to the White House is long, circuitous, and bumpy. It contains numerous hazards and potential dead ends. Those who choose to traverse it—and there are many who do so—need considerable skill, perseverance, and luck to be successful. They also need substantial amounts of time, money, and effort. For most candidates, there is no such thing as a free or easy ride to the presidency.

The framers of the Constitution worked for several months on the presidential selection system, and their plan has since undergone a number of constitutional, statutory, and precedent-setting changes. Modified by the development of parties, the expansion of suffrage, the growth of the news media, and the revolution in communications technology, the electoral system has not only become more open and participatory but also more contentious, complex, and expensive. It has "turned off" many people who, for a variety of reasons, have chosen not to participate.

This chapter is about that system: why it was created; what it was supposed to do; the compromises that were incorporated in the original plan; its initial operation and the changes that have subsequently affected it; the groups that have benefited from these changes; and the overall effect of the presidential electoral process on the parties, the electorate, and American democracy.

This chapter is organized into four sections. The first section discusses the creation of the presidential election system. It explores the motives and intentions of the delegates at Philadelphia and describes the procedures for selecting the president within the context of the constitutional and political issues of that day. The second section examines the development of partisan nominating systems. It explores the three principal methods that have been used to nominate presidential candidates: congressional caucuses, brokered national conventions, and state primaries and caucuses. It also describes the political forces that helped to shape these modes of nomination and, in the case of the first two, destroyed them.

3

The third section focuses on the most controversial election outcomes, ones, those determined by the House of Representatives (1800 and 1824), influenced by Congress (1876), and decided by the Supreme Court (2000). The section also examines elections in the twentieth and twenty-first centuries in which the shift of a relatively small number of votes could have changed the outcome (1960, 1968, 1976, 2004, and 2016). In doing so, this section highlights the strengths and weaknesses of the Electoral College and assesses its consistency with the principles of a democratic electoral process.

The final part of the chapter examines the current operation of the electoral system. It describes its geographic and demographic biases and how they affect national presidential elections. The section also discusses the Electoral College's major party orientation and its adverse impact on third-party and independent candidacies.

The Creation of the Electoral College

Of the many issues facing the delegates at the Constitutional Convention of 1787 in Philadelphia, the selection of the president was one of the toughest. Seven times during the course of the convention the method for choosing the executive was altered. The framers' difficulty in designing electoral provisions for the president stemmed from their need to guarantee the executive's independence and, at the same time, to create a technically sound, politically effective mechanism that would be consistent with a republican form of government. They wanted a representative government based on consent but not a direct democracy in which every adult citizen had an opportunity to participate in the formulation of public policy. Their goal was an electoral system that would choose the most qualified person but not necessarily the most popular.

There seemed to be no precise model to follow; heredity was out of the question, and a direct popular vote was viewed as impractical and undesirable. Three methods of election had been proposed. The Virginia Plan, a series of resolutions designed by James Madison and introduced by Virginia's governor, Edmund Randolph. The plan provided for legislative selection of the president. Eight states chose their governors in this fashion at that time. Having Congress choose the president would be practical and politically expedient. Moreover, members of Congress could be expected to exercise a considered judgment, more so than that of the general public.

The difficulty with legislative selection was the threat it posed to the institution of the presidency. How could the executive's independence be preserved if the election of the president hinged on popularity within Congress and reelection depended on the legislature's appraisal of the president's performance in office? Only if the president were to serve a long term and not be eligible for reelection it was thought, could the institution's independence be guaranteed if Congress was the electoral body. But ineligibility also posed problems because it provided little incentive for outstanding performance in office and denied the country the possibility of reelecting a person whose experience and success demonstrated qualifications that were superior to others.

Reflecting on these concerns, delegate Gouverneur Morris urged the removal of the ineligibility clause on the grounds that it tended to destroy the great motive to good behavior, the hope of being rewarded by reelection.[1] Delegates for a majority of the states agreed. Once the ineligibility clause was deleted, however, the term of office had to be shortened to prevent what the framers feared might become unlimited tenure or, in the words of Thomas Jefferson, "an elective monarchy." With a shorter term of office and permanent reeligibility, legislative selection was not nearly as desirable because it could make the president beholden to the legislature. Moreover, there was still the issue of whether the Congress would vote as one body or as two separate legislative houses. The large states favored a joint vote; the small states wanted separate votes by the House and Senate (because they had equal representation in the upper chamber).

Popular election did not generate a great deal of enthusiasm. It was twice rejected in the convention by overwhelming votes.[2] Lacking confidence in the public's ability to choose the best-qualified candidate, many delegates also believed that the size of the country and the relatively primitive state of its communications and transportation in the eighteenth century precluded a national campaign and election. The geographic expanse was simply too large to allow for proper supervision and administration of a national election. Sectional distrust and rivalry also contributed to the difficulty of conducting it.

A third option, indirect election, in which popular sentiment could be considered but would not necessarily dictate the outcome, was proposed by James Wilson after he failed to generate much support for a direct popular vote. Delegates Luther Martin, Gouverneur Morris, and Alexander Hamilton also suggested an indirect popular election through intermediaries. It was not until the debate over legislative selection divided and eventually deadlocked the delegates, however, that election by electors was seriously considered. Proposed initially as a compromise that incorporated previous convention agreements by a Committee on Unfinished Business, the Electoral College design was viewed as acceptable by weary delegates eager to return home and get the Constitution ratified.

The debate over the Electoral College system was short and to the point. Viewed as a safe, workable solution to the election dilemma, it was deemed consistent with the constitutional and political features of the new government and resistant to the kind of cabal and corruption that might tinge a popular vote. How the electors were to be selected was left to the states to determine. To ensure their independence, the electors could not simultaneously hold a federal government position.

The number of electors was to equal the number of senators and representatives from each state. At a designated time, they would meet, vote, and send the results to Congress, where they would be announced to a joint session by the president of the Senate, the vice president. Each elector had two votes because a president and vice president were to be selected separately at that time. The only limitations on voting were that the electors could not cast both their ballots for inhabitants of their own states[3] nor designate which of the candidates they preferred to be president and which one vice president.[4]

Under the initial plan, the person who received a majority of votes cast by the Electoral College was elected president, and the one with the second highest total, vice president. In the event that no one received a majority, the House of Representatives would choose from among the five candidates with the most electoral votes, with each state delegation casting one vote. If two or more individuals were tied for second, then the Senate would select the vice president Both of these provisions were effectively modified by the Twelfth Amendment to the Constitution.

The electoral system was a dual compromise that incorporated provisions of the large–small state and North–South compromises. Both dealt with representation. The first provided for one legislative body to be based on population (the House of Representatives) and one in which the states were equally represented (the Senate); the other compromise allowed three-fifths of the slave population to be counted in the determination of a state's popular representation. Both compromises protected slave owners in the South by making it difficult for the representatives of the more populous North to determine public policy on their own.

Designating the number of electors to be equal to a state's congressional delegation gave the larger states an advantage in the initial voting for president; casting ballots by state delegations in the House, if the Electoral College was not decisive, benefited the smaller states. It was anticipated that this two-step process would occur most of the time because there would probably not be a consensus national leader other than George Washington. In effect, the large states would nominate, much like the state primaries and caucuses do today, and the small states would exercise equal influence in the final election.[5]

The other compromise between the proponents of a federal system and those who favored a more centralized, national government allowed state legislatures to establish the procedures for choosing electors but had a national legislative body, the House of Representatives, decide among the candidates if there was no Electoral College majority. Finally, limiting the vote to the electors was intended to reduce intrigue, fraud, and cabal, fears that were expressed about the undesirability of state-based, popular voting.

The Development of Nominating Systems

Although the Constitution prescribed a system for electing a president, it made no reference to the nomination of candidates. Political parties had not emerged prior to the Constitutional Convention. Factions existed, and the framers of the Constitution were concerned about them, but the development of a party system was not anticipated. Rather, it was assumed that electors, whose interests were not tied to the national government, would make an independent judgment, and it was hoped they would choose the person they felt was best suited for the job.

In the first two elections, the system worked as intended. George Washington was the unanimous choice of the electors. There was, however, no consensus on the vice president. The eventual winner, John Adams, benefited from some informal lobbying by prominent individuals prior to the vote.[6] A more organized effort to agree on candidates for the presidency and vice presidency was undertaken in

1792. Partisan alliances were beginning to develop in Congress. Members of the two principal groups, the Federalists and the Anti-Federalists, met separately to recommend individuals for whom to vote in addition to Washington. The Federalists chose Vice President John Adams (Massachusetts); the Anti-Federalists picked Governor George Clinton (New York).

With political parties evolving during the 1790s, the selection of electors quickly became a partisan contest. In 1792 and 1796, a majority of the state legislatures chose them directly. Thus, the political group that controlled the legislature also determined the selection of electors. Appointed for their political views, electors were expected to exercise a partisan judgment. When a Pennsylvania elector did not do so in 1796, he was accused of faithless behavior. One critic wrote in a Philadelphia newspaper: "What, do I chuse Samuel Miles to determine for me whether John Adams or Thomas Jefferson shall be President? No! I chuse him to act, not to think."[7] Washington's decision not to serve a third term forced Federalist and Anti-Federalist members of Congress to recommend the candidates in 1796. Meeting separately, party leaders agreed among themselves on the tickets.

The Federalists urged their electors to support John Adams and Thomas Pinckney, whereas the Anti-Federalists (or Democratic-Republicans, as they began to be called) suggested Thomas Jefferson and Aaron Burr. Because it was not possible to specify presidential and vice presidential choices on the ballot, Federalist electors, primarily from New England, decided to withhold votes from Pinckney to make certain that he did not receive the same number as Adams. This strategy enabled Jefferson with sixty-eight votes to finish ahead of Pinckney but behind Adams, who had seventy-one. Four years of partisan differences followed between a president who, though he disclaimed a political affiliation, clearly favored the Federalists in appointments, ideology, and policy, and a vice president who was the acknowledged leader of the opposition party.

Congressional Caucuses

Beginning in 1800, partisan caucuses, composed of members of Congress, met for the purpose of recommending their party's nominees. The Democratic-Republicans continued to choose candidates in this manner until 1824; the Federalists did so only until 1808. In the final two presidential elections in which the Federalists ran candidates, 1812 and 1816, top party leaders, meeting in secret, decided on the nominees.[9] "King Caucus," as the partisan congressional caucuses were called, violated the spirit of the Constitution. Caucuses effectively allowed members of Congress to pick their party's nominees. After the decline of the Federalists, the nominees of the Democratic-Republicans, or simply Republicans as they became known, were, in fact, assured of victory—a product of the dominance of that party in the Congress and the country.

There were competing candidates within the Republican congressional caucus, however. In 1808, Madison prevailed over James Monroe and George Clinton. In 1816, Monroe overcame a strong challenge from William Crawford. In both cases, the electors united behind the successful nominee. In 1820, however, they did not. Disparate elements within the party selected their own candidates.

Although the caucus was the principal mode of candidate selection during the first part of the nineteenth century, the process was never formally institutionalized. How the meetings were called, who called them, and when they were held all varied from election to election, as did attendance. A sizable number of representatives chose not to participate at all. Some stayed away on principle; others did so because of the particular choices they would have to make. In 1816, less than half of the Republican members of Congress were at their party's caucus. In 1820, only 20 percent attended, and the caucus had to adjourn without formally supporting President Monroe and Vice President Daniel D. Tompkins for reelection. In 1824, almost three-fourths of the members boycotted the session.

The 1824 caucus did nominate candidates. But with representatives from only four states constituting two-thirds of those attending, the nominee, William Crawford, failed to receive unified party support. Other candidates were proposed by state legislatures and conventions, and the electoral vote was divided. Because no candidate obtained a majority, the House of Representatives had to make the final decision. John Quincy Adams was selected on the first ballot. He received the votes of thirteen of the twenty-four state delegations.

The caucus system was never resumed. In the end, it was a victim of the Federalist Party's decline, the decentralization of political power within the country, and Andrew Jackson's strong opposition to this method of presidential nomination. As the Republican Party grew from being the majority to the only party, factions developed within it, the two principal ones being the National Republicans and the Democratic-Republicans. In the absence of a viable opposition party, there was little to hold these factions together. By 1830, they had split into two separate groups, one supporting President Jackson and the other opposing him.

Political leadership was changing as well. A relatively small number of individuals dominated national politics for the first three decades following the ratification of the Constitution. Their common experience in the Revolutionary War, the Constitutional Convention, and the early government produced personal contacts, political influence, and public respect that contributed to their ability to agree on candidates and to generate public support for them.[9] Those who followed them in office had neither the tradition nor the national orientation with which to affect the presidential selection process nor the national recognition to build support across the country for their candidates. Most of this new generation of political leaders owed their prominence and political influence to states and regions, and their loyalties reflected these bases of support.

The growth of party organizations at the state and local level affected the presidential nomination system. In 1820 and 1824, it evolved into a decentralized mode of selection, with state legislatures, caucuses, and conventions proposing their own candidates. Support was also mobilized on regional levels. Whereas the congressional caucus had become unrepresentative, state-based nominations suffered from precisely the opposite problem. They were too sensitive to sectional interests and produced too many candidates. Unifying these diverse elements behind a single national ticket proved extremely difficult, although Jackson was successful in doing so in 1828. Nonetheless, a system that was more broadly based than the old caucus and could provide a more decisive and mobilizing mechanism was needed. National nominating conventions filled the void.

National Nominating Conventions

The first nominating convention was held in 1831 by the Anti-Masons. A small but relatively active third party, it held virtually no congressional representation. Unable to utilize a congressional caucus, the party turned instead to a general meeting that was held in a saloon in Baltimore, with 116 delegates from thirteen states attending. These delegates decided on the nominees as well as on an address to the people that contained the party's position on the dominant issues of the day. Three months later, a second convention was held in the same saloon by opponents of President Jackson. The National Republicans (or Whigs, as they later became known) also nominated candidates and agreed on a platform critical of the Jackson administration.

The following year, the Democratic-Republicans (or Democrats, as they were later called) also met in Baltimore. The impetus for their convention was Jackson's desire to demonstrate popular support for his presidency as well as to ensure the selection of Martin Van Buren as his running mate. In 1836, Jackson resorted to another convention—to handpick Van Buren as his successor. The Whigs did not hold a convention in 1836. Believing that they would have more success in the House of Representatives than in the nation as a whole, they ran three regional candidates, who were nominated by the states and competed against Van Buren in their areas of strength. The plan, however, failed to deny Van Buren an electoral majority. He ended up with 170 votes compared with a total of 124 for the other principal contenders. Thereafter, the Democrats and their opponents, first the Whigs and then their Republican successors, held nominating conventions to select their candidates. The early conventions were informal and rowdy by contemporary standards, but they also set the precedents for later meetings. The delegates decided on the procedures for conducting the convention, developed policy statements (addresses to the people), and chose nominees. Rules for apportioning the number of delegates were established before the meetings were held. Generally speaking, the states were accorded as many votes as their congressional representation merited, regardless of the number of actual convention participants.

Party leaders within the states controlled the delegate selection process. Their influence depended on their ability to deliver votes, which in turn required that the convention delegates not exercise their own independent judgment but support their state leader's choice. Much of the bartering was conducted behind closed doors. Actions on the convention floor often had little to do with the wheeling and dealing that occurred in the smaller "smoke-filled" rooms. Because there was little public preconvention activity, many ballots were often necessary to reach the number that was required to win the party's nomination, usually two-thirds of the delegates. The winners owed their selection to the heads of the powerful state organizations and not to their own political prominence and organizational support. But the price they had to pay for the nomination, when calculated in terms of patronage and other political payoffs, was often quite high.

Nonetheless, nineteenth-century conventions served several purposes. They provided a national forum for state party leaders. They constituted a mechanism by which agreements could be negotiated and support mobilized. By brokering interests, conventions helped unify the disparate elements within a party, thereby converting an organization of state parties into a national coalition for the purpose of conducting a presidential campaign.

Popular Primaries and Caucuses

Demands for reform began to be heard at the beginning of the twentieth century. The Progressive Movement, led by Robert La Follett of Wisconsin and Hiram Johnson of California, aimed to break the power of state bosses and their political machines through the direct election of convention delegates or, alternately through the expression of a popular choice by the state's electorate. Florida became the first state to provide its political parties with such an option. In 1904, the Democrats took advantage of it and held a statewide vote for convention delegates. One year later, Wisconsin enacted a law for the direct election of delegates to nominating conventions. Others followed suit. By 1912, fifteen states provided for some type of primary election. Oregon was the first to permit a preference vote for the candidates themselves.

The year 1912 was also the first in which a candidate sought to use primaries as a way to obtain the nomination. With almost 42 percent of the Republican delegates selected in primaries, former President Theodore Roosevelt challenged incumbent William Howard Taft. Roosevelt won nine primaries to Taft's one yet lost the nomination. Taft's support among regular party leaders who delivered their delegations and controlled the convention was sufficient to win renomination. He received one-third of his support from southern delegations, although the Republican Party had won only a small percentage of the southern vote in the previous presidential election.

Partially in reaction to the unrepresentative, "boss-dominated" convention of 1912, additional states adopted primaries. By 1916, more than half of them held a Republican or Democratic contest. Although a majority of the delegates in that year were chosen by some type of primary, most of them were not bound to support specific candidates. As a consequence, primary results did not dictate the outcome of the conventions.

The movement toward popular participation was short-lived, however. Following World War I, the number of primaries declined. State party leaders, who saw primaries as a threat to their own influence, argued against them on three grounds: they were expensive; they did not attract many voters; and major candidates tended to avoid them. Moreover, primaries frequently encouraged factionalism, thereby weakening a party's organization. In response to this criticism, he reformers that supported primaries could not claim that their principal goal, nk-and-file control over the selection of party nominees, had been achieved. blic participation was disappointing. Primaries attracted only a small percentage of those who voted in the general election. The minority party, in particular, suffered from low turnout for an obvious reason: Its candidates stood little chance of winning the general election. In some states, rank-and-file influence was further diluted by the participation of Independents who did not align themselves with a political party.

As a consequence of these factors, some states that had enacted new election laws reverted to their former method of selection. Others made their primaries advisory rather than mandatory. Fewer convention delegates were chosen in them. By 1936, only fourteen states held Democratic primaries, and twelve held Republican ones. Less than 40 percent of the delegates to each convention that year were chosen in this manner. For the next twenty years, the number of primaries and the percentage of delegates hovered around this level.

Theodore Roosevelt's failure in 1912 and the decline in primaries thereafter made them, at best, an auxiliary route to the nomination. Although some presidential aspirants became embroiled in primaries, none who depended on them won. In 1920, a spirited contest among three Republicans (General Leonard Wood, Governor Frank Lowden of Illinois, and Senator Hiram Johnson) failed to produce a convention majority for any of these candidates and resulted in party leaders choosing Warren Harding as the standard-bearer. Similarly, in 1952, Senator Estes Kefauver, who chaired the highly publicized and televised Senate hearings on organized crime, entered thirteen of seventeen presidential primaries, won twelve of them but failed to win his party's nomination.

The reason Kefauver could not parlay his primary victories into a convention victory was that a majority of the delegates were not selected in primaries in 1952. Of those who were, many were chosen separately from the presidential preference vote. Kefauver did not contest these separate delegate elections. As a consequence, he obtained only 50 percent of the delegates in the states in which he actually won the presidential preference vote. Moreover, the fact that most of his wins occurred against little or no opposition undercut Kefauver's claim to being the most popular and electable Democrat. He had avoided primaries in four states in which he feared that he might either lose or do poorly.

Not only were primaries not considered to be an essential road to winning the nomination but running in too many of them was also interpreted as a sign of weakness and not strength. It indicated a lack of national recognition, a failure to obtain the support of party leaders, or both. For these reasons, leading candidates tended to choose their primaries carefully, and the primaries, in turn, tended to reinforce the position of the leading candidates. Those who entered primaries did so mainly to test their popularity rather than to win convention votes. Dwight D. Eisenhower in 1952, John F. Kennedy in 1960, and Richard M. Nixon in 1968 had to demonstrate that being a general, a Catholic, or a once-defeated presidential candidate would not be fatal to their chances. In other words, they needed to prove they could win the general election if nominated by their party.

With the possible exception of Kennedy's victories in West Virginia and Wisconsin, primaries were neither crucial nor decisive for winning the nomination until the 1970s. When there was a provisional consensus within the party, primaries helped confirm it; when there was not, primaries could not produce it.[10] In short, they had little to do with whether the party was unified or divided at the time of the convention.

Primary results tended to be self-fulfilling in the sense that they confirmed the front-runner's status. Between 1936 and 1968, the preconvention leader, the candidate who was ahead in the Gallup Poll before the first primary, won the nomination seventeen out of nineteen times. The only exceptions were Thomas E. Dewey, who was defeated by Wendell Willkie in 1940, and Kefauver, who lost his race for the nomination to Adlai Stevenson in 1952. Willkie, however, had become the public opinion leader by the time the Republican convention met. Even when leading candidates lost a primary, they had time to recoup. Dewey and Stevenson, defeated in early primaries in 1948 and 1956, respectively, went on to reestablish their credibility as front-runners by winning later primaries.

This situation in which the primaries were not the essential route to the nomination changed dramatically after 1968. Largely as a consequence of the tumultuous Democratic nominating convention of that year, in which the party's nominees and platform were allegedly dictated by party "bosses," demands for a larger voice for rank-and-file partisans increased. In reaction to these demands, the Democratic Party began to look into the matter of delegate selection. The party enacted a series of reforms designed to ensure broader representation at its convention. To avoid challenges to their delegations, a number of states that had used caucus and convention systems changed to primaries. The number of primaries began to increase as did the percentage of convention delegates chosen from them.

New finance laws, which provided for government subsidies for preconvention campaigning, and increased news media coverage, particularly by television, also added to the incentive to enter primaries. By 1972, primaries had become decisive. In that year, Senator Edmund Muskie, the leading Democratic contender at the beginning of the process, was forced to withdraw after doing poorly in the early contests. In 1976, President Gerald Ford came close to being the first incumbent president since Chester A. Arthur in 1884 to be denied his party's nomination because of a primary challenge by Ronald Reagan. In 1980, President Jimmy Carter was also challenged for renomination by Senator Edward Kennedy, as was George H. W. Bush by Pat Buchanan in 1992. Bill Clinton, George W. Bush, Barack Obama, and Donald Trump were not challenged for renomination, in part because they raised millions to ensure that a credible candidate would not oppose them. But the threat of a challenge kept them sensitized to the needs and interests of their partisan supporters.

Since the 1970s, primaries have revolutionized the presidential nomination process. They have been used to build popularity rather than simply reflect it. Candidates for a party's nomination can no longer hope to succeed without entering them; incumbents can no longer ignore them if they face major opposition within their own party. The impact of primaries has been significant, affecting the strategies and tactics of the candidates, the composition and behavior of the convention delegates, and the decision-making process at the national conventions. The contests for the nomination have shifted power within the parties. They have enlarged the selection zone of potential nominees but still advantage well-known and well-funded candidates. Popularity with key constituencies within the party's electoral coalition is the key to success.

An extended, divisive nomination process can also adversely affect the party's standard-bearer in the election by depleting the winning candidate's war chest, damaging their leadership image, and forcing that nominee to have taken extreme policy positions, more popular with the base than with the whole electorate. Each of these developments will be discussed in subsequent chapters.

The Evolution of the General Election

The general election has changed as well. The Electoral College no longer operates in the way it was designed. It now has a partisan coloration. There is greater opportunity for the public to participate, but the campaign is not geared to obtaining the most popular votes. Although the system bears a resemblance to its past form, it differs in practice.

Partisan Electors

The development of the party system changed the character of the Electoral College. Only in the first two elections, when Washington was the unanimous choice, did the electors exercise a nonpartisan and presumably independent judgment. Within ten years from the time the federal government began to operate, electors quickly became the captives of their party and were expected to vote for its candidates. The outcome of the election of 1800 vividly illustrates this new pattern of partisan voting.

All electors who had cast ballots for Jefferson also cast them for Burr. Because it was not possible in those days to differentiate the candidates for the presidency and vice presidency on the ballot, the results had to be considered a tie, though Jefferson was clearly his party's choice for president. Under the terms of the Constitution, the House of Representatives, voting by individual state delegations, had to choose the winner.

Congressional Decisions

On February 11, 1801, after the results of the Electoral College tie were announced by the vice president, who happened to be Jefferson, a Federalist-controlled House convened to resolve the dilemma. Because the winners of the 1800 election did not take office until March 4, 1801, representatives from a "lame-duck" Congress would have to choose the next president.[11] Most Federalists supported Burr, whom they regarded as the more pragmatic politician, a person with whom they could deal. Jefferson, on the other hand, was perceived as a dangerous, uncompromising radical by many Federalists. Alexander Hamilton, however, was outspoken in his opposition to Burr, a political rival from New York, whom Hamilton regarded as "the most unfit man in the United States for the office of President."[12]

On the first ballot taken on February 11, 1801, Burr received a majority of the total votes, but Jefferson won the support of more state delegations.[13] Eight states voted for Jefferson, six backed Burr, and two were evenly divided. This result left Jefferson one short of the needed majority. The House took nineteen ballots on its first day of deliberations and a total of thirty-six before it finally reached a majority for Jefferson. Had Burr promised to be a Federalist president, it is conceivable that he could have won.

The first amendment to reform voting procedures in the Electoral College was enacted by the new Congress, controlled by Jefferson's party, in 1803 and ratified by the states in 1804. This amendment to the Constitution, the twelfth, provided for separate voting for president and vice president. It also refined the selection procedures in the event that the president or vice president did not receive a majority of the electoral vote. The House of Representatives, still voting by state delegation, was to choose from among the top three presidential candidates, and the Senate, voting by individual senators, was to choose from the top two vice presidential candidates. If the House could not make a decision by March 4, the amendment provided for the new vice president to assume the presidency until such time as the House could render a judgment.

The next nondecisive presidential vote did not occur until 1824. That year, four people received electoral votes for president: Andrew Jackson (ninety-nine votes), John Quincy Adams (eighty-four), William Crawford (forty-one), and Henry Clay (thirty-seven). According to the Twelfth Amendment, the House of Representatives had to decide from among the top three because no one had a majority. Eliminated from the contest was Henry Clay, who happened to be Speaker of the House. Clay threw his support to Adams, who won. It was alleged that Clay did so in exchange for nomination as secretary of state, a charge that Clay vigorously denied. After Adams became president, however, he chose Clay for secretary of state, a position Clay readily accepted.[14]

Jackson was the winner of the popular vote in 1824. In eighteen of the twenty-four states that chose electors by this method, he received 192,933 votes compared with 115,696 for Adams, 47,136 for Clay, and 46,979 for Crawford. Adams, however, had the backing of more state delegations. A Massachusetts resident, he enjoyed the support of the six New England states, and with Clay's help, the representatives of six others backed his candidacy. The votes of thirteen states, however, were needed for a majority.

New York seemed to be the pivotal state, and Stephen Van Rensselaer, a former Revolutionary War general, the swing representative. On the morning of the vote, Speaker Clay and Representative Daniel Webster tried to persuade Van Rensselaer to vote for Adams. It was said that they were unsuccessful.[15] As the voting began, Van Rensselaer bowed his head as if in prayer. On the floor, he saw a piece of paper with "Adams" written on it. Interpreting this as a sign from on high, he dropped the paper in the box. New York went for Adams by only one vote, providing him with the barest majority.[16]

Jackson, outraged at the turn of events, urged the abolition of the Electoral College. His claim of a popular mandate, however, was open to question. The most populous state at the time, New York, did not permit its electorate to choose electors. Moreover, in three of the states in which Jackson won the electoral vote but lost in the House of Representatives, he had fewer popular votes than Adams.[17]

Opposition to the system mounted, however, and a gradual democratization of the electoral process occurred. More states began to choose their electors directly by popular vote. In 1800, ten of the fifteen states used legislative selection. By 1832, only South Carolina retained this practice. The trend was also toward statewide election of an entire slate of electors. States that had chosen their electors within legislative districts converted to a winner-take-all system to maximize their voting power in the Electoral College. This change, in turn, created the possibility that there could be a disparity between the popular and electoral vote.

The next disputed election did not occur until 1876. In that election, Democrat Samuel J. Tilden received the most votes. He had 250,000 more popular votes and nineteen more electoral votes than his Republican rival, Rutherford B. Hayes. Nonetheless, Tilden fell one vote short of a majority in the Electoral College.

Twenty electoral votes were in dispute. Dual election returns were received from Florida (four votes), Louisiana (eight votes), and South Carolina (seven votes). Charges of fraud and voting irregularities were made by both parties. The Republicans, who controlled the three state legislatures, contended that Democrats had forcibly prevented newly freed slaves from voting. The Democrats, on the other hand, alleged that many nonstate residents participated as did people who were not registered to vote. The other disputed electoral vote occurred in Oregon where a single Republican elector was challenged on the grounds that he held another federal position (assistant postmaster) and, thus, was ineligible to be an elector.[18]

Three days before the Electoral College vote was to be officially counted, Congress established a commission to examine and try to resolve the dispute. The electoral commission was to consist of fifteen members: ten from Congress (five Republicans and five Democrats) and five from the Supreme Court. Four of the Supreme Court justices were designated by the act (two Republicans and two Democrats), and they were to choose the fifth. Their choice, Justice David Davis, a political Independent, was expected to become a member of the commission, but on the day it was created, Davis was appointed by the Illinois legislature to the US Senate. The Supreme Court justices then picked Joseph Bradley, an independent Republican from New Jersey. Bradley sided with his party on every issue. By a strictly partisan vote, the commission validated the credentials of all the Republican electors, thereby giving Hayes a one-vote margin of victory in the Electoral College.[19]

Prior to the elections of 2000 and 2016, the only other one in which the winner of the popular vote was beaten in an undisputed Electoral College vote occurred in 1888. Democrat Grover Cleveland had a plurality of 95,096 popular votes, but only 168 electoral votes compared with 233 for Republican Benjamin Harrison.

The 2020 Electoral College Vote Challenge

Donald Trump and his supporters challenged the official Electoral College results in 2020. They argued that the vote was rigged, that Democrats had to cheat to win. To support their contention, they claimed that more votes were cast than the number of registered voters in some districts, that there were unexplained surges in the popular vote, and that the voting machines themselves were programed in a way to benefit the Democrats, a charge that the company that designed the software, Dominion Voting Systems, vigorously denied. Dominion subsequently sued Fox News for promulgating baseless allegations about its machines. In the closely contested states, some Republicans also said that dead people voted.

Protesting the election results, Republican supporters of Trump instituted sixty-one lawsuits in battleground states. The courts ruled against sixty of these suits on the grounds that insufficient evidence was provided to support the claims of fraudulent voting. Nor did the Justice Department during Trump's presidency find evidence of fraud that would overturn the results of the election in any state.

When Congress met to certify the Electoral College vote, President Trump asked Vice President Pence, the presiding officer of the Senate, to reject the official vote count in five swing states (Arizona, Georgia, Michigan, Pennsylvania, and Wisconsin). Pence refused to do so, arguing that he lacked the constitutional authority. Trump was furious and denounced Pence, calling him a "pussy" and urging his supporters to protest the "rigged election outcome" at a rally on the National Mall in Washington. He then urged them to go to the Capitol to protest. Thousands of people followed his advice, but when they got there, the peaceful protest turned violent. The crowd broke through police barracks, and hundreds entered the locked Capitol building, attacking police and hunting for members of Congress (figure 1.1). Five people died, and many were injured during the riot.

FIGURE 1.1 ★ Crowd of Trump supporters marching on the US Capitol on January 6, 2021.

TapTheForwardAssist/Wikimedia Commons

The insurrection lasted almost five hours. It was covered live on television. Trump watched events unfold in the White House dining room on television; he was prevented from going to the Capitol by his Secret Service detail. For the next three hours and seven minutes, the president stayed glued to TV news coverage but did nothing to quell the insurrection. Members of his family and senior White House aides urged him to make a public statement to stop the violence and tell his supporters to go home. He did not want to do so but finally did in a short video clip. The president not only asked the protestors and rioters to go home, but he also expressed his warm and favorable feelings about them, saying, "we love you, you're very special."

Polls taken after the insurrection indicated that a plurality of Americans believed that Trump bore some responsibility for the insurrection. A congressional committee was formed to investigate the violent protests and the president's role inciting the crowd.[20] The committee conducted extensive hearings, questioning White House staffers, Secret Service agents, Capitol Police, and other federal enforcement officials, and a documentary filmmaker who filmed the riot and talked with some of the protest leaders and others with knowledge of the situation, applicable laws, and individuals who participated in the rally, march, and insurrection. In all, it questioned twelve hundred witnesses.

In addition, the committee reviewed thousands of emails and transcribed thousands of telephone conversations and texts. Trump sought to prevent the release of material from the National Archives, asserting executive privilege, but the Supreme Court ruled unanimously that executive privilege did not extend to former presidents. The committee, in closed and public hearings, revealed Trump's determination to contest the results of the election even though almost all his senior advisors in the White House and Attorney General Barr told him that there was not sufficient evidence of fraudulent voting to overturn the outcome of the vote in any state.

In subsequent months, Trump and his backers tried to change the election certification procedures and the officials responsible for determining the final vote in these and other states. The certification process, however, was reaffirmed when Congress rewrote the electoral count of 1887 and included it an an omnibus appropriation bill in December 2022.

New election laws, ostensibly designed to prevent fraudulent voting, were enacted by Republican-controlled state legislatures, however. Democrats responded to these new laws by challenging them on the grounds that they discriminated against minority voters, impeding their access to vote. Most of the new legislation, however, has been upheld by state courts. The Biden Justice Department has promised to enforce voting rights protected by the Constitution and federal legislation, but the partisan political struggle on voting rights is far from over.

On December 22, 2022, the January 6th Committee issued its final report, accusing former president Trump of inciting the riot and recommending that the Justice Department prosecute him for criminal activities. In his quest for the 2024 Republican nomination, Trump has continued to claim the 2020 election was fraudulent and lauded the January 6th rioters as loyal patriots.

Judicial Determination

The 2000 Electoral College vote was too close to call. Democrat, Al Gore, was ahead in twenty states plus the District of Columbia with a total of 267 electoral votes. Republican, George W. Bush, led in twenty-nine states with a total of 238 electoral votes. The vote in one state, Florida, was in dispute. Out of more than 5.9 million votes cast in that state, only 537 votes separated the two candidates. Both sides alleged procedural irregularities, voter eligibility issues, and vote-counting errors.

Four legal issues marred the Florida election: voter confusion over the design of the ballot in one county, disagreement over eligible voters and absentee ballots in several others, tabulation problems in counties that used punch-card ballots, and the date when the official results had to be certified by the secretary of state.

Voter confusion stemmed from a "butterfly ballot" used in Palm Beach County, where many retirees live. Designed by a Democratic campaign official, the ballot was intended to help senior citizens read the names of the candidates more clearly by using larger type. To fit all the names on a single punch card, however, two columns had to be used, with the punch holes for voting, or "chads" as they are called, between them. Although Democrats Al Gore and Joe Lieberman were listed second on the left-hand column, their chad was positioned third, after the chad of the candidates on the right-hand column, Pat Buchanan and Ezola Foster of the Reform Party.

Some voters, who claimed that they intended to vote for the Democratic candidates, punched out the second rather than the third chad, which registered as a vote for Buchanan. Others, in confusion, pushed out both the second and third chads, automatically voiding their ballots.[21] Aggrieved Democrats in the county immediately filed a lawsuit to contest the vote and demand a new election. A Florida state court, however, rejected their request, effectively terminating the revote option.

The second legal issue concerned ballots that were not properly included in the machine count. Many counties in Florida used a punch-card system of voting in which chads, a small perforated box on the card, must be removed with a specially designed instrument for the vote to be properly cast. The holes in the card were then tabulated by a machine. However, if a chad was not completely removed, the vote may not have been recorded by the voting machine. The Gore campaign alleged that thousands of presidential votes in three Democratic counties (Miami-Dade, Broward, and Palm Beach) were not counted because part or all of a chad was still attached to the ballot. In other words, voters had not punched through the card completely. Democrats appealed to county officials for a hand count of these ballots; Republicans opposed the count, claiming that a selective hand count in some counties was unfair to people in the other counties. Before the courts had rendered a judgment, however, Florida's secretary of state, a Republican appointee, certified the original county vote as the official tally to which only absentee ballots, postmarked no later than election day and received by the counties within one week of the election, could be added. The secretary of state's certification prompted Gore's legal team to go to state court to force the secretary to accept hand-counted votes and an amended vote total submitted after the certification.

Some of the legal issues were resolved by Florida courts. The most contentious one, however, the hand counting of punch cards not tabulated by the voting machines, ended up in the US Supreme Court. Initially, the court remanded the case back to Florida's Supreme Court that had ruled in Gore's favor. When the Florida court reaffirmed its previous decision, Bush's lawyers reappealed to the US Supreme Court.

On December 11, 2000, one day before Florida law required the designation of its electors, the US Supreme Court heard oral arguments in the case known as *Bush v. Gore*, 531 U.S. 93 (2000); it announced its ruling the next evening. The court reversed the Florida Supreme Court's judgment that hand counting could be resumed in three counties. In its decision, the Supreme Court held that the absence of a single standard to be used throughout the state by election officials violated the Fourteenth Amendment, which requires the states to provide all their residents with equal protection of the laws. A majority of the court also went on to conclude that there was not sufficient time, given the state legislature's intent to designate Florida's electors by December 12, to establish and implement such a standard. Hence, the certified vote that had Bush leading by 537 votes was final. Winning Florida gave Bush an Electoral College majority.[22]

Following the disputed election, changes in the election laws occurred on both state and national levels. Florida enacted electoral reforms to prevent a repetition of the problems that occurred in 2000. In 2002, *The Help America Vote Act*, passed by Congress, provided federal funds to the states to help them consolidate and computerize their voter registration lists, but electoral problems have persisted.

As previously noted, Donald Trump had claimed that the electoral process was rigged during his 2016 election campaign. After he won an Electoral College victory, the president appointed a Presidential Commission on Election Integrity, chaired by the Vice President Pence and a Republican state official from Kansas. The commission requested the states to provide detailed information on voters including data on their registration, dates of birth, and social security numbers. Fifteen state election officials refused to do so; others criticized the requirement for personal information. The commission met irregularly; its staff operated behind closed doors; and even some of its members complained that they were kept in the dark. After seven months, Trump abolished the commission but continued to complain about rigged elections by the Democrats.

Other Close Elections

There have been other close elections, however, in which the switch of a relatively small number of people would have altered the results. In 1860, a shift of twenty-five thousand in New York from Abraham Lincoln to Stephen Douglas would have denied Lincoln a majority in the Electoral College. A change of fewer than thirty thousand in three states in 1892 would have given Benjamin Harrison another victory over Cleveland.

In 1916, Charles Evans Hughes needed only 3,807 more votes in California to have beaten Woodrow Wilson. Similarly, Thomas E. Dewey could have denied Harry S. Truman a majority in the Electoral College with 12,487 more California votes in 1948. A change in the votes of fewer than nine thousand people in

Illinois and Missouri in 1960 would have meant that John F. Kennedy would have lacked an Electoral College majority. In 1968, a shift of only 55,000 votes from Richard M. Nixon to Hubert H. Humphrey in three states would have thrown the election into the House of Representatives, which at that time was controlled by the Democrats. In 1976, if 3,687 more voters in Hawaii and 5,559 more in Ohio voted for Ford, he would have won the Electoral College vote.[21] In 2004, George W. Bush received only 0.02 percent more votes (120,000 out of 5.6 million) than John Kerry did in Ohio; had Kerry won Ohio, he would have had an Electoral College majority. In three states that Trump won in 2016 (Michigan, Wisconsin, and Pennsylvania), he received a total of 77,744 more votes than Hillary Clinton out of 13,940,912 cast, a margin of only 0.006 percent. Had Clinton prevailed in these traditional Democratic states, she would have had an Electoral College majority in addition to her popular vote win.

Not only could the results of these elections have been affected by small shifts in voter preferences, but in 1948, 1960, 1968, and 1992, there was the added possibility that the Electoral College vote would not be decisive because of a potentially strong third-party or Independent candidates. In 1948, Henry Wallace (Progressive Party) and Strom Thurmond (States' Rights Party) received almost 5 percent of the total popular vote, and Thurmond won thirty-nine electoral votes. In 1960, fourteen unpledged electors were chosen in Alabama and Mississippi. In 1968, George Wallace of Alabama, running under the American Independent Party label, received almost 10 million popular votes and forty-six electoral votes, and in 1992, H. Ross Perot received 19.7 million popular votes (almost 19 percent of the total) but none in the Electoral College. Four years later, he got 8.1 million popular votes but, again, no electoral votes. Ralph Nader received less than 3 percent of the popular vote in 2000, but his 97,488 votes in Florida probably cost Gore that state and the election.

The Politics of Electoral College Voting

The presidential campaign and election are shaped by the Electoral College. The strategies the candidates pursue, the resources they utilize, and the states in which they place their major efforts are all calculated based on Electoral College politics and not the popular vote. The Electoral College is not neutral. The way the votes are aggregated within it usually works to the advantage of the candidate who has the most popular votes. In 2000 and 2016, it did not, however. (See table 10.1).

Why does the Electoral College usually enhance the margin of the popular vote winner? The reason has to do with the winner-take-all system of voting that adopted by most states. In almost every instance, the presidential and vice presidential candidates who receive a plurality of the popular vote within the state get all its electoral votes.[23] This usually translates into a larger percentage of the Electoral College vote than would have occurred with a direct popular vote.

Advocates of the system see this enlarged Electoral College vote as an advantage for the new or reelected president. They claim that it increases the president's mandate for governing as well as the coalition of supporters on whom the president can rely. According to political analyst Nate Silver, it was the desire for a broad mandate that prompted Clinton to spend her resources in more states than necessary to win an Electoral College victory in what turned out to be a poor strategic decision.[24]

Most states also perceive a benefit from casting their votes as a unit. They believe that it enhances their political clout. In 2004, voters in Colorado soundly defeated a constitutional amendment that would have allocated their state's electoral vote in proportion to the popular vote that the candidates received. Such an amendment would have decreased that state's importance to the presidential candidates and the state's overall impact on the Electoral College vote. Following the 2012 and 2016 elections, Republicans in Virginia and other states suggested the electors be chosen by congressional districts rather than a statewide vote, but only two states, Nebraska and Maine, currently do so.

The large states, theoretically, gain more influence in the Electoral College by winner-take-all voting. The very smallest states do so as well because they receive a minimum of three electoral votes regardless of population. size. Consequently, their citizens have greater voting power than they would have in a direct election system. To illustrate, if Wyoming's population of less than 600,000 were divided by its three electoral votes, there would be one elector for every 200,000 people. Dividing California's population of nearly forty million by its fifty-five electoral votes yields one elector for every 727,000 persons.[25] The medium-sized states are comparatively disadvantaged.

But the advantage that the largest and smallest states reap from the current Electoral College system pales by comparison to the benefit that the most competitive states receive regardless of their size. Since the advent of frequent public opinion polling during the election period, candidates concentrated their time, efforts, and resources in those states that seemed to be up for grabs. Noncompetitive states, large or small, see little of the presidential campaign. The candidates rarely visit them; they spend little, if any, money in them; they run few, if any, political advertisements in their major media markets; and they mount little, if any, grassroots efforts. They are essentially ignored because their Electoral College outcome is predictable.

Moreover, the number of competitive states in presidential elections have declined. In 1960, about half the states were deemed competitive; either of the major party candidates had a realistic chance to win them. In the twenty-first century, less than one-third have been seen as competitive at the beginning of the general election and less than ten at the end and only five or six in 2020. Candidates concentrate their campaign in the small number of battleground states. In short, the one national election in the United States has been reduced to a contest fought in less than 15 percent of the states.

The Electoral College also benefits the two major parties at the expense of third parties and independent candidates. The reason it does so is that the winner-take-all system of voting by the states when combined with the need for a majority of the total electoral vote makes it difficult for third parties to accumulate enough electoral votes to win an election. To have any effect, minor-party candidates must have support that is geographically concentrated, as Strom Thurmond's was in 1948 and George Wallace's in 1968, rather than more broadly distributed across the country, as Henry Wallace's was in 1948 and H. Ross Perot's was in 1992 and 1996.

Given the limitations on third parties, their most realistic electoral objectives would seem to be to defeat one of the major contenders rather than to elect their own. In 1912, Theodore Roosevelt's Bull Moose campaign split the Republican Party, thereby aiding the Democratic Party candidate, Woodrow Wilson. In 2000, Ralph Nader's vote in Florida probably cost Gore the election. Which of the major parties is advantaged by the Electoral College? In 2016, it was definitely the Republicans who won more states but lost the national popular vote.

Summary

The quest for the presidency has been and continues to be influenced by the system designed in Philadelphia in 1787. The objectives of that system were to protect the independence of the institution, ensure the selection of a well-qualified, national candidate, and do so in a way that was politically expedient, technologically feasible, and consistent with the tenets of a republican form of government.

Although many of these objectives remain, the system has changed significantly over the years, primarily because of the creation of political parties. Their development created an additional first step in the process, the nomination, which has influenced the selection and behavior of electors ever since. The nomination process is necessary to the goals of the parties to get their candidates elected. At first, members of Congress, meeting in partisan caucuses, decided on the nominees. After the caucus method broke down, a more decentralized mode of selection, reflective of the increasing sectional composition of the parties, emerged. Controlled by state leaders, the nominations were decided at brokered national conventions. Demands for greater public participation eventually opened up the nomination process and reduced but did not eliminate the influence of party elites and interest group leaders.

Today, candidates compete for their party's nomination in primaries and caucuses. They effectively choose the slates of electors that will vote for them if they win a plurality of the state vote. Thus, the Electoral College reflects the popular vote but does so within the states rather than the country as a whole.

Winner-take-all state voting distorts the national vote. In most elections, it has magnified that vote; in two of the last six elections, it has reversed it. Critics contend that the system is undemocratic, unequal, and unwise. They argue that it does not encourage candidates to campaign nationwide, does not encourage turnout in less competitive states, and does not produce a mandate or an electoral coalition for governing. Considering that a substantial portion of the people do not vote, and the popular vote itself may be close, the winner rarely gains the support of more than one-third of the population, hardly the popular backing one might expect or desire in a democratic electoral system.

Defenders of the Electoral College, on the other hand, say that it is consistent with the country's constitutional design and political tradition, reflects the federal character of the United States, minimizes the extent to which fraudulent electoral activity at the state level affects the overall national results, and produces a quick and conclusive outcome for an extended presidential campaign.

Exercises

1. Prior to the completion of the next nomination process, obtain the most recent schedule of primaries and caucuses for the selection of delegates to the Democratic and Republican national nominating conventions. You can do this on most major news organizations' websites, or *The Green Papers*. Try to figure out which of the declared and undeclared candidates for each party's nomination is most and least advantaged by this schedule and explain why.

2. Get up to speed on the Electoral College by accessing and reviewing information on the Electoral College from the website of the National Archives and Records Administration Use the links available at this site to find out how the electors in your state are selected. These procedures are also available at *The Green Papers*.

3. Access the website, 270 to Win. Explain how the Electoral College maps for the 2016 and 2020 elections differed. Then construct a winning Electoral College strategy for the Democratic or Republican candidate you prefer in 2024. Focus on the likely swing states in your analysis. Why do you think these states may go Democratic or Republican in the next election?

Selected Readings

Bennett, Robert W. *Taming the Electoral College*. Stanford, CA: Stanford University Press, 2006.

Best, Judith. "Presidential Selection: Complex Problems and Simple Solutions." *The Political Science Quarterly* 119 (Spring 2004): 39–59.

Curtis, Michael, "The Pros and Cons of the Electoral College." *American Thinker*, December 24, 2016.

Edwards, George C. III. *Why the Electoral College Is Bad for America*, 3rd ed. New Haven, CT: Yale University Press, 2019.

Fortier, John C., ed. *After the People Vote: A Guide to the Electoral College*. Washington, DC: The AEI Press, 2004.

Issacharoff, Samuel. "Law, Rules, and Presidential Selection." *Political Science Quarterly* 120 (Spring 2005): 113–29.

Jones, Bradley. "Majority of Americans Continue to Favor Moving away from the Electoral College." Pew Research Center, January 21, 2021.

Levinson, Sanford, Daniel Lowenstein, and John McGinnis. "Should We Dispense with the Electoral College?" *University of Pennsylvania Law Review* 156 (2007): 10–37.

Longley, Lawrence D., and James D. Dana Jr. "The Biases of the Electoral College in the 1990s." *Polity* 25 (Fall 1992): 123–45.

Panagopoulos, Costas. "Electoral Reform." *Public Opinion Quarterly* 68 (Winter 2004): 623–40.

Presidential Election Inequality: The Electoral College in the 21st Century. Fair Vote.

Ross, Tana. *Why We Need the Electoral College*. Washington, DC: Regnery Gateway, 2021.

Rakove, Jack. "Presidential Selection: Electoral Fallacies." *Political Science Quarterly* 119 (Spring 2004): 21–38.

Troy, Gil. *See How They Ran: The Changing Role of the Presidential Candidate*. New York, NY: Free Press, 2012.

Wallison, Peter J. "Why We Need the Electoral College." *Real Clear Politics*, December 6, 2016.

Notes

1. Gouverneur Morris, *Records of the Federal Convention*, ed. Max Farrand (New Haven, CT: Yale University Press, 1921), II: 2, 33.
2. The first proposal for direct election was introduced in a timid fashion by James Wilson, a delegate from Pennsylvania. James Madison's *Journal* describes Wilson's presentation as follows: "Mr. Wilson said he was almost unwilling to declare the mode which he wished to take place, being apprehensive that it might appear chimerical. He would say, however, at least that in theory he was for an election by the people; Experience, particularly in N. York & Massts, shewed that an election of the first magistrate by the people at large, was both convenient & successful mode." Farrand, *Records of the Federal Convention*, I: 68.
3. This provision was intended to decrease parochialism and facilitate the selection of a national candidate.
4. It forced Dick Cheney, George W. Bush's choice to be his vice presidential running mate in 2000, to move his official residence from Texas to Wyoming so that Texas's electors could vote for the entire Republican ticket if Bush and Cheney won the popular vote in that state, which they did.
5. So great was the sectional rivalry, so competitive the states, and so limited the number of people with national reputations, that it was feared electors would tend to vote primarily for residents of their own states. To prevent the same states, particularly the largest ones, from exercising undue influence in the selection of both the president and vice president, this provision was included.
6. George Mason declared, "Nineteen times out of twenty, the President would be chosen by the Senate." Farrand, *Records of the Federal Convention*, II: 500. The original proposal of the Committee on Unfinished Business was that the Senate should select the president. The delegates substituted the House of Representatives, fearing that the Senate was too powerful with its appointment and treaty-making powers. The principle of equal state representation was retained. Choosing the president is the only occasion on which the House of Representatives votes by state.
7. Thomas R. Marshall, *Presidential Nominations in a Reform Age* (New York, NY: Praeger, 1981), 19.
8. Neal R. Peirce and Lawrence D. Longley, *The People's President* (New Haven, CT: Yale University Press, 1981), 36.
9. Marshall, *Presidential Nominations*, 20.
10. Ibid., 21.
11. Louis Maisel and Gerald J. Lieberman, "The Impact of Electoral Rules on Primary Elections: The Democratic Presidential Primaries in 1976," in Louis Maisel and Joseph Cooper, eds., *The Impact of the Electoral Process* (Beverly Hills, CA: Sage, 1977), 68.
12. Until the passage of the Twentieth Amendment, which set early January as the time that members of Congress took their oaths of office and convened, it was the second session of the preelection Congress that met after the election.
13. Lucius Wilmerding, *The Electoral College* (New Brunswick, NJ: Rutgers University Press, 1953), 32.
14. There were 106 members of the House (fifty-eight Federalists and forty-eight Republicans). On the first ballot, the vote of those present was Burr, 53, and Jefferson, 51.
15. In those days, being secretary of state was considered a stepping-stone to the presidency. With the exception of Washington and John Adams, all the people

who became president prior to Andrew Jackson had first held appointment as secretary of state.

16. Peirce and Longley, *People's President*, 51.

17. Marquis James, *The Life of Andrew Jackson* (Indianapolis, IN: Bobbs-Merrill, 1938), 439.

18. He captured the majority of electoral votes in two of these states because the electors were chosen on a district rather than on a statewide basis. William R. Keech, "Background Paper," in *Winner Take All: Report of the Twentieth Century Fund Task Force on Reform of the Presidential Election Process* (New York, NY: Holmes & Meier, 1978), 50.

19. The act that created the commission specified that its decision would be final unless overturned by both houses of Congress. The House of Representatives, controlled by the Democrats, opposed every one of the commission's findings. The Republican Senate, however, concurred. A Democratic filibuster in the Senate was averted by Hayes's promise of concessions to the South, including the withdrawal of federal troops. Tilden could have challenged the findings of the commission in court but chose not to do so.

20. The Committee consisted of seven Democrats and two Republicans. It was supposed to be bipartisan, but after Speaker Nancy Pelosi rejected two of Kevin McCarthy's nominees, the Republican minority leader refused to appoint any more Republicans to the committee. The two who joined the committee, Liz Cheney and Adam Kinzinger, had voted in favor of impeaching Donald Trump. Bennie Thompson (D-MS) chaired the committee and Liz Cheney (R-WY) was vice chair.

21. The vote tabulated in this county provided some evidence of the confusion. Buchanan's vote was larger in Palm Beach than in any other Florida county. Palm Beach had a large, elderly Jewish population unlikely to have supported Buchanan. Moreover, Palm Beach had a larger percentage of ballots in which no presidential vote was recorded than all but two of the other sixty-seven counties in the state.

22. Four justices dissented from the decision that time had run out. Two of these justices believed that the deadline for the designation of electors specified by US law, the first Monday following the second Wednesday in December (the 18th in 2000), took precedence over the state legislature's date of December 12 and thus provided sufficient time for the state supreme court to establish a single standard for recounting the votes. The two other dissenters felt that the Florida Supreme Court had acted properly, that the vote count was legal, and that it should not have been halted by the US Supreme Court.

23. Two states, Maine and Nebraska, do not always vote as a bloc because they do not select all their electors on an at-large basis. Two are chosen at large and the remaining ones are elected in each of the states' congressional districts. In 2008, Nebraska's electoral vote was divided, with Republican John McCain winning four and Democrat Barack Obama winning one. McCain won the popular statewide vote as well as the vote in two of the state's three congressional districts. In 2016, Trump won one of the two congressional districts in Maine and Clinton the other as well as the overall state vote. Thus, she received three electoral votes to Trump's one in that state; in 2020 Maine split its electoral votes, 3 to 1 for Biden; Nebraska voted 4 in favor of Trump.

24. Nate Silver, "Donald Trump Had a Superior Electoral College Strategy," *Five Thirty Eight*.

25. The 2017 population estimates are from the US Census Bureau.

Chapter ★ ★ ★ ★ ★ 2 Campaign Finance

Introduction

Running for office, especially for the presidency, is expensive. The millions, even billions, spent on presidential candidates pose serious problems for presidential candidates who must raise considerable sums, closely watch their expenses, make important allocation decisions, and conform to the intricacies of finance laws during both the nomination and general election campaigns. In addition, the candidates must coordinate their financial activities with party leaders who must also solicit, distribute, and spend money—more than $1.5 billion in the 2019–2020 election cycle—on behalf of their nominees for national and state office.[1] Such large expenditures raise important issues for a democratic selection process. This chapter explores some of those issues.

The chapter is organized into four sections. The first details the rising costs of running for president. The next section discusses Congress's attempts to regulate federal elections and the Supreme Court's decisions on such laws enacted by Congress since the 1970s. In the third section, the explosion of money in the form of candidate contributions and expenditures as well as the activities of party and nonparty groups are examined. In the fourth and final section, the relationship between money and electoral success is explored.

The Rising Costs of Running for President

Candidates have always spent money in their quest for the presidency, but it was not until they started personal campaigning across the country that these costs began to increase sharply.

When electioneering was conducted within a highly partisan press environment before the Civil War, there were few expenses other than for the occasional biography and campaign pamphlet printed by the party and sold to the public at less than cost. With the advent of more active public campaigning toward the middle of the nineteenth century, candidate organizations turned to buttons, billboards, banners, and pictures to symbolize and illustrate their campaigns.[2] By the beginning of the twentieth century, the cost of this type of advertising in each election exceeded $150,000, a lot of money then but a minuscule amount by contemporary standards.[3]

In 1924, radio was used in presidential campaigns for the first time. The Republicans spent approximately $120,000 that year, and the Democrats spent only $40,000.[4] Four years later, however, the two parties together spent more than $1 million. Radio expenses continued to equal or exceed a million dollars per election for the next twenty years.[5]

Television emerged as a vehicle for presidential campaigning in 1952. Both national party conventions were broadcast on television and on radio. Although there were only nineteen million television sets in the United States at that time, almost one-third of Americans were regular TV viewers. The number of households with television sets rose dramatically over the next four years. By 1956, an estimated 71 percent had television, and by 1968, the figure was close to 95 percent; today, it exceeds 98 percent, with most homes having two or more sets.

The first commercials for presidential candidates also appeared in 1952. They became regular fare thereafter, contributing substantially to campaign costs. Film biographies, interview shows, political rallies, town meetings, and other campaign-related events have all been seen with increasing frequency since then. In 1948, no money was spent on television by either party's candidate. Twenty years later, the cost for television ads was $13 million, approximately one-fourth of the total expenditures of the 1968 campaign. More than fifty years later, billions were spent on television, radio, and social media. The advent of the electronic campaign following World War II was the principal reason campaign costs skyrocketed. In 1960, John Kennedy and Richard Nixon each spent a hundred times the amount Abraham Lincoln had spent one hundred years previously. In the twelve years following the 1960 general election, expenditures increased from about $20 million to more than $90 million, an amount that far outstripped the inflation rate during that period. Table 2.1 lists the costs of the major party candidates in presidential elections from 1860 to 1972, the last general election before Congress enacted legislation to regulate campaign finance.

Prenomination costs have risen rapidly. Until the 1960s, large expenditures were the exception, not the rule, for gaining the party's nomination. General Leonard Wood spent an estimated $2 million in an unsuccessful quest to head the Republican ticket in 1920. The contest between General Dwight D. Eisenhower and Senator Robert A. Taft in 1952 cost about $5 million, a total that was not exceeded until 1964, when Nelson Rockefeller and Barry Goldwater together spent approximately twice that amount.

Before the 1970s, running in the primaries and caucuses were optional; now it is mandatory even for incumbent presidents. They raise and spend money even when they are not seriously challenged. In 1984, the Reagan campaign committee spent almost $28 million during the nomination period, much of it on voter registration drives for the general election; in 1992, it cost George H. W. Bush more than $27 million to defeat Pat Buchanan, a conservative newspaper columnist. Subsequently, incumbents have spent millions running unopposed: Bill Clinton

TABLE 2.1 ★ Costs of Presidential General Elections, Major Party Candidates, 1860–1972

Year	Democratic	Cost	Republican	Cost
1860	Stephen Douglas	$50,000	Abraham Lincoln*	$100,000
1864	George McClellan	50,000	Abraham Lincoln*	125,000
1868	Horatio Seymour	75,000	Ulysses Grant*	150,000
1872	Horace Greeley	50,000	Ulysses Grant*	250,000
1876	Samuel Tilden	900,000	Rutherford Hayes*	950,000
1880	Winfield Hancock	335,000	James Garfield*	1,100,000
1884	Grover Cleveland*	1,400,000	James Blaine	1,300,000
1888	Grover Cleveland	855,000	Benjamin Harrison*	1,350,000
1892	Grover Cleveland*	2,350,000	Benjamin Harrison	1,700,000
1896	William Jennings Bryan	675,000	William McKinley*	3,350,000
1900	William Jennings Bryan	425,000	William McKinley*	3,000,000
1904	Alton Parker	700,000	Theodore Roosevelt*	2,096,000
1908	William Jennings Bryan	629,341	William Taft*	1,655,518
1912	Woodrow Wilson*	1,134,848	William Taft	1,071,549
1916	Woodrow Wilson*	2,284,950	Charles Evans Hughes	2,441,565
1920	James Cox	1,470,371	Warren Harding*	5,417,501
1924	John Davis	1,108,836	Calvin Coolidge*	4,020,478
1928	Alfred Smith	5,342,350	Herbert Hoover*	6,256,111
1932	Franklin Roosevelt*	2,245,975	Herbert Hoover	2,900,052
1936	Franklin Roosevelt*	5,194,751	Alfred Landon	8,892,972
1940	Franklin Roosevelt*	2,783,654	Wendell Willkie	3,451,310
1944	Franklin Roosevelt*	2,169,077	Thomas Dewey	2,828,652
1948	Harry Truman*	2,736,334	Thomas Dewey	2,127,296
1952	Adlai Stevenson	5,032,926	Dwight Eisenhower*	6,608,623
1956	Adlai Stevenson	5,106,651	Dwight Eisenhower*	7,778,702
1960	John Kennedy*	9,797,000	Richard Nixon	10,128,000

TABLE 2.1 ★ Costs of Presidential General Elections, Major Party Candidates, 1860–1972 *continued*				
Year	Democratic	Cost	Republican	Cost
1964	Lyndon Johnson*	8,757,000	Barry Goldwater	16,026,000
1968†	Hubert Humphrey	11,594,000	Richard Nixon*	25,042,000
1972	George McGovern	30,000,000	Richard Nixon*	61,400,000

*Indicates winner.

†George Wallace spent an estimated $7 million as the candidate of the American Independent Party in 1968.

Source: Data based on Herbert E. Alexander, *Financing Politics: Money, Elections, and Political Reform*, 3rd ed. (Washington DC: Congressional Quarterly Press, 1984). *Financing Politics: Money, Elections, and Political Reform*, 3rd ed. By Herbert E. Alexander. Copyright 1984 by Congressional Quarterly, a division of SAGE Publications, Inc.

almost $35 million, George W. Bush over $250 million, Barack Obama $211 million, and Donald Trump $835 million before 2020 and $500 million after it. Table 2.2 lists the costs of major party nominations from 1964 through 2020.

Throughout most of US electoral history, parties and candidates depended on large contributions from individual donors. Now they depend on candidate-oriented political action committees (PACs), often funded by billionaires, to do so.

The Regulation of Campaign Finance

Reacting to these issues, in the 1970s Congress enacted far-reaching legislation designed to reduce dependence on large donors, increase the transparency of revenues and expenditures, discourage illegal contributions, broaden the base of public giving, and control escalating costs at the presidential level. Additionally, the Democratically controlled Congress that passed these laws designed them to equalize the funds available to the nominees of both parties.

The Federal Election Campaign Act

The Federal Election Campaign Act (FECA), enacted in 1971, set ceilings on the amount of money presidential and vice presidential candidates and their families could contribute to their own campaigns. It allowed unions and corporations, which had been prohibited from contributing, to form PACs, consisting of their members, employees, and stockholders, to solicit voluntary contributions for candidates or parties. The FECA also established procedures for public disclosure of contributions given to nonparty groups over a certain amount.

A second statute, the Revenue Act of 1971, created tax credits and deductions to encourage private contributions. It also provided for public funding by creating a presidential election campaign fund. Financed by an income tax check-off provision, the fund initially allowed taxpayers to designate one dollar of their federal income taxes to a special presidential election account.

TABLE 2.2 ★ Costs of Presidential Nominations, 1964–2020 (in millions)		
	Expenditures	
Year	Democrats	Republicans
1964	(uncontested)	$10.0
1968	$25.0	20.0
1972	33.1	*
1976	40.7	26.1
1980	41.7	86.1
1984	107.7	28.0
1988	94.0	114.6
1992	66.0†	51.0
1996	41.8	182.0
2000	95.8	247.2
2008	1,043.9	450.2
2012	211.4	283.2
2016	834.7	667.5
2020	1,424.3	1,579.2

*During a primary in which Richard M. Nixon's renomination was virtually assured, Representative John M. Ashbrook spent $740,000 and Representative Paul N. McCloskey $550,000 in challenging Nixon.

†Estimates based on Alexander and Corrado, *Financing the 1992 Elections*, Tables 2.1 and 2.4.

Sources: 1964–1972, Herbert E. Alexander, *Financing Politics* (Washington, DC: Congressional Quarterly, 1976), 45–47, Copyright © 1984 by Congressional Quarterly Press, a Division of SAGE Publications, Inc. Reprinted by permission; 1976–1984, Federal Election Commission, "Reports on Financial Activity, 1987–88," *Presidential Pre-Nomination Campaigns* (August 1989), Table A.7, 10; Herbert E. Alexander, "Financing the Presidential Elections" (paper presented at the Institute for Political Studies in Tokyo, Japan, September 8–10, 1989), 4, 10; 1988–1992, Herbert E. Alexander and Anthony Corrado, *Financing the 1992 Elections* (Armonk, NY: Sharpe, 1995), Copyright © 1995 by M. E. Sharpe, Inc. Reprinted with permission of the publisher; 1996–2020, updated by author from data published by the Federal Election Commission, "Presidential Pre-Nomination Campaign Disbursements."

These laws began a period of federal government regulation of national elections that has continued into the twenty-first century. The history of that regulation is a history of good intentions built on political compromise but marred by unintended consequences of the legislation and its implementation as candidates, parties, and nonparty groups have tried and succeeded in circumventing the letter and spirit of the law to gain electoral advantage.

Partisan compromises in the enactment of campaign finance legislation were evident from the outset. Although the original funding provision was enacted in 1971, it did not go into effect until the 1976 presidential election.

Most Republicans, including President Nixon, opposed the policy of government financial support and regulation. In addition to conflicting with the Grand Old Party's (GOP) belief that the national government's role in the conduct of elections be limited, the legislation offset the Republicans' traditional fundraising advantage. President Nixon was persuaded to sign the public funding bill, however, after Democrats agreed to delay the date the law would go into effect until after his likely reelection.

The 1972 election was marked by heavy-handed fundraising tactics. The Nixon campaign in that election cycle raised more money than in any other previous presidential campaign. In addition to aggressive solicitation, the expenditures of the Nixon reelection effort also became an issue, albeit after the election. Investigative reporting by *Washington Post* and hearings conducted by a Senate committee revealed that the Committee to Reelect the President, referred to by Nixon's opponents as CREEP, had spent some of its funds on "dirty tricks" and other unethical and illegal activities, such as the break-in at the Democratic National Committee's (DNC's) headquarters at the Watergate office building. These revelations aroused public ire and created the incentive for a Democratically controlled Congress to enact new and even more stringent legislation.

In 1974, the FECA was amended to include public disclosure provisions, contribution ceilings for individuals and groups, spending limits for the campaigns, federal subsidies for major party candidates in the nomination process, and complete funding for them in the general election. The law also restricted the amount candidates could contribute to their own campaign and the amount that others could spend independently on their behalf. Finally, it established a six-person commission, the Federal Election Commission (FEC), to implement and enforce the law.

The 1974 amendments were highly controversial. Critics immediately charged a federal giveaway as a raid on the Treasury. Opponents of the legislation also argued that the limits on contributions and spending violated their constitutionally guaranteed right to freedom of speech, that the funding provisions unfairly discriminated against third-party and independent candidates, and that Congress's appointment of some of the commissioners violated the separation of powers.

The *Buckley v. Valeo* Decision

In 1976 in the landmark case of *Buckley v. Valeo*, 424 U.S. 1 (1976), the Supreme Court upheld the right of Congress to regulate campaign contributions and expenditures but negated the overall limits on spending by individuals and nonparty groups and the appointment by Congress of four of the six election commissioners. The majority opinion in that case contended that by placing restrictions on the amount of money a person or an organization could spend during a campaign, the law directly and substantially restrained freedom of speech, a freedom protected by the First Amendment.

The Supreme Court did allow limits on contributions to candidates for federal office, however, and limits on expenditures of those candidates who accepted public funds but not those who refused these funds. By holding that contributions and expenditures of presidential candidates could be limited, the justices acknowledged that large, often secret contributions and rapidly increasingly expenditures did pose problems for a democratic election process, problems that Congress could address.

The court's decision required that the election law be amended once again. It took Congress several months to do so. In the spring of 1976, during the presidential primaries of that year, amendments to the legislation were enacted that continued public funding of the presidential nomination and election campaigns, based on a figure of $10 million in 1974 to be adjusted for inflation, but did so on a voluntary basis. Candidates did not have to accept government funds, but if they did, they were limited in how much they and others could contribute to their own campaigns and how much those campaigns could spend. The FEC was reconstituted with all six members to be nominated by the president and appointed subject to the advice and consent of the Senate. The law required that three commissioners be Democrats and three be Republicans to ensure that the commission would be fair to both major parties.

With limited amounts of money available, the candidates opted to spend most of it on television advertising. Gone were the buttons, bumper stickers, and other election paraphernalia that had characterized previous campaigns. Fewer resources were directed toward grassroots organizing. Turnout fell. The national parties lost influence. Congress was concerned.

The Soft Money Loophole and Other Amendments

In 1979, additional amendments to the FECA were enacted to rectify these problems. To encourage voluntary activities and higher voter turnout, the amendments allowed party committees at the national, state, and local levels to raise and spend unlimited amounts of money for party-building activities such as registration and getting out the vote. Known as the soft money provision, this amendment, as interpreted by the FEC, created a gigantic loophole in the law. It permitted, even encouraged, the major parties to solicit large contributions and distribute the money to their state and local affiliates as they saw fit. Pandora's box had been opened, although it took another decade and a half to exploit it fully. Later amendments to the FECA increased the base grant for nominating conventions of the major parties to $3 million in 1979 and $4 million in 1984 (adjusted to inflation). Congress eliminated this grant entirely in 2014.

It was not until 1993 that the law was amended again to increase the amount of money in the fund used to subsidize candidates for their party's presidential nomination and provide general election grants. Congress's failure to tie the amount of money taxpayers could designate for the fund to inflation, the decline in the percentage of taxpayers making such a designation, and the increasing number of candidates vying for their party's nominations all contributed to a treasury shortfall that was only expected to get worse in the years ahead. To rectify the problem, Congress increased the income tax checkoff from $1 to $3, a little less than the cost-of-living adjustment since the provision had originally gone into effect. However, the portion of taxpayers designating a payment to the fund had fallen significantly from its high of 28.7 percent in 1980 to about 5 percent in 2020.

A new problem of a different magnitude emerged in 1996—the exploitation of the soft money loophole to circumvent the law's intended contribution and expenditure limits. This exploitation resulted from a creative interpretation of the 1979 amendments by President Clinton's political advisers, the major parties, subsequently the FEC, and finally, the courts. Here's what happened.

In 1995, Clinton and his advisers began planning for the president's reelection campaign. Their strategy was to position Clinton as a centrist by airing a series of advertisements that touted his record and favorably contrasted it with that of the congressional Republicans. The ad campaign was costly. After $2 million was spent by the president's reelection committee in summer 1995, the president's advisers feared that there would not be sufficient funds left to handle a challenge for the Democratic nomination if one developed and also respond to a strong Republican opponent prior to the nominating conventions. They resolved this dilemma by turning to soft money. Since the commercials that the Clinton administration aired were policy oriented and did not specifically and directly urge the president's reelection, the president's advisers (and Democratic Party lawyers) contended that the party could pay for the ads with soft money, which the president would help raise.

What followed was a frantic, no-holds-barred fundraising effort in which the president and the vice president actively participated. Inducements to contribute included dinners with the president and vice president at expensive Washington hotels, sleepovers in the Lincoln bedroom in the White House, state dinners with world leaders, rounds of golf with Clinton, trips on Air Force One, VIP treatment at Democratic Party functions such as its 1996 nominating convention, and even invitations to join the commerce secretary on official US trade missions abroad. Naturally, Republicans were outraged by these activities, particularly the use of public office for partisan purposes. Their party officials and elected leadership protested and congressional investigations followed, but no action was taken. In the end, the Republicans resorted to the same tactics as the Democrats, using their control of Congress as leverage to raise soft money. They eventually netted more of it than did the Democrats.

The Bipartisan Campaign Reform Act

The soft money issue reemerged during the 2000 nomination campaign. Republican candidate John McCain and Democrat Bill Bradley promised, if elected, to support a ban on soft money. Although neither candidate's bid for their party's nomination was successful, the campaign finance issue remained salient; it put presidential candidates, George W. Bush and Al Gore, on the defensive and led to cries for reform. In April 2001, the Senate enacted the Bipartisan Campaign Reform Act (BCRA) to close the soft money loophole. The legislation also restricted the use of the principal instrument by which nonparty advocacy groups had tried to affect the election's outcome—issue advocacy advertising. Nine months later, the House of Representatives followed suit, and in March 2002, the legislation became law.

The BCRA banned the national party committees from raising soft money, but to compensate, the new law also raised individual and overall federal contribution limits to candidates and parties and restricted the use of issue advocacy ads, in which candidates were cited by name, to periods that exceeded thirty days before a primary and sixty days before the general election. Exemptions, however, remained for tax-exempt organizations.

Opponents of the law immediately questioned its constitutionality. Such disparate groups as the National Rifle Association, the American Civil Liberties Union, and the Christian Coalition argued that the ban on issue advocacy advertising in the final days of the nomination and general election campaign violated the First Amendment's protections of freedom of speech and the press. The Republican National Committee claimed that the prohibition on soft money violated the state parties' right to raise money to organize and mobilize voters in elections, while groups representing poorer Americans contended that the increase in amount of money that could be contributed by individual donors violated the rights of less wealthy people under the Fifth Amendment's equal protection clause. Supporters of the legislation included the FEC, Common Cause and other public interest groups, and twenty-one state attorneys general.

Anticipating a constitutional challenge, the drafters of the legislation included a provision for a quick judicial review. One year later, on December 10, 2003, as the nomination process was underway, the Supreme Court issued its ruling in the case of *McConnell v. FEC*, 540 U.S. 93 (2003). By a 5–4 vote, the justices upheld most of the provisions of the BCRA, including the ban on soft money solicitation by the national parties and the limits placed on issue advocacy ads that identified specific candidates in the closing month of primaries and sixty days or less in the general election. It was left to the FEC to regulate enforcement.

The FEC issued a series of regulations, some of which were contentious, that the courts invalidated. One of the most controversial involved "nonpolitical" organizations, which the FEC had indicated were not subject to the soft money restrictions. But how was nonpolitical to be defined? Did it mean that the group could not engage in political activities, that most of its expenditures could not be devoted to electioneering, or that its primary purpose could not be to elect a specific candidate?

The question was more than a theoretical one. It had practical and immediate consequences. The reason is that Democrats, fearing that the prohibition on soft money would place their party at a competitive disadvantage, had turned to nonprofit, nonpartisan groups to raise unlimited amounts of money and spend it on election-related activities. Sponsors of the BCRA and their supporters urged the

FEC to regulate these groups in accordance with the intent of the law to prohibit soft money in national elections. Republicans who had previously opposed the law also urged the FEC to issue new regulations to prohibit nonparty groups from engaging in these activities. However, the commission voted 4–2 not to do so.

After the election, and with prodding from a federal judge, the commission said that it would regulate these groups on an ad hoc basis rather than prescribe general rules for all of them. It fined four of the groups, two Democratic and two Republican, a total of $1.38 million for not registering as political organizations and for accepting contributions that exceeded the legal amount. Because the groups raised millions, the fines were considered minimal—the cost of doing business. It has not deterred similar "nonpolitical" groups from large-scale fundraising during subsequent presidential campaigns.

Although the Supreme Court upheld Congress's right to prohibit advocacy ads in which candidates are identified by name in the final days before the election, the issue came up again in 2006 after a pro-life group in Wisconsin sued the FEC for ruling that the group's advocacy ads violated the sixty-day rule before the election. During fall 2006, the group had urged people to write to their senators opposing the confirmation delay of several of President George W. Bush's judicial nominations. Mentioned in the ad were the names of the state's two senators, Russell Feingold and Herbert Kohl, but not their voting records on nomination or abortion-related issues. Feingold was running for reelection that year. A three-judge federal court reversed the FEC's ruling on the grounds that the group's freedom of speech was violated. In 2007, the Supreme Court agreed to review the lower court ruling.

The Court's *Citizens United* Decision

One year later, during the 2008 nomination campaign, a conservative, nonprofit corporation, Citizens United, produced a documentary film attacking Hillary Rodham Clinton. The film was made available to movie theaters and sold as a DVD. Citizens United also wanted to distribute it on cable television as a paid-for video and intended to run advertisements informing the public of the film's availability. The FEC, however, ruled that a movie produced by a corporation at its expense violated the ban on corporate spending in federal elections. The commission also indicated that advertising for the film would be subject to the disclosure provision of the BCRA. A lower court that considered the controversy also ruled against Citizens United, prompting the corporation to appeal the case to the Supreme Court.

That court heard oral arguments on both cases, the Wisconsin "pro-life" group and Citizens United, in March 2009 and then asked the parties to reargue the case in September of that year. Solicitor General Elena Kagan, later nominated by President Obama to the Supreme Court, defended the government's position validating the election law. In January 2010, the Supreme Court issued its decision in the case of *Citizens United v. Federal Election Commission*, 558 U.S. 310 (2010).

A 5–4 majority concluded that corporations have free speech rights that are protected by the First Amendment. In the words of the justice who wrote the majority opinion, Anthony Kennedy, "If the First Amendment has any force, it prohibits Congress from fining or jailing citizens, or associations of citizens, for simply engaging in political speech."[6] Justice John Paul Stevens, author of the dissent, retorted, "At bottom, the Court's opinion is . . . a rejection of the common sense of the American people who have recognized a need to prevent corporations from undermining self-government since the founding, and who have fought against the distinctive corrupting potential of corporation electioneering since the days of Theodore Roosevelt."[7] The Court did not invalidate the BCRA's disclosure requirements or the limits that the law placed on the size of contributions to candidates in federal elections (table 2.3).

The *Citizens United* decision was criticized by Democrats who feared that groups with access to large amounts of money would be able to exercise undue influence on American elections. Republicans contended that freedom of speech, a basic right of Americans, individually and collectively, had been preserved.

Following the court's decision, a unanimous Court of Appeals ruled that the *Citizens United* judgment also applied to other nonparty groups. This ruling enabled the candidates, or more precisely their aides, friends, and financial backers, to establish their own, candidate-oriented groups, called Super PACs. As a consequence, money poured into the 2012 campaign.

In 2014, the Supreme Court went further. In the case of *McCutcheon v. FEC*, 572 U.S. 185 (2014), another 5–4 majority ruled that the aggregate limits the law placed on individual contributions to all federal candidates, party committees, and nonparty groups abridged freedom of speech and was thus unconstitutional. This decision raised the question about whether the court might revisit (and revise) its 1976 *Buckley v. Valeo* judgment that permitted Congress to limit the amounts contributed to candidates for federal office.

The Money Explosion

The BCRA, the *Citizens United* decision, and the revolution in communications technology have significantly affected campaign finance. They have permitted the amount of money raised and spent by candidates to increase as well as the number of donors, both large and small, to these campaigns. The rise in individual contribution limits (from $1 to $3 and adjusted for inflation) increased the incentive for campaigns to expand their fundraising activities among the public, but the percentage of taxpayers willing to have their tax dollars used for public funding declined markedly.

Candidate Revenues

Candidates for their party's nomination in 2004 were the first to benefit from the change. In that competitive Democratic nomination, $347.5 million was received from 338,735 individual donors. President George W. Bush, running unopposed for the Republican nomination, took in $257.4 million from 190,332 contributors. In 2008, with campaigns in both parties, Republican candidates raised a total of $405.1 million and Democrats $689.9 million prior to their party's political conventions. In 2012, with no opposition, Obama raised $409 million prior to the

TABLE 2.3 Contribution Limits for the 2023–2024 Election Cycle

Donor	Recipient				
	Candidate Committee	PAC† (SSF and nonconnected)	Party committee: state/district/local	Party committee: national	Party committee: national
Individual	$3,300* per election	$5,000 per year	$10,000 per year (combined)	$41,300* per year	$123,900* per year
Candidate committee	$2,000 per election	$5,000 per year	Unlimited transfers	Unlimited transfers	
PAC: multicandidate	$5,000 per election	$5,000 per year	$5,000 per year (combined)	$15,000 per year	$45,000 per year
PAC; non-multicandidate	$3,300* per election	$5,000 per year	$10,000 per year (combined)	$41,300* per year	$123,900* per year
Party committee: state/district/local	$5,000 per election	$5,000 per year	Unlimited transfers	Unlimited transfers	
Party committee: national	$5,000 per election**	$5,000 per year	Unlimited transfers	Unlimited transfers	

* Indexed for inflation in odd-numbered years.

† "PAC" here refers to a committee that makes contributions to other federal political committees. Independent-expenditure-only political committees (sometimes called "Super PACs") may accept unlimited contributions, including from corporations and labor organizations.

‡ The limits in this column apply to a national party committee's accounts for: (i) the presidential nominating convention; (ii) election recounts and contests and other legal proceedings; and (iii) national party headquarters buildings. A party's national committee, Senate campaign committee and House campaign committee are each considered separate national party committees with separate limits. Only a national party committee, not the parties' national congressional campaign committees, may have an account for the presidential nominating convention.

Source: Federal Election Commission. "Contribution Limits for 2023–2024." https://www.fec.gov/resources/cms-content/documents/contribution_limits_chart_2023-2024.pdf

Democratic convention and $337 million after it (a total of $746 million); many of his contributors were small donors. Romney raised almost $90 million before and during the competitive phase of the Republican caucuses and primaries and a little more than $500 million after it (a total of $596 million). During the 2015–2016 election cycle, Clinton raised $563.8 million and Trump $333.1 million, of which $66.1 million came from his own personal wealth. Four years later, Trump's revenues totaled $789.8 thousand, but he did not contribute to his own campaign. Biden's total for the nomination and election was $1.1 billion in 2020.[8]

Funds raised but not spent by candidates in their campaigns for other federal offices can be used in their quest for the presidential nomination. John McCain transferred $2 million from his Senate account to fund the initial stages of his 2000 campaign for the Republican nomination and $22 million in 2008. Hillary Clinton transferred $10 million in 2016 as did most Democratic candidates in 2020. The ability to tap these funds encourages potential candidates in the House and Senate to raise as much money as they can prior to an anticipated bid for their party's presidential nomination.

The FECA provides public funding to presidential candidates, matching grants for the nomination process, and a general grant for the election. George W. Bush did not accept government grants in 2000. The reason he did not do so is because accepting federal funds places limits on candidate spending.

The three to five months that usually separate the contested phase of the nominations from the national nominating conventions put a primary winner who accepted federal funds at a considerable financial disadvantage during this period, making them dependent on the support of the party and nonparty groups. In 2000, George W. Bush was the first major party candidate to refuse preconvention funds for these reasons. Beginning in 2004, it became standard practice for most nominees of the major parties to do so. In 2016, only Democrat Martin O'Malley and Green Party candidate Jill Stein accepted public funds that totaled $1.5 million. The law also restricts general election funding to the size of the federal grant. Unless the law is changed, spending limits increased, and supplementary private contributions allowed, the only major party candidates likely to accept public funds in the future will be those who have no other viable options.

Minor party candidates are also eligible to receive federal funds in the general election, but only an amount equal to their proportion of the popular vote, provided it is 5 percent or more. They get this grant after the election unless their party received the minimum percentage or more in the previous election. Using his own wealth to fund his 1992 presidential campaign, H. Ross Perot, a candidate of his newly created Reform Party, received 19 percent of the popular vote, making his party eligible for $29 million in the next election. Perot accepted these funds for his 1996 campaign. The Reform Party candidate in 2000, Pat Buchanan, received $12.6 million in 2000 but fell short of the 5 percent threshold needed to be eligible for automatic federal funds thereafter. No minor party candidate since then has received the required percentage to be eligible for federal funds.

Campaign Expenditures

Candidates

More than $4 billion was spent on the 2019–2022 presidential campaign. Slightly more than half of that amount was spent by the candidates' campaigns; outside groups spent the balance. For the candidates, the largest single item on which money was spent was mass media. About 60 percent of total campaign expenditures was directed toward the production and airing of advertisements on radio, television, and the internet, plus the cost charged by media consultants and their firms. Other costs included fundraising as salaries, travel, computing, and office rentals.

Political Parties

The national party organizations tend to remain neutral during the primaries and caucuses. They impose the rules that frame the process, but their leadership usually remains on the sideline until the nominee has been effectively decided. In 2016, the DNC did not and provided behind-the-scenes help to Hillary Clinton in her quest against Bernie Sanders. State party leaders, on the other hand, frequently endorse individual candidates and help bolster their campaigns with organizational support and access to financial resources.

Once the nominee is effectively determined, the national party gets involved. It coordinates fundraising with its future standard-bearer, a coordination that is necessary because both presidential campaign and party solicit contributions from the same base of donors. Although national parties can no longer accept soft money, they can accept individual and group contributions that are indexed to inflation. The amount that can be contributed to national party organizations was substantially increased by Congress in 2014, the same year in which federal grants to parties for their conventions was eliminated. In addition, each party's House and Senate campaign committees raise money as do state and local party organizations.

Once a candidate has been officially nominated, the political party can coordinate spending with its presidential candidate's campaign as well as spend unlimited money independently on its nominee's behalf. The national party committees have raised and spent record amounts during the last four presidential election cycles. Table 2.4 lists their revenues in recent election cycles.

Until the Supreme Court's *Citizens United* decision, corporations and labor unions were prohibited from making direct contributions to political candidates. Unions got around this restriction in 1944 by asking their members to make voluntary contributions into a separate political fund to help reelect Franklin D. Roosevelt. The fund maintained its own bank account and administrative structure. It was the first PAC that operated in the presidential electoral process.

TABLE 2.4 ★ National Party Revenues and Expenditures in Recent Election Cycles (in Millions)

Year	Democrats		Republicans	
	Revenue	Expenditure	Revenue	Expenditure
2007–2008	$763.3	746.5	792.9	766.1
2011–2012	800.1	784.1	803.5	786.9
2015–2016	870.2	843.3	752.4	706.7
2019–2020	1,527.5	1,424.3	1,662.0	1,579.2

Source: Federal Election Commission, "Federal Financial Activity of Party Committees."

Political Action Committees

The campaign finance legislation enacted in the 1970s, and revised in 2002, opened this activity to corporation employees and stockholders, people associated with trade associations, and other nonconnected groups, those that did not have a formal business or labor tie. The legislation also placed limits on the size of the contributions they could make ($5,000 per candidate; $15,000 per party) and receive ($5,000 from an individual donor). PACs had to register with the FEC and file periodic reports.

Because of the limited size of the contributions they could accept, PACs have not become a major source of funding for presidential candidates. Prospective presidential candidates regularly set up their own Leadership and Advocacy PACs to help support their preelection activity, paying for staff and consultants, travel, and other incidental expenses as well as making contributions to other candidates whose support they hope to gain for a presidential campaign. These PACs help establish a donor base and generate visibility for their ideas and policy positions.

Nonpolitical Groups

When the soft money spigot was turned off in 2002 by the BCRA, party activists and interest group leaders looked for other ways to solicit large contributions from the wealthy individuals and groups to use in federal campaigns. They turned to nonpolitical groups, such as social welfare and nonprofit organizations, to do so. These groups are allowed to accept unrestricted contributions and involve themselves in political activities as long as their primary purpose is not political. They must spend less than half their budget on election activities. Organized under provisions 527 and 501c of the Internal Revenue code, the groups must receive government approval for tax-exempt status.

Although the 521 and 501c nonpolitical groups were allowed to accept unlimited contributions, the Supreme Court's *Citizens United* decision allowed corporations, labor unions, and candidate-centered groups, termed Super PACs, to do the same. They are deemed independent expenditure groups. They cannot contribute to a candidate's campaign nor coordinate their electoral activities with those campaigns, but they can raise and spend unlimited amounts of money in federal elections.

They do not have to identify their donors, a reason why many Super PACs have established their own 501c groups to provide anonymity to donors who want it. The term used to describe these contributions is "dark money." These groups played a major role in the buildup to the 2024 Republican nomination. Donald Trump, Ron DeSantis, Mike Pence, Nikki Haley, Tim Scott, and other Republicans raised and spent millions in 2021 and 2022 to position themselves for a possible run for the GOP's 2024 nomination.

The proliferation of regular Super PACs and 501c PACs has focused early fundraising on large donors, which in turn, has contributed to the public's belief that wealthy interests exercise disproportionate undue influence on candidates and election outcomes. Big contributors gain more access to elected officials, receive more invitations to government briefings and social events, and more appointments to public office.

Money and Electoral Success

The relationship between money and electoral success has spurred considerable debate in recent years and generated much criticism from those who believe unequal resources undermine democratic elections in the United States. Do those with more money have an advantage? Do they usually win? The simple answer is usually yes, but the longer answer is more complicated. First, who has or gets the money? Second, what difference does the money make in the election?

Two types of candidates tend to have more resources at their disposal: those who are personally wealthy and those who are well-known and well-connected public figures. Wealth can buy public recognition, as it did for Ross Perot in the 1992 and 1996 general elections and Steve Forbes in 1996 and 2000 Republican primaries and Michael Bloomberg in 2020, but it obviously cannot buy an election victory, as they also found out. Similarly, party front-runners, can raise more money because they are perceived as likely to win their party's nomination, but again there are advantages but no guarantees for victory.

Money matters most when the candidates are least known to the voters, when they do not receive a lot of news coverage, and when paid advertising, which, is expensive, can bring recognition and enhance images, factors more prevalent during the nomination process than during the presidential election. As the race begins, money buys name recognition, organizational support, computer equipment and analysts, and campaign consultants; over the course of the campaign, it purchases advertising, digital outreach, and a grassroots operation.

In general elections, the candidates with the largest bankrolls have generally been more successful, although it is difficult to determine precisely whether money contributed to victory or simply flowed to the likely winner. Between 1860 and 1972, more money was spent on the winner of the presidency than the loser twenty-two out of thirty elections. Republican candidates have spent more than their Democratic opponents in twenty-five out of thirty elections during this period. The five times they did not, the Democrats won.

The correlation between money and electoral success has continued in the contemporary period. In the 1980s, considerably more was spent on behalf of Republican nominees than on their Democratic opponents, and the GOP won each presidential election during this period. In the 1990s, the Democrats benefited from substantial expenditures by organized labor, which helped to equalize resources for both major parties' presidential candidates.

George W. Bush was financial as well as electoral victor in 2000; in 2004, however, the amount of money each side had in the general election was about equal and the results of the vote were very close. In 2008, Obama had a significant financial advantage and probably enlarged his general election victory as a consequence. In 2012, he raised more money than did Romney, but outside groups spent more on the Romney campaign. In 2016, spending more did not help Hillary Clinton win in the Electoral College although it might have contributed to her popular vote victory. In 2020, Biden's larger war chest contributed to his victory, particularly in the swing states.

What do all these trends suggest? According to political scientist Larry Bartels, "campaign spending has had a significant electoral impact in presidential elections from 1952 to 2004."[9] It has benefited the party that has spent the most, the Republicans. Bartels concludes that campaign spending increases the probability of voter support, particularly among the most affluent voters.[10] The closer the election, the more the disparity in funds can make a difference.

Summary

Campaign finance became an important aspect of presidential elections by the end of the nineteenth and the beginning of the twentieth centuries. In recent years, however, it has become even more significant because costs have escalated, and legal restrictions have limited large gifts to candidates but not to outside groups. As a consequence, more money donated by more people to more groups has supplemented presidential campaigns but has also magnified the difficulty of candidates controlling their own campaigns because the largest contributions go to PACs supporting them or the policies they advocate than to their campaigns.

In the early and mid-twentieth century, candidates of both major parties turned to large contributors for financial support. Their dependence on a relatively small number of large donors, combined with spiraling costs, created serious problems for a democratic election process. The 1972 presidential election, with its high expenditures, "dirty tricks," and illegal campaign contributions, vividly illustrated these problems and generated public pressure on Congress to regulate campaign finance.

In the 1970s, Congress enacted and amended the Federal Election Campaign Act to bring donors into the open, to limit the size of their contributions, and to provide government subsidies to reduce the burdens of fundraising. These reforms were designed to produce a less costly, more equitable, more visible, and candidate-centered presidential selection process. The Federal Election Commission was also established to monitor the election financial activities and oversee compliance of the laws.

The legislation was only partially successful, however. It increased the importance of having a large base of contributors during the preconvention period but did not reduce the time and energy spent on fundraising nor the incentive to "max out" donors. It produced greater equity by limiting the size of contributions and by providing federal subsidies but did not level the playing field evenly among the candidates. During the nomination stage, well-known and well-funded candidates were still advantaged.

The campaign finance laws also contributed to fractionalization of the major parties by providing financial incentives for candidates who might otherwise not have had have not had the money to run. Moreover, it has encouraged the formation and involvement of nonparty groups, which supplement the campaigns of the major party candidates but cannot coordinate their efforts with the candidates and their parties. Finally, the law has increased public information about campaign finance but has also forced campaigns to engage in additional bookkeeping and reporting procedures, which in turn have increased the costs of their campaigns.

In the 1980s, Congress amended the law to allow the parties to solicit unlimited contributions for party-building activities. This loophole undermined the equity goal of the original legislation and generated a "no-holds-barred" race to tap the wealthy. The Bipartisan Campaign Reform Act of 2002 sought to end this race by banning the national parties from soliciting these types of donations. To compensate the parties for this loss of revenue, the law doubled individual contribution limits and indexed them to inflation.

Along with the development of the internet as a cheap, quick, and broad-based fundraising tool, the candidates were incentivized to rely on private funding solely rather than accept federal funds and the limits those funds imposed, effectively undermining public funding of presidential elections.

The Supreme Court's decision in the *Citizens United* case opened the door further to large individual and group nonparty contributions and expenditures, reigniting the debate over the influence of the wealthy on campaigns and elections. The increasing proportion of the electorate that contributes to campaigns, the explosion of Super PACs and the expansion of their election activities, and the demise of federal funding have contributed to the rise in expenditures in presidential as well as congressional elections, but in 2012 and 2016, the candidates that had the most money spent on their behalf lost. In 2020, they did not. Having more money helps, but it obviously does not guarantee victory.

Exercises

1. During the preelection period, see if you can identify the Leadership and Super PACs that potential Republican and Democratic candidates have created for their presidential campaigns. You can find these groups on the website of open secrets.org. Note the amount of money these groups have raised and how they have spent it.

2. Compile a running summary of revenue and expenditures as filed with the FEC (www.fec.gov) by candidates who have officially declared themselves for

their party's 2024 presidential nomination. Does the differential in their war chests explain their respective campaign activities or their position in the public opinion polls?

3. List the funds raised and spent by the major party candidates in the 2024 general election. Note how the news media have reported these revenues and expenditures as part of their narrative on status of the candidates in the preelection polls and the election results.

Selected Readings

"President Trump, with RNC, Helped Raised More Small Donor Money than President Obama, as Much as Clinton and Sanders Combined." Campaign Finance Institute, February 21, 2017.

Christenson, Dino P., and Corwin D. Smidt. "Following the Money: Super PACs and the 2012 Presidential Nomination." *Presidential Studies Quarterly* 44 (September 2014): 410–30.

Corrado, Anthony. "Party Finance in the Wake of BCRA: An Overview." In Michael J. Malbin, ed., *The Election after Reform: Money, Politics and the Bipartisan Campaign Reform Act*. Lanham, MD: Rowman and Littlefield, 2006.

Corrado, Anthony, Michael J. Malbin, Thomas E. Mann, and Norman J. Ornstein. *Reform in an Age of Networked Campaigns*. Washington, DC: Campaign Finance Institute, Brookings Institution, and the American Enterprise Institute, 2010.

Drutman, Lee. "The Political 1% of the 1% in 2012." Sunlight Foundation, June 24, 2013.

Gilens, Martin. *Affluence and Influence: Economic Inequality and Political Power in America*. Princeton, NJ: Princeton University Press, 2012.

Koerth-Baker, Maggie. "How Money Affects Elections." *Fivethirtyeight.com*, September 10, 2018.

Malbin, Michael J. "Small Donors, Large Donors and the Internet." Campaign Finance Institute, March 25, 2010.

———, ed. *The Election after Reform: Money, Politics and the Bipartisan Campaign Reform Act*. Lanham, MD: Rowman and Littlefield, 2006.

Malbin, Michael J., and Brendan Glavin. "CFI's Guide to Money in Federal Elections—2016 in Historical Perspective." Campaign Finance Institute, 2018.

Mayer, Jane. *Dark Money: The Hidden History of the Billionaires behind the Rise of the Radical Right*. New York, NY: Doubleday, 2016.

Mutch, Robert E. *Campaign Finance; What Everyone Needs to Know*. New York, NY: Oxford University Press, 2016.

Notes

1. Federal Election Commission, "Statistical Summary of Campaign Activity."
2. Herbert E. Alexander, "Making Sense about Dollars in the 1980 Presidential Campaigns," in Michael J. Malbin, ed., *Money and Politics in the United States* (Washington, DC: American Enterprise Institute/Chatham House, 1984), 24.
3. Ibid.
4. Edward W. Chester, *Radio, Television, and American Politics* (New York, NY: Sheed & Ward, 1969), 21.

5. Herbert E. Alexander, *Financing Politics: Money, Elections, and Political Reform*, 3rd ed. (Washington, DC: Congressional Quarterly, 1984), 11–12.

6. *Citizens United v. Federal Election Commission*, 558 U.S. 310 (2010).

7. Ibid.

8. Anna Massoglia, "Trump's Political Operation Raises over $500 million after 2020 Election, Despite Increased Scrutiny." Open Secrets. September 8, 2022.

9. Larry M. Bartels, *Unequal Democracy: The Political Economy of the New Gilded Age*. (Princeton, NJ: Princeton University Press, 2008), 120.

10. Ibid., 120–22.

Chapter

3

The Political Environment

Introduction

The nature of the electorate influences the content, images, and strategies of the campaign and affects the outcome of the election—an obvious conclusion to be sure, but one that is not always appreciated. Campaigns are not conducted in ignorance of the voters. Rather, they are calculated to appeal to the needs and desires, attitudes and opinions, and associations and interactions of the electorate within the environment in which the election occurs.

Voters do not come to the election with completely open minds. They come with preexisting views. They do not see and hear the campaign in isolation. They observe it and absorb it as part of their daily lives. In other words, people's attitudes and associations affect their perceptions and influence their behavior. Preexisting beliefs and opinions make it important for students of presidential elections to examine the formation of political attitudes and the patterns of social interaction.

Who votes and who does not? Why do people vote for certain candidates and not others? Do campaign appeals affect voting behavior? Are the responses of the electorate predictable? Political scientists have been interested in these questions for some time. Politicians have been interested in them for even longer.

A great deal of social science research and political savvy has gone into finding the answers to these questions. Spurred by the development of sophisticated survey techniques, methods of data analysis, and experimental research, political scientists, sociologists, and social psychologists have uncovered a wealth of information about public reactions and the electorate's behavior during a campaign. They have examined correlations between demographic characteristics and voter turnout. They have explored psychological motivations, social influences, and political pressures that contribute to voting decisions. They have even done research on the genetic components of attitudes, participation, and voting. This chapter discusses some of their findings.

Organized into three parts, the chapter first looks at who votes. After describing the expansion of suffrage in the nineteenth and twentieth centuries, it then discusses recent voting trends late in the twentieth and early in the twenty-first centuries. Turnout is influenced by personal feelings and beliefs, especially partisanship; social factors such as age, education, and group association and situational variables, such as the state of domestic and foreign affairs, the competitiveness of the election, the weather, and the efforts by candidate campaigns, parties, and nonparty groups to generate enthusiasm and get out the vote. Turnout is also affected by state and national laws that govern the conduct of elections, especially registration requirements, early and absentee voting, and the locations and hours of polling places, especially the time it usually takes for people in different precincts to vote. The impact of these variables, singularly and together, on the decision of whether to cast a ballot is the principal focus of this section.

The second and third parts of the chapter study influences on the vote. First, the partisan basis of politics is examined. How have political attitudes changed over the years, and how do they affect the ways people evaluate the candidates and their campaigns and shape their voting decisions? Models of voting behavior are presented and then used to help explain contemporary voting patterns.

Next, the chapter analyzes the social basis of politics. Here we look at the electorate's demography, its socioeconomic divisions, and the public's various beliefs and the values on which those beliefs are based. Our objective is to discuss the relationship between groups within the electorate and their voting trends. Primary emphasis is placed on the formation and evolution of the major parties' electoral coalitions. The chapter concludes with a description of the groups that comprise contemporary Republican and Democratic parties.

Turnout

Who votes? In one sense, this is a simple question to answer. Official election returns indicate the number of voters and the states, even the precincts, in which people voted. By easy calculation, the percentage of the voting age population (VAP) that cast ballots for president can be determined: 50.0 percent (2000), 55.4 percent (2004), 56.9 percent (2008), 53.6 percent (2012), 54.7 percent (2016), and 61.5 percent in 2020.[1] But there is a problem with using the VAP as a basis for determining voting turnout. The VAP includes people who are old enough to vote but may not be eligible to do so: noncitizens; most of the people who are currently incarcerated or institutionalized; in some states, ex-felons and ex-military who were dishonorably discharged from the armed forces; citizens who do not meet their state's residence requirements; and people who are not registered to vote.[2] If these people are excluded, then the percentage voting increases a little.[3] Professor Michael P. McDonald, a political scientist who studies turnout figures, concluded that 60.1 percent of the voting eligible population (VEP) actually did so in 2004, 61.6 percent in 2008, 58.7 percent in 2012, 60.2 percent in 2016, and 66.1 percent in 2020. For the 2022 midterm elections, it was 46.8 percent, which is quite high for a midterm.[4]

The Evolution of Voting in American Elections ───────────

Voting turnout in the United States has varied markedly over the years. Several legal, social, and political factors have contributed to this variation. The next section documents these shifts and explains them within the context of the political environment of the times.

The Constitution empowers the states to determine the time, place, and manner of holding elections for national office. Although it also gives Congress the authority to alter such regulations, Congress did not do so until after the Civil War. Thus, states were free to restrict suffrage, and most did. In some of them, property ownership was a requirement for exercising the franchise; in others, a particular religious identity was necessary. In most, it was essential to be white, male, and twenty-one years of age or older.[5] Only about 11 percent of the adult population participated in the first national election. The percentage voting for president was even lower because most of the electors were designated by the state legislatures and not chosen directly by the people. Prior to 1824, voters remained a relatively small percentage of the then eligible population, in the range of 20–25 percent. Without a tradition of participation in politics or a well-entrenched party system during this period, the public deferred to the more politically prominent members of the society in choosing their state's elected officials.

Spurred by a political reform movement known as Jacksonian Democracy, turnout began to increase in the 1820s. This movement advocated a greater role for the public in the electoral process. By the 1830s, most states had eliminated property and religious restrictions, thereby extending suffrage to approximately 80 percent of the adult white male population. Turnout expanded accordingly. The rise of competitive, popular-based parties in the 1840s, along with campaigns directed at the entire electorate, boosted participation. Professor Walter Dean Burnham estimated turnout in the range of 70–80 percent of eligible voters throughout the remainder of the nineteenth century, although these percentages may be misleading because of the coercive and sometimes fraudulent practices that occurred during the era of machine party politics, a period during which the parties ran the elections, provided the ballots (distinguished by color), oversaw the voting, mobilized their partisans, and got them to the polls early and sometimes often.[6]

Reforms at the end of the nineteenth and beginning of the twentieth centuries, however, reduced some of the more flagrant attempts to influence election outcomes. States began to monitor the conduct of elections more closely and more impartially. They adopted the Australian ballot and instituted secret voting; no longer could party poll watchers know how people voted by looking at the color of the ballot they used. Registration procedures were introduced to prevent nonresidents and noncitizens from voting. These reforms not only improved the integrity of the electoral process, but they also reduced the percentage of the eligible population that voted.

Following the Civil War, and the removal of federal troops in the South, one-party Democratic politics dominated the southern electorate. Despite the ratification of the Fifteenth Amendment in 1870, which removed race and color as qualifications for voting, there was decreased turnout in the South, a consequence of restrictive state laws, such as poll taxes, literacy tests, and "private" primaries in which only whites could participate, as well as the imposition of more restrictive residence requirements.

Decreasing competition between the major parties in the North and West at the end of the nineteenth century had much the same effect. It reduced the percentage of the adult population that voted, as did the extension of suffrage to women in 1919. Although the number of the eligible electorate doubled, turnout declined because newly enfranchised citizens do not vote with the same regularity as do people who have been exercising the franchise for years. In 1924, only 44 percent of the voting age population cast ballots. Within a period of thirty years, turnout had declined almost 40 percent.

Although voter participation grew moderately during Franklin Roosevelt's presidency and the post–World War II era, it decreased again following the 1960 presidential election, an election in which 64 percent of the adult population voted. Part of the decline had to do with the expanding base of the electorate, especially among the young and new immigrants; part with growing voter disillusionment, heightened by the war in Vietnam, the Watergate scandal, and a series of lackluster presidential candidates; and part with the weakening of the major parties' grassroots organizations and their increased dependence on television advertising for mobilizing the vote.

Beginning in the 1960s, suffrage rights were expanded. In 1961, the District of Columbia was granted three electoral votes, thereby extending to its residents the right to vote in presidential elections (Twenty-Third Amendment); in 1964, the collection of a poll tax was prohibited for national elections (Twenty-Fourth Amendment); in 1971, the right to vote was extended to all citizens eighteen years of age and older (Twenty-Sixth Amendment).

Moreover, the Supreme Court and Congress began to eliminate the legal and institutional barriers to voting. In 1944, the court outlawed the white-only primary. In the mid-1960s, Congress passed the Civil Rights Act (1964) and the Voting Rights Act (1965). The latter banned literacy tests in federal elections for all citizens who had at least a sixth-grade education in a US school. Federal officials were sent to facilitate registration in districts in which less than 50 percent of the population was registered to vote. Amendments to the Voting Rights Act have also reduced the residence requirement for presidential elections to a maximum of thirty days. In 2002, the Help Americans Vote Act, designed to improve the accuracy of registration lists and allow provisional voting in cases in which controversies over registration occurred at the time of voting, was enacted. The legislation also created the Election Assistance Commission to facilitate registration procedures nationwide.

Although these legal initiatives broadened the opportunities for people, particularly minority ethnic and racial groups, to participate in the electoral process, they also engendered pushback from state officials fearing that fraudulent voting practices could result and that the party in power might lose its dominance.

Following the 2004 presidential election, several states, controlled by Republican legislators and governors, enacted laws that required citizens to show government-issued identification cards to vote. In 2008, the Supreme Court, in the case of *Crawford v. Marion Election Board*, 533 U.S. 181 (2008), upheld the state of Indiana's right to do so. These laws, ostensibly designed to prevent fraudulent voting, have since proliferated, especially after the 2020 election. Today more than half of the states have some type of voter ID laws; fifteen of them require photo identification. Democrats perceive these state laws as discriminatory, designed to reduce the vote of racial and ethnic minorities and lower-income citizens, people that are more apt to lack these credentials. Many states have also eliminated or restricted weekend and evening voting hours, ostensibly to save money. However, Democrats contend that these restrictions also disproportionately affect minorities and people with lower incomes who find it easier to vote during nonworking days and hours. States that have enacted such restrictions tend to have histories of racial discrimination and expanding minority populations.

Democratic Party officials, citizen advocacy groups, and the Obama administration challenged the new state election laws, arguing that the Voting Rights Act required election law preclearance by the Department of Justice. The suits reached the Supreme Court in 2012. In the case of *Shelby County v. Holder*, 570 U.S. 2 (2013), the court held that the 1965 preclearance requirement for states that had engaged in racial discrimination, mostly in the South, was outdated; Congress needed to establish new criteria for determining discrimination. The political battle over state regulations on voting continues within both the congressional and judicial arenas.

Table 3.1 indicates turnout levels in recent presidential elections based on VAP.

TABLE 3.1 ★ Suffrage and Turnout in the Twenty-First Century			
Year	VAP	Turnout	Percentage of the VAP
2000	205,815,000	105,586,284	51.3
2004	215,694,000	122,295,345	56.7
2008	230,898,029	132,645,504	56.9
2012	240,926,957	130,292,355	53.6
2016	250,585,915	138,846,571	54.7
2020	257,605,088	159,738,337	61.9

VAP, voting age population.

Sources: Population figures from 1988 to 2004 were compiled from official election returns supplied by the Federal Election; 2008–2020 data from Michael P. McDonald, "General Election Turnout Rates,: *The Election Project*.

Influences on Turnout

Why don't people vote? Some citizens have lost their right to vote. People who are incarcerated or institutionalized usually do not vote. Those who have been convicted of a felony or dishonorably discharged from military service may not be allowed to vote in some states. These regulations prevent almost 6 million people from voting, disproportionately affecting African Americans, particularly men.

Congress tried to deal with voter registration problems in 1993 with the enactment of the "Motor-Voter" bill, legislation that requires states to permit registration by mail and make the forms for it available at motor vehicle offices. Oregon was the first state to automatically register eligible citizens. States that permit automatic or same-day registration have had the largest increase in the percentage of registered voters.

In addition to the registration, states that have facilitated the availability of absentee ballots and early voting generally have higher turnout. Since 2012, approximately one-third of the electorate vote before election day. The length of time during which voting is permitted and the accessibility of voting precincts naturally make it easier for people to vote. On the other hand, being away from home at school, jobs, or out-of-town trips makes voting more difficult.

The absence of peer pressure may also be a problem, especially for first-time voters. Finding the correct location, getting to the polls, and figuring out how to use the machines or punch cards are no longer major obstacles once a person has voted. For people with limited English language skills, various mental and physical handicaps, and those that lack required identification, voting can still be difficult. Older citizens vote at higher rates than do younger ones.

Personal feelings and beliefs are an important motivating factor. Interest in the election, concern over the outcome, feelings of civic pride, and political efficacy (the belief that one's vote really counts) influence how regularly people vote. The decline in personal efficacy, distrust of government, and suspicion of elected officials have all depressed turnout despite the effort of candidate-oriented campaigns, political parties, and outside groups to maximize their vote.

Several demographic factors also correlate with turnout. They include education, income, and occupational status, which also correlate with one another. As people become more educated, as they move up the socioeconomic ladder, and as they gain more professional jobs higher in status and income, they are more likely to vote. (See table 3.2.)

Given the relationship of education to turnout, why did the rate of turnout decline from the 1960s through most of the 1990s as the general level of education increased in the United States during this period? The answer is that the attitudinal factors of weakening partisanship in the 1970s and declining efficacy during this time countered the increase in education. Had educational levels not increased, turnout would have been even lower.

Finally, situational variables and external conditions help explain fluctuations in the vote. Even the weather may be a factor. Three political scientists, Brad T. Gomez, Thomas G. Hansford, and George A. Krause, examined the impact of weather on turnout and found that precipitation reduces turnout by about 1 percent per inch of rain.[7]

TABLE 3.2 ★ Social Characteristics and Voting in 2016 and 2020 (in Thousands)

Characteristic	2016	2020
United States		
Total, voting age	**245,502**	**252,274**
Total voted	137,537	154,628
Percentage voted	56.0	61.3
Race and Hispanic Origin		
White	58.2	63.7
White non-Hispanic	64.1	69.8
Black	55.9	58.7
Asian and Pacific Islander	33.9	42.8
Hispanic (of any race)	32.5	38.8
Sex		
Male	53.8	59.5
Female	58.1	63.0
Age		
18 to 24 years	39.4	48.0
25 to 44 years	49.0	55.0
45 to 64 years	61.7	65.5
65 years and older	68.4	71.9
Northeast, Midwest, and West		
Total, voting age	**153,528**	**156,253**
Total voted	87,015	97,564
Percentage voted	56.7	62.4
Race and Hispanic Origin		
White	59.6	65.4
White non-Hispanic	65.1	70.9
Black	53.6	58.3
Asian and Pacific Islander	34.5	42.9
Hispanic (of any race)	33.8	40.6

TABLE 3.2 ★ Social Characteristics and Voting in 2016 and 2020 (in Thousands) *continued*		
Characteristic	2016	2020
South		
Total, voting age	**91,973**	**96,022**
Total voted	50,522	57,064
Percentage voted	54.9	59.4
Race and Hispanic Origin		
White	55.8	60.7
White non-Hispanic	62.1	67.6
Black	57.7	59.0
Asian and Pacific Islander	32.0	42.2
Hispanic (of any race)	30.5	36.0

Source: US Census, Table A-9.

Turnout and Democracy

What difference does it make that many people do not vote? A great deal! Turnout affects perceptions of how well the democratic electoral system is functioning. Low turnout suggests that people may be alienated, lack faith in the candidates and parties, think that the government is and will remain unresponsive to their needs and interests, and, most importantly, believe that they cannot achieve change through the electoral process.

Low turnout also impacts representation and public policy decisions. "Who gets what" relates in large part to the influence some people and groups have on election outcomes and government decisions. The connection between low economic status and not voting results in a class bias that undercuts the democratic character of the American political system by widening the participation gap between the haves and have-nots. This gap has produced an electorate that is not representative of the whole population, that is older, and that has higher incomes than the general public. To the extent that elected officials respond to the electorate that supported them, rather than to the entire population, means that government policies take on a "have" rather than "have-not" coloration.

This class bias in voting produces a tragic irony in American politics. Those who are most disadvantaged and need to change conditions the most vote the least. Those who are the most advantaged, benefit from existing conditions, and presumably benefit from the public policy that contributes to those conditions vote more often. Obviously, turnout has partisan implications as well. Because the Democratic Party draws more of its electoral support from those in the lower socioeconomic groups, lower turnout tends to hurt that party more than the GOP, particularly during midterm elections.

The common wisdom is that, all things being equal, the larger the turnout, the better the Democrats will do. In 1960 and 1976, increases in turnout did favor the Democrats and resulted in two close victories. The relatively high Democratic turnout in these two elections overcame the advantage the Republicans usually gain from having a larger proportion of their rank-and-file voter. Similarly, in the 2000 presidential election, a late surge of support for Al Gore gave him a popular vote victory although he lost in the Electoral College.

Republican strategists, surprised by the larger turnout the Gore campaign generated, studied the Democrats' election day tactics, particularly the efforts of organized labor and leadership within the African American community to increase the number of voters likely to vote for their party's candidates in that election. Determined not to be outmaneuvered again, the Republicans devised a turnout strategy for 2004 in which potential Republican voters were targeted, canvassed, and contacted by local volunteers within seventy-two hours before they voted. That strategy was successful. Republican turnout increased more than Democratic turnout in that election.

Personal contact, strong feelings, and partisan allegiances are keys to maximizing the vote. But why do people vote as they do? Considerable research has been conducted to answer this question. Initially, much of it was done with data collected from surveys by the Center for Political Studies at the University of Michigan. Beginning in 1952, that center conducted nationwide surveys during presidential elections, surveys now called American National Election Studies (ANES). To identify the major influences on voting behavior, a random sample of the electorate is interviewed before and after the election (table 3.3). Respondents are asked a series of questions designed to reveal their attitudes toward the parties, candidates, and issues.

Voting Behavior

One of the earliest and most influential theories of voting behavior based on the Michigan survey data was presented in the book *The American Voter* (1960).[8] The model on which the theory was based assumed that individuals are influenced by their partisan attitudes and social relationships in addition to the political environment in which the election takes place. According to that theory, people develop attitudes early in life, largely as a consequence of interacting with their families, particularly their parents and other significant elders. These attitudes, in turn, tend to be reinforced by neighborhood, school, and religious associations.

Psychologically, it is more pleasing to have beliefs and attitudes supported than challenged. Socially, it is more comfortable and safer to associate with like-minded people with similar economic, cultural, educational, and religious backgrounds than with others who do not share the same values, beliefs, and experiences. This desire to increase one's "comfort level" in social relationships explains why the environment for most people reinforces rather than challenges their values and beliefs most of the time.

Attitudes mature and harden over time. The older people become, the less amenable they are to change. They are more set in their ways and their beliefs.

Although scholars have offered modifications to this model of attitude development, most of the political science literature has remained focused on

TABLE 3.3 ★ Party Identification of the American Electorate, 1952–2020

Party ID	1952	1956	1960	1964	1968	1972	1976	1980	1984	1988	1992	1996	2000	2004	2008	2012	2016	2020
SD	23	22	21	27	20	15	15	18	17	18	18	18	19	17	19	20	21	23
WD	26	24	26	25	26	25	25	23	20	18	17	19	19	16	15	15	13	12
ID	10	7	8	9	10	11	12	11	11	12	14	14	15	17	17	12	12	12
II	5	9	10	8	11	15	16	15	13	12	13	10	13	10	11	14	14	12
IR	8	9	7	6	9	10	10	10	12	13	12	12	13	12	12	12	12	10
WR	14	15	14	14	15	13	14	14	15	14	14	15	12	12	13	12	12	11
SR	14	16	16	11	10	10	9	9	12	14	11	12	12	16	13	15	17	21
N	1,689	1,690	1,864	1,536	1,531	2,695	2,833	1,612	2,228	2,026	2,473	1,706	1,790	1,194	2,293	5,894	4,248	8,280

SD, Strong Democrat; SR, Strong Republican; WD, Weak Democrat; WR, Weak Republican; ID, Independent Democrat; IR, Independent Republican; II, Independent Independent.

"Generally speaking do you usually think of yourself as a Republican, a Democrat, an Independent, or what?" (IF Republican or Democratic) "Would you call yourself a strong (Republican or Democrat) or a not very strong (Republican or Democrat)?" (IF Independent or other) "Do you think of yourself as closer to the Republican or Democratic party?"

Sources: American National Election Studies, "The ANES Guide to Public Opinion and Electoral Behavior."

external factors within the environment that shape how people think and behave politically. Another line of research, however, has taken a different approach, a biological one. This research postulates that the genes people inherit from their biological parents affect the beliefs they develop and the behavior they exercise within the electoral arena. Two researchers have gone so far as to identify specific genes that they believe affect turnout. These findings, however, have been difficult to replicate.[9] Genetic research, neuroscience, biological politics, and postulating causal relationships based on genetic sequencing is still in its early stages of development. Although the nature–nurture debate is likely to continue, the impact of socialization on how political attitudes are shaped over time is clearer.

Of all the external factors that contribute to the development of a political attitude, identifying with a political party seems to be the most important. It affects how people see campaigns, how they evaluate candidates and issues (as well as how they assess elected officials), and how they vote on election day. Party identification operates as a conceptual framework, a mindset, a lens through which information is digested and analyzed, and the campaign is understood. Partisan allegiances provide cues for interpreting the issues, judging the candidates, and deciding whether to vote. If the decision is to vote, partisanship influences for whom the vote is cast. The stronger these attitudes, the more compelling the cues; conversely, the weaker the attitudes, the less likely they will affect perceptions during the campaign and influence voting. When identification with a party is weak or nonexistent, other factors, such as the personalities of the candidates, their issue positions, and external conditions, are correspondingly more important.

Partisanship is stable but can be modified or even changed over time. Although partisan allegiances affect perceptions of the candidates and issues, perceptions of the candidates and issues also affect allegiances toward the parties. It is a two-way street in which people's perceptions can be reinforced or challenged by what happens before, during, and after campaigns. To summarize, partisanship is stable but not static; it can vary in intensity.

Partisan orientation may even be a factor for those who identify themselves as Independent. There are more people in the electorate who claim to be an Independent than vote in an independent manner. Political scientists have found most Independents lean in a partisan direction.

So then, why would so many people claim to be Independents? The reason may be that they believe they can make an enlightened and rational judgment, one that will be in the public interest rather than some narrower partisan or parochial one requires independence. The empirical evidence, however, indicates that there are patterns of partisan voting behavior, even among Independents.

People form general impressions based on what they know about candidate qualifications, experience, and character. Challengers are judged primarily on their potential for office and incumbents on their performance in office. Even when incumbents are not running, their record usually affects their party's standard-bearer. Reagan's positive evaluations in 1988 helped Republican George H. W. Bush, whereas George W. Bush's negative ones hurt Republican John McCain in 2008.

Personal attributes, such as trustworthiness, integrity, and empathy, may also be relevant, depending on the nature of the times. In the aftermath of a presidency mired in scandal or lacking in candor, integrity and honesty assume more importance than at other times when the problem has been weak or unsuccessful leadership. Once these attributes are associated with candidates, this image is hard to change.

Candidates' stands on the issues, unless misinformed, objectionable, or in other ways out of the mainstream, seem less critical than their partisan affiliation and leadership capabilities. To be important, issues must be salient. They must attract attention; they must hit home. Without personal impact, they are unlikely to be primary motivating factors for voting.

In addition, candidates must discuss a multitude of issues over the course of the election cycle. To the extent that their policy positions are not known or clearly indistinguishable from one another, voters tend to rely more on their own partisanship and perceptions of their personal character in making a voting decision. Ironically, that portion of the electorate that can be more easily persuaded, weak partisans and Independents, tends to have the least politically relevant information. Conversely, the most committed also tend to be the most informed. They use their information to support their partisanship.

The relationship between partisan loyalties and political knowledge has significant implications for a democratic society. The traditional view of a democracy holds that information and awareness are necessary to make an enlightened voting decision. However, the finding that those who have the most information are also the most committed, and that those who lack this commitment also lack the incentive to get more information, has upset some of these democratic perquisites. Do people think and vote rationally? According to political scientist Morris Fiorina, they do. In his study *Retrospective Voting in American National Elections* (1981), Fiorina used a rational choice model adopted from economics to argue that voting decisions are calculations people make based on their accumulated political experience.[10] They make these calculations by assessing the past performance of the parties and their elected officials in light of the promises they made, positions they took, and actions in office and the impact of those actions on the country. Fiorina called this a retrospective judgment.

Retrospective judgments are not only important for influencing voting in an election but are also important for shaping partisan attitudes, which Fiorina defined as "a running tally of retrospective evaluations of party promises and performance."[11] In other words, the running tally is a summary judgment of how well the parties and their leaders have done. Over time, that judgment can change, which in turn affects people's evaluations of the parties.

Shifts in Partisanship

When the first studies on voting behavior were published in the middle of the twentieth century, about three-fourths of the electorate identified with one of the major parties, half of them strongly. Both major parties were heterogeneous.

Although they differed on economic and social issues, the divide was not as deep as it is today. The Democrats had been in the majority beginning in the 1930s and controlled government for most of the period from 1932 to 1968. Much has changed in the political environment since then.

Radio, television, and social media have become primary communication links between candidates and the electorate. Accompanying the changes in communication technology have been significant international and domestic developments.

Beginning in the mid-1960s, the war in Vietnam and the civil rights movement at home divided the country and hurt the Democrats. The Watergate scandal, culminating in President Nixon's resignation and his pardon by President Ford, adversely affected the Republicans in the 1970s. During this period, partisan intensity and identification declined. More people claimed to be Independents.

Elections became more candidate-oriented with candidate organizations competing with party committees for money, staff, and influence. More emphasis was placed on personal imagery with television used to project it. Media gurus began to replace grassroots organizers as key campaign operatives.

Not only were campaigns more candidate-focused, but they also became more issue-oriented. Ideological differences between the parties began to emerge on social issues in the 1960s in addition to the economic and foreign policy ones that already existed. These divisions carried over into the 1980s.

In the short run, the Republicans benefited. Weakening support for the dominant party, the Democrats, and the greater emphasis put on personal qualifications and experience of the candidates allowed Republicans to run for office without hiding their political affiliation. The GOP's more conservative policies, and especially its opposition to preferential treatment for minorities, coincided with the views of many white Americans, especially those living in the South. As the country prospered and the middle class grew, people became more conservative, evidencing less sympathy for policies that urged major social, economic, and political reform. They also became leery of legislating social and economic policy at the national level.

The Democrats lost their status as the majority party by the end of the 1970s and their partisan plurality began to shrink in the 1980s. By the 1990s, the parties were at rough parity with one another. The electorate has remained at or near parity since then with economic conditions at home and international conflicts abroad affecting electoral outcomes.

As the partisan policy differences became clearer in the 1980s, two distinct governing philosophies emerged. The Republican blueprint, articulated by Ronald Reagan in his presidential campaigns; Newt Gingrich, House Speaker, in the Republican's "Contract with America" in 1994; George W. Bush and Tea Party activists during the Obama administration; and Donald Trump contending that the national government had gotten too large, too expensive, and too invasive. They argued that it should play a smaller and less regulatory role in the economic and social spheres while focusing more on domestic order and national security issues; in contrast, the Democrats' position is that government remains an important instrument for addressing social and economic inequities and for redistributing resources, especially for closing the gap between the rich and the poor. The New Deal and Great Society programs of Franklin D. Roosevelt and Lyndon B. Johnson embodied these beliefs. So did the legislative activism of the first two years of the Obama and Biden administrations.

The differences have been less pronounced in foreign and national security policy. Democrats agreed with Republicans on the need for a strong defense during the Cold War. After the Cold War ended, the Democrats have been more reluctant than Republicans to rely primarily on the use of military force to promote the country's interests and security. In general, they have placed greater emphasis on diplomacy, international organizations, and multilateral agreements in the conduct of US foreign policy, while Republicans have been more willing to act unilaterally and, if necessary, employ military actions to further US values, interests, and beliefs.

These diverging domestic and foreign perspectives have contributed to the aligning of partisan attitudes along ideological lines. The convergence of ideology and partisanship has made the two major parties more internally cohesive and externally distinctive from one another. It has also generated more political animosity among their adherents.

Partisan cleavages within government also became more pronounced with more party-line voting in Congress, more partisan divisions over judicial appointments, more strident political rhetoric, and less civility among elected officials in government. The number of moderates elected to Congress has declined. Conservative Southern Democrats, who frequently sided with the Republicans on budget and tax matters, were replaced by even more conservative Republicans, and moderate Republicans, especially from the Northeast, who sided with the Democrats on some social issues, have been replaced by liberal Democrats.

Not only has political polarization deeply divided elected officials, but it has also divided the American electorate, although political scientists disagree on how deep and wide that division is. There are two schools of thought on this question. One, put forth by Professor Morris Fiorina and some of his colleagues at Stanford University, argues that the polarization is not nearly as extensive or as deep within the general population as it is among those in power. The Fiorina School attributes the shift of public policy issues along ideological lines to elite sorting, to the diverse political choices the public faces when voting.

In contrast, the polarization school adherents believe that the ideological divisions run deep within the body politic. They point to the persistence of partisan voting patterns and partisan presidential evaluations since the end of the 1980s and the effectiveness of base-oriented campaign strategies since 2004 in maximizing the vote. They also rely on empirical findings of recent surveys that indicate that the partisan gap on values and issues has doubled over the last three decades.

Political polarization in America has serious implications for politics and government. For the parties, it calls into question the extent to which they can accommodate the diversity of views and interests within the whole country, and can claim to be big tents, large enough to attract and welcome all of those that choose to enter. At its core, the issue is the ability of the two-party system to sustain itself in an increasingly diverse and multicultural society.

For candidates, the dilemma is who and how to represent their electorate. Should they take moderate stands to appeal to a broader range of electoral constituencies or direct their messages to their core supporters, those who nominated them and are most likely to vote for them in the general election? The dilemma is similar for those in government. Should elected officials compromise or adhere to their partisan political beliefs that they articulated in their campaign for office? Since the 1990s, candidates and government officials have increasingly reflected their partisan and ideological beliefs. In summary, partisan orientation remains a strong influence on how people evaluate candidates and issues, on how they vote, and how they assess government.

Attitudes and opinions are also influenced by the associations people have with one another and by the groups with which they are affiliated. Although much attention has been given to the effect of partisanship on voting since the 1960s, research by political scientists also indicate that the social context in which elections occur matters. Intermediaries between the candidates and voters—individuals, traditional news outlets, social media, and interest groups—provide information that contributes to voters' decisions. Communicating information and conveying enthusiasm about candidates, parties, and issues informs and energizes the electorate; it brings into the electoral arena people who might otherwise have avoided it. Social media has played an important role in expanding and heightening political debate among the general population.

As we have emphasized in this chapter, personal contact is important in turning out voters. Politicians have believed this proposition for a long time, and more recently, experimental and field research by political scientists Donald P. Green and Alan Gerber has confirmed it. "As a rule of thumb," they write, "one additional vote is produced for every fourteen people who are successfully contacted by canvassers."[12]

We now turn to these intermediaries and their influences on voting behavior, specifically to the demographic and social groups that are part of the major parties' electoral coalitions. Three primary factors, the group's size, cohesiveness, resources and voting orientation, affect its impact on the party's electoral base.

The Social Basis of Partisanship

Political coalitions form during periods of partisan realignment. The last time a classic realignment occurred was in the 1930s.

New Deal Realignment

Largely because of the Great Depression, the Democrats emerged as the dominant party. Their electoral coalition, held together by a common belief that the government should play a more active role in addressing the nation's economic problems, supported Franklin Roosevelt's New Deal program. Those in the most dire economic circumstances generally subscribed to this view; they had few other options. On the other hand, many of the owners and executives of still solvent businesses saw government intervention in the private sector as a threat to the capitalist system. They opposed much of Roosevelt's domestic legislation and remained Republican in attitude and vote. The Democrats became the majority party during this period by expanding their base. Since the Civil War and the withdrawal of federal troops in the South, the Democrats had enjoyed solid support in that region of the country. White Protestants living in rural areas dominated the southern electorate; African Americans were largely excluded. Only in the election of 1928 when Al Smith, the Catholic governor of New York, ran as the Democratic candidate was there a sizable southern vote for a Republican presidential candidate. As a Catholic and an opponent of prohibition, Smith was unacceptable to many white Protestants.

Catholics, living primarily in the urban centers of the North and Midwest, became an increasingly important component of the Democrats' electoral coalition. Facing difficult economic circumstances, social discrimination, and, for many, language barriers, Catholic immigrants turned to big-city bosses for help; in return, they were expected to support the boss and the candidates that the party organization ran for office. In 1928, for the first time, a majority of voters living in cities voted for Democratic candidate Al Smith for president.

The harsh economic realities of the Great Depression enabled Roosevelt to expand his base even further by appealing to people in the lower socioeconomic strata, people with less education and income, and those who were unemployed, underemployed, or had lower-paying jobs. Organized labor, in particular, became reliably Democratic. In addition to establishing a broad-based, blue-collar, working-class coalition, Roosevelt also lured specific racial and ethnic groups, such as African Americans and Jewish Americans, from their former Republican roots. African Americans who lived outside of the South voted Democratic for economic reasons, and Jewish Americans supported Roosevelt's liberal domestic programs and his anti-Nazi foreign policy. Neither of these groups provided the Democratic Party of the 1930s with many votes, but their long-term allegiances to that party have continued. Although the Republicans did retain the backing of the business and professional classes, which grew after World War II, their working-class base eroded. Republican strength remained concentrated in the Northeast.

Evolving Political Coalitions, 1950-1970

The coalitions that were restructured during the 1930s and 1940s held together for the next twenty years. With minority racial, ethnic, and religious groups increasing their identification with and support of Democratic candidates. Protestants remained Republican except for less-educated, lower-income fundamentalist and evangelical groups that voted Democratic, largely for economic reasons through the 1970s.

Prior to the 1980s, there were no major partisan distinctions in gender preferences, although some cleavages among different age cohorts were evident. Younger voters, attracted by the liberal policies of Democratic candidates and older Americans who had benefited from these policies, particularly Social Security, backed the Democrats during this decade.

The civil rights movement, however, began to erode the Democrats' electoral base, first in the South and later in other parts of the country. In 1948, Harry

Truman won 52 percent of the southern vote, compared with Roosevelt's 69 percent four years earlier. Although Adlai Stevenson and John Kennedy carried the South by reduced margins, the southern white Protestant vote for president went Republican for the first time in 1960 and has continued to do so since then.

Rising economic prosperity also made the Republicans' policy positions more attractive to a growing middle class. That middle class became more conservative in its political view, which was reflected in the Republicans' policy positions. Coincidentally, the Democrats' labor base began to shrink.

Electoral Coalitions: The Last Fifty Years

The 1980s saw the end of Democratic dominance and the growth of the Republican Party to near parity with the Democrats. It also saw changes in composition and intensity of each party's electoral coalition.

Since the 1980s, southern whites have become increasingly Republican. In the 1994 midterm elections, GOP congressional candidates won a majority of the southern vote for the first time since Reconstruction. In subsequent elections, the Republicans enlarged their congressional southern majority. And even though the Democrats ran two southern candidates in 1992 and 1996 (Bill Clinton and Al Gore), the white vote in the South has remained solidly Republican. In 2008, Barack Obama made inroads in the South, winning the electoral vote of three southern states (Florida, North Carolina, and Virginia). He won two of them (Florida and Virginia) four years later. Only Virginia voted Democratic at the presidential level in 2016 and 2020; Biden narrowly won Georgia in 2020.

Beginning in the 1980s, Protestant fundamentalists and evangelical Christians shifted their political allegiances to the Republican Party, largely because of that party's position on social issues. Mainline Protestants remained Republican but have not been as supportive of Republican candidates as their fundamentalist and evangelical brethren. This "traditionalist–modernist" distinction within the Protestant religious community extends to other religion groups. In general, people who have the greatest involvement in religious activities, who attend services regularly, and who subscribe to more literal readings and interpretations of the Bible are more likely to vote Republican than those whose theological views are more nuanced, who are less engaged in church-related activities, and who attend services less often, if at all. The movement of Protestant fundamentalists to the Republican Party has left the Democrats with a more secular base. Except for Hispanic Catholics, Muslims, and Jews, the Democrats lack the strong religious support it had in past.

Although the socioeconomic class distinctions of the New Deal and Great Society eras have become more muted, racial, ethnic, and gender differences have become more distinct. The white majority has become increasingly Republican, whereas most minority groups have remained solidly Democratic. A product of the growing multiculturalism in American society and national government policies designed to help the economically and socially disadvantaged, these trends have produced a deep partisan divide, often referred to as *identity* politics. Differences in the voting behavior of men and women have also expanded, producing a gender gap that has ranged from single to double digits and is still growing. Women have become more active politically.

Age and education distinctions have also emerged within each party's electoral coalition. Older and less formally educated whites lean more toward the Republicans, whereas younger people with more formal education lean more toward the Democrats.

Summary

The electorate is not neutral. People do not come to campaigns with completely open minds. Rather, they come with preexisting attitudes and accumulated experiences that color their perceptions and affect their judgments. Stimuli from the campaign tend to reinforce rather than challenge those attitudes and experiences. Of the political beliefs people possess, partisanship has the strongest impact on turnout and voting behavior. It provides a perspective for evaluating the campaign and for deciding whether and how to vote. It is also a motive for being informed and getting involved.

Toward the end of the 1960s, there was a decline in the proportion of the population that professed loyalty to a major political party. This decline, a product of disillusionment with both major parties, contributed to lower voter turnout. It also increased the importance of short-term factors on voting behavior. During this period, more people identified themselves as Independents; there was more candidate and issue voting; and, consequently, more split-ticket ballots.

The use of television as the primary channel through which candidates and parties communicated to the electorate, the weakening of the major parties' grassroots organizations, and the creation of separate candidate and party organizations for the presidential election required by the Federal Election Campaign Act all worked to reduce the influence of the parties on voting behavior. By the 1980s, however, that influence was strengthening again even though the proportion of the population identifying themselves as political partisans had declined.

Since the 1980s, the parties have also become more ideological, with the Republicans much more conservative than the Democrats. Diverse ideologies have also divided the electorate and the government. How wide and deep these divisions are within the body politick has been debatable, although the growth in the proportion of self-identified Independents suggests that many people may be "turned off" by the extreme beliefs and behavior of party leaders and elected officials. Nonetheless, the parties remain close to electoral parity. That parity has been reflected in relatively close presidential elections with frequent shifts in the control of the White House and Congress.

Group ties to the parties have shifted as well. The Democratic Party has lost the support of a majority of southern whites, non-Hispanic Catholics, and Protestant fundamentalists and evangelicals. The Democratic labor base shrunk as union laborers declined as a proportion of the population. Racial minorities, however, such as African Americans and Hispanics, have increased their loyalty to the Democrats, and Jewish Americans have retained theirs. Women have become much more supportive of Democratic candidates, as have people with secular views and younger voters. The party has improved its proportion of the vote in the Northeast, Pacific Coast, and more recently, the Southwest—the latter a result of Hispanic immigration.

The Republicans have made inroads among older people who came of age after the New Deal, people with sectarian beliefs that are the most active within their religious communities, and voters with less formal education. The Republicans' emphasis on family, traditional values, and law and order has attracted more support from married heterosexuals, white men, and older voters. In addition to most of the South, the GOP has maintained support in most of the mountain states and, increasingly, the Midwest.

The changes within the political environment have important implications for presidential politics. They have produced a more ideologically based party system and created more animosity among partisans, and they have also alienated moderate voters who find it difficult to identify with the policies and candidates of either major party. Self-identified Independents have increased. Ideological polarization has also produced a more divisive government in which Republicans and Democrats find it difficult to work together, much less agree, on national public policy. Divided government has become increasingly dysfunctional.

Exercises

1. If you are a US citizen, eighteen years of age or older, and haven't already done so, begin your registration process by accessing the Election Assistance Commission's website and downloading the National Voter Registration form. Complete it, and send it to your state election officials.

2. How can the differences between the voting age population (VAP) and voting eligible population (VEP) be reduced? Is higher turnout feasible? Is it desirable? Does higher turnout make for a more representative electorate, a more informed one, and greater legitimacy in the outcome? Would it produce a more or less effective government?

3. Go to the websites of the candidates who are running for president in the election to determine what they are doing to mobilize their supporters. Based on what you can determine from their websites, which candidates seem to have the most comprehensive and creative turnout campaigns? Which of them do you think will be able to turn out the most supporters to vote?

4. Describe the composition of the major parties' electoral coalitions today. Use data from recent national surveys and exit polls to do so. Based on your description, identify interest groups that represent groups of supporters. Access the websites of these groups and note what they have done or plan to do to mobilize their supporters in the forthcoming election.

Selected Readings

America Goes to the Polls. "Nonprofit Vote and the U.S. Elections Project." April 2017.

Abramowitz, Alan I. *The Disappearing Center: Engaged Citizens, Polarization, and American Democracy.* New Haven, CT: Yale University Press, 2010.

Abramowitz, Alan, and Steven Webster. "The Rise of Negative Partisanship and the Nationalizations of US Elections in the 21st Century." *Electoral Studies* (March 2016): 12–22.

Aldrich, John H., Jamie Carson, Brad T. Gomez, and David W. Rohde. *Change and Continuity in the 2020 Elections*. Lanham, MD: Rowman and Littlefield, 2023.

Brater, Jonathan, Kevin Morris, Myrna Perez, and Christopher Delozio. "Purges: A Growing Threat to the Right to Vote." Brennan Center, July 20, 2018.

Campbell, Angus, Philip E. Converse, Warren E. Miller, and Donald E. Stokes. *The American Voter*. New York, NY: Wiley, 1960.

Fiorina, Morris, Samuel J. Abrams, and Jeremy C. Pope. *Culture War? The Myth of a Polarized America*. New York, NY: Longman, 2006.

Gerber, Alan S., Donald P. Green, and Christopher W. Larimer. "Social Pressure and Voter Turnout: Evidence from a Large-Scale Field Experiment." *American Political Science Review* 102 (February 2008): 33–48.

Holbrook, Thomas M., and Scott D. McClurg. "The Mobilization of Core Supporters: Campaigns, Turnout, and Electoral Composition in United States Presidential Campaigns." *American Journal of Political Science* 49 (October 2005): 689–703.

Iyengar, Shanto, and Sean T. Westwork. "Fear and Loathing Across Party Lines: New Evidence of Group Polarization." *American Journal of Political Science* 59 (July 2015): 690–707.

Lewis-Beck, Michael S., William G. Jacoby, Helmut Norpoth, and Herbert F. Weisberg. *The American Voter Revisited*. Ann Arbor: University of Michigan Press, 2008.

Martinez, Michael, and Jeff Gill. "The Effects of Turnout on Partisan Outcomes in U.S. Presidential Elections, 1960–2000." *Journal of Politics* 67 (November 2005): 1248–74.

Nivola, Pietro S., and David W. Brady, eds. *Red and Blue Nation? Characteristics and Causes of America's Polarized Politics*. Washington, DC: Brookings Institution, 2006.

Patterson, Thomas E. *The Vanishing Voter*. New York, NY: Knopf, 2002.

Persily, Nathaniel, ed. *Solutions to Political Polarization in America*. New York, NY: Cambridge University Press, 2015.

Sances, Michael, and Stewart, Charles. "Partisanship and Confidence in the Vote Count: Evidence from US Elections Since 2000." *Electoral Studies*, December 2015: 176–88.

Sides, John, Michael Tesler, and Lynn Vavreck, *Identity Crisis: The 2016 Presidential Campaign and the Battle for the Meaning of America*. Princeton, NJ: Princeton University Press, 2018.

Wald, Kenneth D., and Allison Calhoun-Brown. *Religion and Politics in the United States*, 8th ed. Lanham, MD: Rowman and Littlefield, 2018.

Weiser, Wendy R., and Max Freeman. "The State of Voting 2018." Brennan Center, June 5, 2018.

Notes

1. Michael P. McDonald, "2020 November General Election Turnout Rates," United States Election Project.
2. 'The Diversifying Electorate—Voting Rates by Race and Hispanic Origin in 2020 (and Other Recent Elections)," US Census Bureau.
3. Michael P. McDonald and Samuel L. Popkin, "The Myth of the Vanishing Voter," *American Political Science Review* 95 (December 2001): 963–74; Samuel L. Popkin and Michael P. McDonald, "Turnout's Not as Bad as You Think," *The Washington Post* (November 5, 2000), B1, B2; Michael P. McDonald, "The Return of the

Voter: Voter Turnout in the 2008 Presidential Election," *The Forum: A Journal of Applied Research in Contemporary Politics* 6, no. 4, article 4 (2008.)

4. Michael P. McDonald, "2020 November General Election Turnout Rates," 2022 November General Election Turnout Rates.

5. Although some states initially permitted all landowners to vote, including women, by 1807, every state limited voting to men. Michael X. Delli Carpini and Ester R. Fuchs, "The Year of the Woman: Candidates, Voters, and the 1992 Election," *Political Science Quarterly* 108 (Spring 1993): 30.

6. Despite these allegations, Walter Dean Burnham still maintains that the high turnout percentages were real, "not artifacts of either census error or universal ballot stuffing." (117). Walter Dean Burnham, "The Turnout Problem," in A. James Reichley, ed., *Elections American Style* (Washington, DC: Brookings Institution, 1987), 112–17.

7. Brad T. Gomez, Thomas G. Hansford, and George A. Krause, "The Republicans Should Pray for Rain: Weather, Turnout, and Voting in U.S. Presidential Elections," *Journal of Politics* 69 (August 2007): 649–63.

8. Angus Campbell, Philip Converse, Warren Miller, and Donald Stokes, *The American Voter* (New York, NY, Wiley, 1960).

9. John R. Alford, Carolyn I. Funk, and John R. Hibbing, "Are Political Orientations Genetically Transmitted? *American Political Science Review* (May 2005): 153–67; J. F. Fowler and C. T. Dawes, "Two Genes Predict Voter Turnout," *Journal of Politics* (July 2008): 570–94.

10. Morris P. Fiorina, *Retrospective Voting in American National Elections* (New Haven, CT: Yale University Press, 1981): 65–83.

11. Ibid.

12. Donald P. Green and Alan S. Gerber. *Get Out the Vote: How to Increase Voter Turnout.* (Washington DC: Brookings, 2002).

PART TWO

The Nomination

Party Rules and Their Impact

★ ★ ★ ★ ★

Chapter 4

Introduction

Presidential nominees are selected by delegates who attend their party's national convention. The manner in which these delegates are chosen, however, influences the choice of the nominees and affects the influence of the state and its party leaders.

State law determines the dates, processes, rules, and voter requirements for state elections. The parties also decide their calendar, procedure, and rules for nominating candidates for office. Sometimes states and parties disagree on these aspects of the nomination process, producing political controversies and legal challenges. Recent presidential nominations have been affected by these conflicts.

Prior to the 1970s, statutes passed by the state legislature buttressed the position and clout of state party leaders. Although primary elections were held, many of them were advisory; the actual selection of the delegates was left to caucuses, conventions, or committees, which were more easily controlled by party officials. The selection of favorite-son candidates, tapped by state party leaders, prevented meaningful contests in many states. There were also impediments to delegates getting on the ballot: high fees, lengthy petitions, and early filing dates. Winner-take-all provisions gave a great advantage to candidates backed by the party organization, as did rules requiring delegates to vote as a unit.

Popular participation in the selection of convention delegates has been a relatively recent phenomenon in the history of national nominating conventions. It began in the 1970s when the Democratic Party adopted a series of reforms that affected the period during which delegates could be selected, the procedures for choosing them, and ultimately their actions at that party's national nominating convention. Although these Democratic rules limited the states' discretion, they did not result in uniform voting practices in primaries and caucuses. Considerable variation still exists in how delegates are chosen, how the vote is apportioned, and who participates in the selection.

This chapter explores these rules and their consequences for the nomination process. It is organized into three sections: the first section details the changes in party rules beginning in the 1970s, the second section considers the legal challenges to those rules and the Supreme Court's decisions on them, and the third section examines the impact of the rules changes on the parties, their leaders, their candidates, and their electorate.

Reforming the Nomination Process: Democrats Take the Initiative

The catalyst for the changes in the delegate selection rules was the tumultuous Democratic convention in 1968, a convention in which Senator Hubert Humphrey won the nomination without actively campaigning in the party's primaries. Yet the primaries of that year were important. They had become the vehicle by which Democrats could protest the Johnson administration's conduct of the war in Vietnam. Senator Eugene McCarthy, the first of the antiwar candidates, had challenged Lyndon Johnson in the New Hampshire primary. To the surprise of many political observers, McCarthy received 42.4 percent of the vote, almost as much as President Johnson, who got 49.5 percent.[1]

Four days after McCarthy's unexpectedly strong showing, Senator Robert Kennedy, brother of the late president, John F. Kennedy, and a political rival of Johnson, declared his candidacy for the nation's highest office. With protests about the war mounting and divisions within the Democratic Party intensifying, Johnson bowed out, declaring that he did not want the nation's involvement in Vietnam to become a divisive political issue.

Johnson's withdrawal cleared the way for Hubert Humphrey, the vice president, to run. Humphrey, however, waited almost a month to announce his candidacy. His late entrance into the Democratic nomination process intentionally precluded a primary campaign because filing deadlines had expired in most of the states. Like Johnson, Humphrey did not want to become the focal point of antiwar opposition, nor did he have a grassroots organization to match McCarthy's and Kennedy's. What he did have was the support of most national and state Democratic leaders, including the president.

The last big-state primary in 1968 was California's. In it, Kennedy scored a significant win, but during the celebration that followed, he was assassinated. His death left McCarthy as the principal anti-establishment, antiwar candidate, but he was far short of a convention majority. Despite the last-minute entrance of Senator George McGovern, who hoped to rally Kennedy delegates to his candidacy, Humphrey easily won the nomination. McCarthy and Kennedy's delegates felt victimized by the process, the result, and the party's continued support of military action in Vietnam. They demanded changes in the way Democrats chose their presidential nominee.

Compounding the divisions within the convention were demonstrations outside of it. Thousands of youthful protestors, calling for an end to the Vietnam War, congregated in the streets of Chicago. The police under the direction of the mayor, used strong-arm tactics to disperse the crowds and maintain order. Clashes between police and protesters followed (figure 4.1). Television news

FIGURE 4.1 ★ Young "hippie" standing in front of a row of National Guard soldiers, across the street from the Hilton Hotel at Grant Park, at the Democratic National Convention in Chicago, August 26, 1968.

Leffler, Warren K./Library of Congress

crews filmed these confrontations, and the networks showed them during their convention coverage. The spectacle of police beating demonstrators further inflamed emotions and led to calls for party reform, not only from those who attended the convention but also from those who watched it on television.

To try to unify a divided party, Humphrey and his supporters agreed to the demands of dissident delegates to establish a commission to study procedures for electing and seating convention delegates and to propose ways of improving the selection process. Initially chaired by Senator George McGovern, the commission recommended a series of reforms aimed at encouraging greater rank-and-file participation during the nomination stage and the selection of convention delegates more representative of the party's electorate. They also desired them to be chosen in the year of the general election, not before, and wanted the entire process to be accessible to a wider range of candidates.

To achieve these objectives, the commission proposed that delegate selection be a *fair reflection* of the Democratic electorate's sentiment within the state and, implicitly, less closely tied to the wishes of state party leaders. Rules were approved by the party to make it easier for individuals to run as delegates, to limit the size of the districts from which they could be chosen, and to require that the number of delegates elected be proportional to the popular vote that they, or the candidates to whom they were pledged, received. A requirement that delegates be chosen no earlier than the calendar year of the election was also established.

In addition, Democrats tried to prevent Independents, and especially partisans of other parties, from participating in the selection of Democratic delegates. The difficulty, however, was to determine who was a Democrat because some states did not require or even permit registration by party.

When implementing this rule, the national party adopted a broad interpretation of partisan affiliation. People that identified themselves as Democrats at the time of voting, or those requesting Democratic ballots were considered Democrats for the purpose of participating in the primaries. Self-identification by voters allowed Republicans and Independents to cross over and vote in the Democratic primaries in some states. The only primaries that the Democratic rules effectively prohibited were those in which voters were given the ballots of both major parties and told to discard one and vote on the other. California had such a primary. (See box 4.1 for the basic types of primaries and caucuses which states hold.)

BOX 4.1 ★ Rules for State Caucuses and Primaries

Who Can Vote?
Closed Caucuses and Primaries
Only registered voters can participate in their party's nomination process.

Open Caucuses and Primaries
Any voter, regardless of party registration, may participate in one and only one party's nomination process.

Modified Caucuses and Primaries
In addition to party registrants, Independents may participate in one party's primary.

How the Vote Is Conducted
Caucuses are multitiered events. The first round is usually held at the local level at individual homes, offices, government, or religious institutions. They are scheduled on a specific date and begin at a certain time, usually early in the evening. Only those present and eligible can participate in the selection. The primary purpose of the caucus is to choose delegates to represent the local unit at the next level, frequently the county. County caucuses then chose delegates to represent them at the next level, sometimes congressional districts or directly at the state convention. It is the convention at the state level that makes the final selection of the delegates that will represent the state at the party's national convention. The caucus process may take several months to complete. Most of the delegates chosen are on record as pledged to particular candidates. The state party establishes the caucus procedures. In most states, people speak in support of candidates and then vote. The voting may be secret, by show of hands, or by participants gathering into specific candidate groups.

Caucuses and primaries are elections in which people cast ballots for the candidates or for delegates pledged to candidates. Some states permit eligible participants to also write in names that are not on the official ballot. Voting is secret as in general elections. It usually occurs on a particular date and during hours established by the state. There are various kinds of primaries that are usually distinguished based on the eligibility of the electorate, the units in which the vote is cast (statewide, congressional districts, or local precincts), and the methods for calculating the results.

BOX 4.1 ★ Rules for State Caucuses and Primaries *continued*

Types

There are basically five types. The Conference of State Legislatures describes the different types and the states that subscribe to each as follows.

- **Closed**

  In general, a voter seeking to vote in a closed primary must first be a registered party member. Typically, the voter affiliates with a party on their voter registration application. This system deters "cross-over" voting by members of other parties. Independent or unaffiliated voters, by definition, are excluded from participating in the party nomination contests. This system generally contributes to a strong party organization.

- **Partially Closed**

  In this system, state law permits political parties to choose whether to allow unaffiliated voters or voters not registered with the party to participate in their nominating contests before each election cycle. In this type of system, parties may let in unaffiliated voters, while still excluding members of opposing parties. This system gives the parties more flexibility from year to year about which voters to include. At the same time, it can create uncertainty about whether certain voters can participate in the primaries in a given year.

- **Partially Open**

  This system permits voters to cross party lines, but they must either publicly declare their ballot choice or their ballot selection may be regarded as a form of registration with the corresponding party. Iowa asks voters to choose a party on the state voter registration form, yet it allows a primary voter to publicly change party affiliation for purposes of voting on primary election day. Some state parties keep track of who votes in their primaries to identify their backers.

- **Open to Unaffiliated Voters**

  Several states allow only unaffiliated voters to participate in any party primary they choose but do not allow voters who are registered with one party to vote in another party's primary. This system differs from a true open primary because a Democrat cannot cross over and vote in a Republican party primary, or vice versa. New Hampshire requires that unaffiliated voters declare affiliation with a party at the polls to vote in that party's primary. In Colorado, unaffiliated voters must return just one party's mail ballot or state which party ballot they want at the polls. The choice is public information, although it does not change the voter's unaffiliated status.

- **Open**

  In general, but not always, states that do not ask voters to choose parties on the voter registration form are "open primary" states. In an open primary, voters may choose privately in which primary to vote. In other words, voters may choose which party's ballot to vote, but this decision is private and does not register the voter with that party. This permits a voter to cast a vote across party lines for the primary election.

Source: The Conference of State Legislatures, "Types of Primaries."

Democratic rules require proportional voting for all pledged delegates. Republican rules also require it but only for the states that are permitted to go early and only for the first two weeks of their official nomination calendar. After that Republican state parties have more discretion in determining the mode of selection. Some use a winner-take-all method or one that the winner gets a disproportional share of the vote. Democratic rules specify, however, that no more than 25 percent of a state's delegates can be chosen on a statewide vote. For an extended discussion of different types of primaries and caucuses, see *The Green Papers*.

In addition to translating public preferences into delegate selection, another major objective of the reforms was to improve representation of the party's rank and file in the state delegations themselves. Three groups in particular—African Americans, women, and people younger than thirty—had protested their underrepresentation on party councils and at the nominating conventions. Their representatives and others sympathetic to their plight pressed the party for greater equity. The reform commission reacted to these pressures by proposing a rule requiring that all states represent these groups in reasonable relationship to their presence in the state's population. Failure to do so was viewed as prima facie evidence of discrimination. In fact, the party had established group quotas. Considerable opposition developed to the application of this rule during the 1972 nomination process, and it was subsequently modified to require that states implement affirmative action plans only for groups that had been subject to past discrimination.

Still another goal of the reforms, to involve more partisans in the selection process, was achieved not only by the fair reflection rule but also by making primaries the preferred method of delegate selection. To avoid a challenge to the composition of their delegation, many states switched to primary elections.

Caucuses in which party regulars selected the delegates were still permitted, but they, too, were redesigned to encourage more rank-and-file involvement. No longer could state party leaders vote many proxies for the delegates of their choice. Caucuses had to be publicly announced with adequate time given for campaigning. Moreover, they had to be conducted in stages, and three-fourths of the delegates had to be chosen in districts no larger than those for members of Congress. Iowa traditionally conducts the first caucus.

The rules changes, which were approved by the DNC, achieved some of these initial objectives. Turnout increased; representation of the Democratic electorate at the party's convention improved; more candidates sought the nomination; and two candidates not associated with the national Democratic leadership, George McGovern (1972) and Jimmy Carter (1976), won their party's presidential nomination.

Problems remained, however. Rank-and-file participation in the primaries was not as large as anticipated; the states that held their contests early received disproportionate attention from the candidates and news media, had higher turnouts, and exercised more influence on the selection of the nominee. It took longer than in the past to determine a winner, which, in turn, extended divisions within the party that became harder to heal for the general election. The amount of money needed to run for the nomination increased substantially. In addition, tensions emerged between the winning candidate and the national party organization on policy priorities, organizational matters, and financial needs.

Finally, and most importantly, even though the Democrats constituted a partisan plurality in the electorate in the 1970s, they lost two of three presidential elections by large amounts after the reforms were implemented and had difficulty governing when they were in power from 1977 through 1980. From the perspective of the party leadership, the new delegate selection rules needed to be modified to address its three principal problems: the disproportionate influence of the early states, the continuing representation inequality at the national conventions, and the decreasing clout of party leaders over the selection of the nominee.

Fixing the Calendar

The nomination calendar was becoming front-loaded. The attention given to the states that held their contests early by the candidates and the press created incentives for other states to schedule their primary or caucus toward the beginning of the nomination period. In 1996, almost two-thirds of all the Democratic convention delegates were chosen by the end of March; in 2000 and 2004, two-thirds were chosen by mid-March; in 2008, almost 60 percent were chosen by the first Tuesday in February, although the process did not end until June.

From the party's perspective, front-loading was undesirable for several reasons. Some states separated their presidential primary from the primaries for other statewide and national offices, thereby increasing election costs and potentially damaging party unity.

Partisan learning suffered. The sequential nature of the nomination process facilitates information acquisition more than a compressed process does. In recent nominations, by the time people turned their attention to the presidential nomination campaign, the field of candidates has been narrowed and many of the issues debated. Moreover, once a front-runner emerged with a sizable delegate lead, turnout declined, thereby reducing the proportion of partisans who had a voice and voted in the selection of the party's standard-bearer.

A front-loaded nomination process reinforces and magnifies resources inequity among the candidates. It gives those candidates that have the most money a strategic advantage. They can wage a media-oriented, multistate campaign, whereas others who are less well-known with a smaller war chest must focus on the few early states. And even if these candidates who are not front-runners are successful, they have less time to take advantage of their good fortune in one or two of the early contests to raise additional funds in a highly compressed nomination calendar. In addition, the front-loaded calendar forces all candidates to begin running a year or two before the nomination to raise the money and gain the visibility they need to compete.

To gain greater involvement of rank-and-file partisans, achieve better representation for all groups within the party, and provide more opportunities for a larger field of candidates, the Democrats tried to impose a "window" during which primaries and caucuses could be held. Initially, the Democrats allowed states to hold their presidential nominations from the second Tuesday in March to the second Tuesday in June. In 2008, they began a month earlier but have since reverted to the first Tuesday in March.

What to do with those states, such as Iowa and New Hampshire, whose laws require them to start earlier than others, has been a perennial issue.[2] Conceding that its national party could not conduct the selection process in these states, the Democrats initially decided that the best they could do was grant Iowa and New Hampshire exceptions to its calendar. Naturally, Democrats in other states complained, noting that Iowa and New Hampshire were not representative of African Americans and Hispanics that comprised much of the party's electoral base. To improve these groups' representation, the party also granted calendar exceptions to Nevada to hold its caucus after Iowa's and South Carolina to hold its primary after New Hampshire's. When Michigan and Florida also scheduled their primaries before the official beginning of the Democrats' calendar in 2008, the party pressured candidates for its nomination not to campaign in these states and initially indicated that they would not seat delegates chosen in elections that violated party rules. After the nomination was decided, however, the party recanted, giving Michigan and Florida half their allocated delegates because both states were deemed critical in the general election. In addition to imposing sanctions, the party also tried to encourage states to hold their nomination contests later by offering them more convention delegates if they did so—the later the date, the more delegates they would receive. However, few states have taken advantage of this opportunity for additional delegates.

President Biden proposed changes for the 2024 Democratic nomination calendar to reflect and better represent diversity within the party. He proposed that South Carolina with its large African American population go first in February, followed by New Hampshire and Nevada three days later, then Georgia, and finally Michigan (see table 4.1). Iowa and New Hampshire officials strongly opposed the changes. The DNC approved the changes, which also required "go-early" states' approval. The Republican Party had previously decided to adhere to the 2020 schedule. Consequently, the 2024 primary calendar is even more front-loaded than previous nomination processes.

Improving Representation

A second problem concerns the fair reflection principle and its application. The formulas that the states initially used to convert the popular vote into convention delegates votes did not always reflect the wishes of most of the voters that participated in their state's nomination process, in part because state officials feared that straight proportionality would reduce their state's collective influence on the outcome of the nomination.

The issue of proportionality came to a head in the 1980s when Democratic front-runners, Walter Mondale (1984) and Michael Dukakis (1988), each received a larger proportion of the convention delegates than the popular vote they won. Rev. Jesse Jackson, another candidate, in the contest, did less well in delegates than his popular support would have merited. Jackson's complaints led the national party to impose strict proportionality in applying the fair reflection

TABLE 4.1 ★ Chronological Cumulation Allocation of Convention Delegates, 2024

Date	Democratic				Republican			
	Jurisdiction (delegates)	Delegates Each Date	Cumulative Delegates	Delegates Remaining	Jurisdiction (delegates)	Delegates Each Date	Cumulative Delegates	Delegates Remaining
Monday 5 February 2024					Iowa (40)	40	40	1.62%
Tuesday 6 February 2024	Nevada (48); New Hampshire (33)	81	144	3.19%				
Tuesday 13 February 2024	Georgia (124)	124	268	5.93%	New Hampshire (22)	22	62	2.51%
Saturday 24 February 2024					Nevada (26); South Carolina (50)	76	138	5.59%
Tuesday 27 February 2024	Michigan (140)	140	408	9.03%	Michigan (55)	55	193	7.82%
March 2024	Iowa (46)	46	454	10.05%				

(continued)

TABLE 4.1 ★ Chronological Cumulation Allocation of Convention Delegates, 2024 *continued*

Date	Democratic				Republican			
	Jurisdiction (delegates)	Delegates Each Date	Cumulative Delegates	Delegates Remaining	Jurisdiction (delegates)	Delegates Each Date	Cumulative Delegates	Delegates Remaining
Tuesday 5 March 2024	Alabama (59); American Samoa (11); Arkansas (37); California (497); Colorado (86); Democrats Abroad (17); Maine (32); Massachusetts (116); Minnesota (92); North Carolina (132); Oklahoma (40); Tennessee (70); Texas (272); Utah (34); Vermont (24); Virginia (118)	1,637	2,091	46.28%	Alabama (49); Alaska (28); Arkansas (40); California (169); Colorado (37); Maine (20); Massachusetts (40); Minnesota (39); North Carolina (75); Oklahoma (43); Tennessee (58); Texas (162); Utah (40); Vermont (17); Virginia (48)	865	1,058	42.89%
Saturday 9 March 2024	Northern Marianas (11)	11	2,102	46.53%	Guam (9); Kansas (39); Wyoming (29)	77	1,135	46.01%

Date								
Sunday 10 March 2024				Northern Marianas (9); Puerto Rico (23)	32	1,167	47.30%
Tuesday 12 March 2024	Idaho (24); Mississippi (40); Missouri (71); Washington (111)	246	2,348	51.97%	Hawaii (19); Idaho (32); Mississippi (39); Missouri (54); Washington (43)	187	1,354	54.88%
Tuesday 19 March 2024	Arizona (85); Florida (250); Illinois (174); Ohio (143)	652	3,000	66.40%	Arizona (43); Florida (125); Illinois (64); Ohio (78)	310	1,664	67.45%
Wednesday 20 March 2024					American Samoa (9)	9	1,673	67.82%
Saturday 23 March 2024	Louisiana (56)	56	3,056	67.64%	Louisiana (46)	46	1,719	69.68%
Tuesday 26 March 2024					Georgia (59)	59	1,778	72.07%
Friday 29 March 2024					North Dakota (29)	29	1,807	73.25%
Sunday 31 March 2024	Puerto Rico (56)	56	3,112	68.88%				

(continued)

TABLE 4.1 ★ Chronological Cumulation Allocation of Convention Delegates, 2024 *continued*

Date	Democratic				Republican			
	Jurisdiction (delegates)	Delegates Each Date	Cumulative Delegates	Delegates Remaining	Jurisdiction (delegates)	Delegates Each Date	Cumulative Delegates	Delegates Remaining
Tuesday 2 April 2024	Wisconsin (87)	87	3,199	70.81%	Wisconsin (41)	41	1,848	74.91%
Saturday 6 April 2024	Alaska (19); Hawaii (31); North Dakota (17); Wyoming (16)	83	3,282	72.64%				
Tuesday 23 April 2024	Delaware (33); Maryland (104); Pennsylvania (173); Rhode Island (30)	340	3,622	80.17%	Delaware (16); Maryland (37); Pennsylvania (67); Rhode Island (19)	139	1,987	80.54%
Tuesday 30 April 2024	Connecticut (63); New York (259)	322	3,944	87.30%	Connecticut (28); New York (91)	119	2,106	85.37%
Saturday 4 May 2024	Guam (12); Kansas (39)	51	3,995	88.42%				

Date	States	No.	Cumulative	%	States	No.	Cumulative	%
Tuesday 7 May 2024	Indiana (76); West Virginia (25)	101	4,096	90.66%	Indiana (58); West Virginia (31)	89	2,195	88.97%
Tuesday 14 May 2024	Nebraska (34)	34	4,130	91.41%	Nebraska (36)	36	2,231	90.43%
Tuesday 21 May 2024	Kentucky (51); Oregon (68)	119	4,249	94.05%	Kentucky (46); Oregon (31)	77	2,308	93.55%
Saturday 25 May 2024					Virgin Islands (9)	9	2,317	93.92%
Tuesday 4 June 2024	District of Columbia (48); Montana (22); New Jersey (127); New Mexico (41); South Dakota (19)	257	4,506	99.73%	District of Columbia (19); Montana (31); New Jersey (49); New Mexico (22); South Dakota (29)	150	2,467	100.00%
Saturday 8 June 2024	Virgin Islands (12)	12	4,518	100.00%				
July 2024	Unassigned (0)							

Source: The Green Papers

rule. Today, candidates receive delegates in proportion to the vote they receive, provided they get at least 15 percent of the total. This percentage, referred to as a *threshold*, is designed to discourage frivolous candidates from running and keeping the party divided for an extended period.

Democratic rules also specify that no more than 25 percent of the delegates can be selected on a statewide basis. The rest are chosen in districts that can be no larger than congressional districts. The allocation of at-large and district delegates is based on the population and the Democratic vote in the last three presidential elections. This allocation formula advantages the most Democratic areas, which tend to be districts with large proportions of minority voters. Barack Obama designed a nomination strategy in 2008 to take advantage of higher concentrations of Democratic delegates in urban districts, a strategy that contributed to his success in winning the nomination. Since then, other Democratic candidates have done so as well.

Another representational problem with which the Democrats had to address initially was the selection of more men than women as convention delegates. To rectify the balance and achieve gender equality, the Democrats required the elected delegates to consist of equal proportions of men and women. This requirement was slightly modified in 2018 by not forcing delegate to declare their gender as male or female. The change, instituted to recognize the difficulty that transgender delegates might encounter, now requires equality among the genders declared by delegates. The equality rule, in effect, forces the candidates to choose approximately the same number of men and women for their slates of pledged delegates.

Despite the changes designed to reflect more accurately partisan voting preferences during the nomination process, inequities still exist. Hillary Clinton received a higher proportion of the popular vote in the 2008 Democratic primaries than the proportion of pledged delegates she received. There was less discrepancy in her caucus popular and delegate vote; in 2016, Clinton received more votes and won more state primaries than did her principal opponent, Bernie Sanders, as did Joe Biden in 2020.

Empowering the Leadership

The third unintended consequence of the Democratic rule changes that the party revisited was the decreasing number of party leaders and elected officials who were chosen as delegates. Unhappy with their loss of influence over the presidential selection process as well as their decreasing visibility at the nominating conventions, state and national party leaders convinced the party after the 1980 election to establish a new category of "super" delegates, which included these political leaders and elected officials (PLEOs), all members of the DNC, all Democratic governors and members of Congress, plus a number of other national, state, and local officials. PLEOs were to be *unpledged*. It was thought that this group of distinguished Democrats might be able to hold the balance of power if the primaries did not produce a winner. They have not done so, however.

Nonetheless, the fear that the super delegates could have reversed the results of Obama's victory in 2008 and undermined Bernie Sanders's chances in 2016—Hillary Clinton, the Democratic front-runner, in both nominations initially received the endorsements of most of the "supers"—prompted the Democrats to modify the rule for 2020 to prevent PLEOs from voting on the first convention ballot. If no candidate receives a majority from the pledged delegates on that ballot, the "supers" will then be permitted to vote on subsequent ballots.

The Democrats also approved rule changes that expanded the use of primaries, same-day registration, and increased transparency, all to increase partisan participation in the 2020 nomination process.

Technically, all Democratic pledged delegates can still vote for whom they want at the national convention; since 1980, the Democrats adopted a rule that allows delegates to vote their consciences rather than simply redeem their campaign pledges. However, the requirement that people who want to be convention delegates indicate their presidential preference in writing before they are officially placed on candidate slates in the caucuses and primaries makes it highly unlikely that many of them will change their minds at the convention, unless the candidate to whom they are pledged encourages them to do so.

Republican Reforms

Although the Republicans initially did not alter their rules as quickly or as extensively as the Democrats, they still were affected by the Democratic rules changes because most of the state legislatures that enacted laws governing party nominations were controlled by the Democrats in the 1970s and 1980s when the reforms were initiated. Some of the rules were forced on the Republicans by Democratic state legislatures. Subsequently, the Republicans modified their rules to eliminate discrimination and prevent a small group from controlling the nomination process. Nonetheless, it has been the philosophy of the GOP to give states more discretion in determining their delegate selection procedures than the Democrats. The national party determines the number of delegates per state based on a formula that includes state size and a bonus for the election of Republicans on the national and state level.[3]

The Republican convention formally approves the rules for choosing delegates for the next Republican convention. This practice has effectively prevented rule changes between convention years. In 2008, however, the rules adopted by the Republican National Convention authorized the creation of a committee to examine the schedule and process for delegate selection and to make recommendations to the national committee.[4]

Beginning in the 2011–2012 election cycle, the party approved a revised calendar that designates the first Tuesday after the first Monday in March as its official starting time with exceptions given to Iowa, New Hampshire, Nevada, and South Carolina to hold their contests in February. The party also imposed a penalty for states violating its calendar or other rules. The penalty reduces the number of delegates for the state at the party's national convention.

Another change, which the Republicans implemented prior to their 2012 nomination process, was a proportional voting rule for states that held their selection process prior to April of the election year. Intended to discourage early winner-take-all primaries that greatly advantaged front-runners, the new rule slowed but did not threaten Mitt Romney's win in 2012.[5] In 2016, the proportional voting requirement was applied to states that held their caucuses and primaries before March 14. After that date, they had discretion to decide on their own delegate allocation formulas. Some adopted winner-take-all or winner-take-most systems to maximize their influence on the selection of the nominee.

Whereas the Democrats prescribe a minimum threshold to receive delegate support, the Republicans do not. Their threshold varies from state to state.[6] Nor do Republicans have special categories of delegates for party leaders and elected officials, although each state's national committee members are automatically part of the state's delegation. Nonetheless, elected state and national leaders traditionally attend the convention. In 2016, however, some of those who opposed Donald Trump's nomination did not do so.

The Republicans also do not have a requirement for gender equality. Since the 1980s, the proportion of women delegates at Republican conventions has ranged around from 30 to 44 percent.

Legality of Party Rules

As previously mentioned, party reforms, to be effective, must be enacted into law. Most states have complied with party rules. A few have not, sometimes resulting in confrontation between these states and the national party. When New Hampshire and Iowa refused to move the dates of their respective primary and caucuses into the Democrats' window period in 1984, the national party backed down. But previously, when Illinois chose its 1972 delegates in a manner that conflicted with newly designed Democratic rules, the party sought to impose these rules on the state.

The conflict between the DNC and Illinois also presented an important legal question: Which body—the national party or the state—has the higher authority on delegate selection? In its landmark decision *Cousins v. Wigoda*, 419 U.S. 477 (1975), the Supreme Court ruled in favor of the national party. The court stated that political parties were private organizations with rights of association protected by the US Constitution. Moreover, choosing presidential candidates was a national requirement that states could not abridge unless there were compelling constitutional reasons to do so. Although states could establish their own primary laws, the party could determine the criteria for representation at its national convention.

Crossover voting in open primaries prompted still another court challenge between the rights of parties to prescribe rules for delegate selection and the rights of states to establish their own election laws. Democratic rules prohibit open primaries in which any voter can request the ballot of any party. When

Wisconsin refused to change its open primary law, the party took the issue to court. Citing the precedent of *Cousins v. Wigoda*, the Supreme Court held in the case of *Democratic Party of the U.S. v. Wisconsin ex. rel. La Follette*, 450 U.S. 107 (1981) that a state had no right to interfere with the party's delegate selection process unless it demonstrated a compelling reason to do so. The court ruled that Wisconsin had not demonstrated such a reason; hence, the Democratic Party could refuse to seat delegates who were selected in a manner that violated its rules.

In the case of *California Democratic Party v. Jones*, 530 U.S. 567 (2000), the Supreme Court reiterated its judgment by invalidating California's "blanket" primary system, which voters had approved in a 1996 ballot initiative. The initiative required state officials to provide a uniform ballot in which voters, regardless of their partisan affiliation, could vote for any candidate of any party for any elected position. Naturally, the parties were upset by the possibility that their nominees could be decided by the votes of Independents and partisans of the opposition party. Four California state parties, including the Democrats and Republicans, challenged the constitutionality of the initiative, claiming that it violated their First Amendment right to freedom of association. The Supreme Court agreed and held the California initiative unconstitutional.

Although these court decisions have given the political parties the legal authority to design and enforce their own rules, the practicality of doing so is another matter. Other than going to court if a state refuses to change its election law, a party, particularly a national party, has only two other viable options: Require the state party to conduct its own delegate selection process in conformity with national rules and penalize it if it does not do so, or grant the state party an exemption so that it can abide by the law of the state.[7]

The rule for allocating a specific number of delegates to the states has also generated legal controversy, but in this case, within the Republican Party. The formula that the Republicans use contains a bonus for states that voted Republican in the previous presidential election.[8] Opponents of this rule contend that it discriminates against the large states because bonuses are allocated regardless of size. Moreover, they argue that the large states are apt to be more competitive and thus less likely to receive a bonus. Particularly hard hit are states in the Northeast and on the Pacific Coast, which have gone Democratic in recent elections. The Ripon Society, a moderate Republican group, has twice challenged the constitutionality of this apportionment rule, but it has not been successful. The Democratic apportionment formula, which results in larger conventions than the Republicans, has also been subject to some controversy, although not in recent years.

The Impact of the Rule Changes

The reforms to the nomination process have produced some of their desired results. They have opened up the process by encouraging more candidates to run and more people to participate. They have broadened representation at the conventions. But they have also weakened the ability of state party leaders to determine the delegates and control their voting at the nominating conventions. Party elites and nonparty group leaders still exercise influence on the process as they did for Hillary Clinton in 2008 and 2016, but they do not dictate its outcome, as Barack Obama in 2008 and Donald Trump in 2016 can attest.

Turnout

One objective of the reforms was to involve more of the party's rank and file in the delegate selection process. This goal has been partially achieved. In 1968, before the reforms, only 12 million people participated in primaries, approximately 11 percent of the voting age population (VAP). In 1972, the first nomination contest held after the changes were made, that number rose to 22 million. For the next three decades, turnout rose and fell depending on the level of competition within the major parties and the number of weeks or months it took to effectively determine a winner.

Turnout in the primaries and caucuses has been highest in 2008 and 2016 with competitive nominations in both parties. In the 2008 primaries, it was almost 58 million people, approximately 30 percent of the voting age population; in 2016, it was 57.6 million, about 28.5 percent of eligible voters.[9] (In only one state, New Hampshire, did turnout in both these nomination years exceed more than half of the eligible electorate.)

The level of participation varies with the type of election, the amount of competition, and voter eligibility. It is much greater in primaries than in caucuses and larger when the process people who voted in the nomination contests were not demographically representative of their party's rank and file. Part of the rationale for the most recent Democratic rules changes was to better represent Hispanic Americans and African Americans, two groups that constitute major components of the Democrats' electoral coalition.

A related issue is whether those participating in the caucuses and primaries are representative of rank-and-file partisans in that state. Studies of voters in the 2008 and 2012 Iowa caucuses indicated that they were. Still the proportion of the electorate that vote in their party's presidential nominations is much smaller than in the general election.[10]

The demographic composition of each party's convention delegates still does not accurately reflect its rank and file, much less the general electorate. Ideologically, Democratic delegates have overrepresented liberals and moderates within their party's electoral coalition; Republican delegates have overrepresented conservatives. Regular churchgoers were overrepresented at both major party conventions, although the greater religiosity of the Republican delegates is also indicative of voters in that party's electoral base. Although the Democrats better represent women and minorities than do the Republicans, women and racial and ethnic groups constitute a much larger proportion of the Democrats' base of voters.

Party Organization and Leadership

Weakening the state party organizations and their leadership was not a goal of party reforms, but to some extent, it has been a product of it in recent nomination processes. The proliferation of candidates along with the requirements of the campaign finance legislation has produced separate electoral organizations, especially candidate-based Super PACs, that can rival the regular party organization and other large nonparty groups for money and campaign activities.

Party leaders can still use their influence with their state legislatures to help determine the date on which their nomination contest occurs and the rules by which it is conducted, but they can no longer dictate the composition of their state delegation and their votes at the national nominating convention. State leaders, however, can also work with interest group leaders, party donors, and partisan-oriented media to endorse candidates and mobilize support for them during the nomination which helps but does not guarantee victory.

Referred to as party elites, the leaders and their activist supporters band together to pursue a range of overlapping and disparate policy goals.[11] Their influence is greatest in the first stage of the contest, the so-called invisible primary, when political endorsements and resources effectively narrow the field, identify the front-runners, gain news media attention for them, and begin to inform and shape public opinion.

Do partisan divisions, created and inflated by the nomination process, adversely affect the party's chance in the general election? Some political scientists have argued that they do, claiming that the longer and more divisive the nomination process, the more likely that it will hurt the party's nominee in the general election.[12] Yet the election of Bill Clinton (1992), Barack Obama (2008), Donald Trump (2016), and Joe Biden (2020) after extended nomination battles, suggests that there is more that unifies partisan voters in the general election than divides them.

The passage of time, the healing efforts of the winning candidates, and shared political beliefs and perspectives of the candidate and their fellow partisans, particularly in an era of political polarization, can overcome a divisive nomination, especially one that focuses as much on personal as on policy differences. Economic, social, and political factors can also shape the electoral environment, the quality of the candidates, and situational events.

Winners and Losers

Rules changes are never neutral. They usually help one group at the expense of another. Similarly, they tend to help certain candidates and hurt others. That is why candidates have tried to shape the rules and why the rules themselves have been changed so frequently. Candidate organizations and interest groups have put continuous pressure on state and national parties to modify the calendar, eligibility rules, and vote allocation formulas to increase their influence in the selection process.

Clearly, the prohibition of discrimination, the requirement for affirmative action, and the rule requiring gender equality have improved the representation of women and minorities for the Democrats.

The openness of the process and the greater participation by the party's rank and file have encouraged those who have not been party regulars to become involved and have created opportunities for outsiders to seek their party's nomination. Some, such as Jimmy Carter (1972), Michael Dukakis (1988), Barack Obama (2008), and Donald Trump (2016) have won. Bernie Sanders came close in 2016. On the other hand, the more the process concentrates primaries at the beginning of the calendar, the greater the resource inequality among the candidates, and the amount of the news coverage, political endorsements, and organizational support they receive, the more likely that the well-known and well-regarded front-runners will be advantaged.

All of this has affected the candidates' quests for the nomination and their ability to govern if elected. It has extended campaigning and made it more arduous and more expensive. It has also made governing more difficult because it creates incentives for candidates to promise more than they can deliver and project leadership images that do not comport with the operation of the country's constitutional system. Thus, the quest for the nomination and what it takes to win may ultimately weaken a newly elected president by hyping performance expectations and then generating discontent when these expectations are not met. Outsiders that win their party's nomination, such as Donald Trump, are particularly prone to this type of problem in their first years in office because they may lack close personal and professional ties to other elected national officials.

Summary

The delegate selection process has changed dramatically over the past five decades. Originally dominated by state party leaders, it has become more open to the party's rank and file because of the reforms designed to broaden the base of public participation, improve representation of the party's rank and file, and give partisan activists more influence over the selection of the party's nominees. Initiated by the Democrats, these reforms have affected the Republicans as well, even though the GOP has not mandated as many national guidelines as the Democrats. Supreme Court decisions have given the parties the authority to dictate rules for their nominating conventions; increasingly, public pressure to reflect popular sentiment and improve representation has led to a greater number of primaries and more delegates selected in them, a trend that is likely to continue.

Turnout has increased, although the proportion of the partisan electorate that participates varies from one nomination to another. The date of the contest, the level of intraparty competition, the amount of money spent, and other candidate-related factors help explain these variations. But the democratic bottom line is that even in highly contested nominations many fewer people follow the nomination contests closely and vote in them than in the general election. The lower the turnout, the more influential party activists and interest group leaders tend to be.

Exercises

1. Both national parties have been trying to impose a nomination calendar that is less front-loaded. Why have they been unable to do so? What are the incentives for states to schedule their nominations early? Do these incentives undermine a democratic nomination process? What changes would you suggest to make the nomination process less compressed or more likely to result in the selection of a stronger, more popular nominee?

2. Devise what you consider fair and equitable rules for the major parties for the selection of their presidential nominees. How could the national parties encourage states to abide by these fair and equitable rules?

3. Should Independents be permitted to vote in a party's primary election? Should they be permitted to run for a party's nomination as Bernie Sanders, elected to the Senate as an Independent from Vermont, did in 2016? Explain why or why not (in 2020 he ran as a Democrat).

Selected Readings

Altschuler, Bruce E. "Selecting Presidential Nominees by National Primary: An Idea Whose Time has Come?" *The Forum: A Journal of Applied Research in Contemporary Politics* 5 (4): Article 5 (2008).

Cohen, Marty, David Karol, Hans Noel, and John Zaller. *The Party Decides: Presidential Nominations Before and After Reform.* Chicago, IL: University of Chicago Press, 2008.

Donovan, Todd, and Rob Hunsaker. "Effects of Early Elections in the US Presidential Nomination Contests." *PS: Political Science and Politics* 42 (January 2009): 45–54.

Kamarck, Elaine C. *Everything You Need to Know about How America Nominates its Presidential Candidates.* Washington DC: Brookings Institution, 2018.

Jewitt, Catlin. *The Primaries, Rules, Parties, Voters, and Presidential Nominations.* Ann Arbor: University of Michigan Press, 2019.

Noel, Hans. "The Activists Decide: The Preferences of Party Activists in the 2016 Presidential Nomination." *Journal of Elections, Public Opinion, and Parties* 28, no. 2 (April 2018): 225–44.

Norrander, Barbara. *The Imperfect Primary: Oddities, Biases, and Strength of US Presidential Nomination Politics.* New York, NY: Routledge, 2019.

Polsby, Nelson W. *The Consequences of Party Reform.* New York, NY: Oxford University Press, 1983.

Redlawsk, David P., Caroline Tolbert, and Todd Donovan. *Why Iowa? How Caucuses and Sequential Elections Improve the Presidential Nomination Process.* Chicago, IL: University of Chicago Press, 2011.

Steger, Wayne P. *A Citizen's Guide to Presidential Nominations: The Challenge of Leadership.* New York, NY: Routledge, 2015.

Tolbert, Caroline, and Peverill Squire, eds. "Reforming the Presidential Nomination Process." *PS: Political Science and Politics* 42 (January 2009): 27–79.

Wayne, Stephen J. *Is This Any Way to Run a Democratic Election?* 7th ed. New York, NY: Routledge, 2020.

———. "When Democracy Works: The 2008 Presidential Nominations." In William J. Crotty, ed., *Winning the Presidency* (pp. 48–69). Boulder, CO: Paradigm Publishers, 2009.

Notes

1. McCarthy's name was on the ballot, but the president's name was not. The regular Democratic organization in New Hampshire had to conduct a campaign to have Democrats write in Johnson's name.

2. The principal reasons that Iowa and New Hampshire precedent and laws require them to hold the first caucus and primary respectively is the attention they receive from the news media and the candidates, the money that results from the early campaigns in these states, and the influence their electorate perceives it gains in choosing the nominee.

3. See *The Green Papers* for the GOP's allocation formula.

4. Under the new Republican rules, states with thirty or more delegates would be reduced to just twelve while states with less than thirty would be reduced to nine.

5. In 1988, George H. W. Bush won 59 percent of the popular vote in states holding winner-take-all primaries but 97 percent of the delegates from these states; in 2008, John McCain received 38 percent of the Republican vote in winner-take-all primaries on or before February 5, but 81 percent of the delegates.

6. The threshold cannot exceed 20 percent.

7. In December 1986, in the case of *Tashjian v. Republican Party of Connecticut*, 479 U.S. 208 (1986), the Supreme Court voided a Connecticut law that prohibited open primaries. Republicans, in the minority at the time in Connecticut, had favored such a primary as a means of attracting independent voters. Unable to get the Democratically controlled legislature to change the law, the state Republican Party went to court, arguing that the statute violated its First Amendment rights of freedom of association. In a 5–4 ruling, the Supreme Court agreed and struck down the legislation.

8. The formula Republicans use to determine the size of each state delegation is complex. It consists of three criteria: statehood (six delegates), House districts (three per district), and support for Republican candidates elected within the previous four years (one for a Republican governor, one for each Republican senator, one if the Republicans won at least half of the congressional districts in one of the past two congressional elections, and a bonus of four and one-half delegates plus 60 percent of the electoral vote if the state voted for the Republican presidential candidate in the previous election).

9. "After a Long Decline, Primary Turnout Rebounds," Pew Research Center, June 9, 2016.

10. Drew Desilver, "Turnout was High in the 2016 Primary Season, but Just Short of 2008 Record," Pew Research Center, June 10, 2016.

11. Marty Cohen, David Carol, Hans Noel, and John Zaller, *The Party Decides: Presidential Nominations Before and After Reform* (Chicago, IL: University of Chicago Press, 2008): 232.

12. James I. Lengle, "Divisive Presidential Primaries and the Party Electoral Prospects, 1932–1976," *American Politics Quarterly* 8 (1980): 261–77; James I. Lengle, Diana Owen, and Molly Sonner, "Divisive Nomination Campaigns and Democratic Party Electoral Prospects," *Journal of Politics* 57 (1995): 370–83.

Campaigning for the Nomination

5

Chapter
★ ★ ★ ★ ★

Introduction

Rules changes, finance laws, and press coverage have affected the strategies and tactics of the candidates. Today, entering primaries is essential for everyone, even an incumbent president who may be challenged by a fellow partisan (figure 5.1). No longer can a front-runner safely sit on the sidelines and wait for the call. The winds of a draft may be hard to resist but, more often than not, it is the candidates and their backers who are tending to the bellows.

FIGURE 5.1 ★ Biden speaking at the campaign's kickoff event in Philadelphia, Pennsylvania.

Michael M. Stokes/Wikimedia Commons

In the past, candidates carefully chose the primaries they entered and concentrated their efforts where they thought they would do best. Today, they have less discretion, particularly at the beginning of the process, when press coverage elevates the importance of the early contests. Planning for a nomination run starts years in advance. Candidates usually establish exploratory committees following the midterm elections. These committees help them test the water and raise the money they need for travel, staff, and other expenses, such as designing a website, building a donor base, hiring campaign consultants, and gaining endorsements and nonparty group support.

Basic Strategic Guidelines

Every nomination campaign must make a number of strategic decisions:

- when to begin the quest for the nomination;
- what type of organization to create;
- how to raise and spend the necessary funds;
- which issues to stress, slogans to use, messages to emphasize, and images to create;
- how to design a communication strategy that attracts favorable news coverage, supplements it with effective advertising, and also reaches voters directly online;
- what groups to target, appeals to make, and how to personalize them;
- how to criticize one's nomination opponents yet be in a position to gain their support after becoming the de facto nominee; and finally, how to campaign in the months after effectively winning the nomination but before the national nominating conventions are held.

Plan Far Ahead

Creating an organization, devising a strategy, and raising the funds needed to conduct a broad-based campaign all takes time. These needs have prompted potential aspirants for their party's nomination to set up Leadership PACs, Issue PACs, Super PACs, and 501c nonpartisan, nonprofit PACs in the early months of the election cycle, and sometimes even before it. George McGovern started running for the 1972 Democratic nomination in January 1971; similarly, Jimmy Carter began his quest in 1974, almost two years before the 1976 Democratic convention; Donald Trump declared his candidacy for 2024 in December 2022.

Even incumbents plan for their renomination well in advance of the election year. President Clinton began his reelection bid in winter 1994, following his party's defeat in the midterm elections.[1] President George W. Bush, anxious to avoid his father's belated and unsuccessful quest for reelection, began planning his 2004 campaign from almost the moment he was declared the winner of the 2000 election.[2] Barack Obama started raising money and positioning himself for reelection in the aftermath of his party's defeat in the 2010 midterm elections.

Donald Trump filed papers for the 2020 election on the day he was inaugurated as president, forty-seven months before the election, and his reelection committee started raising money immediately. In February 2017, Trump appointed Brad Parscale, the head of his digital campaign in 2016, as his 2020 campaign manager. By the beginning of 2019, the Trump organization had more than thirty full-time staffers and a coordinated media campaign. Two years later, it had almost one hundred people working for the campaign. It had raised more than $130,000 million and spent much of it expanding its donor list, sponsoring digital advertising, and paying for administrative costs associated with other campaign activities.

With staff in place, money raised, and an initial strategy designed, Trump wanted to discourage other Republicans from challenging his renomination. The first Democrat to declare his candidacy for the party's 2020 nomination, former member of the House of Representative, John Delany, announced his intention to run on July 27, 2017. Other Democrats began testing the waters even before the 2018 midterm elections and declaring their candidacies. By May 2019, twenty-one had done so. They too began to staff their campaigns and build a war chest. The press regarded the amount of the contributions they received as an indication of their potential political support.

> **BOX 5.1 ★ The Start of the 2024 Race for Party Nominations**
>
> Preparations for the 2024 presidential campaign began even before the 2022 midterm election. Donald Trump actively endorsed and supported MAGA candidates in their primary and general election campaigns, ridiculed a potential nomination rival, Governor Ron DeSantis of Florida, calling him "Ron DeSanctimonious," and officially announced his own candidacy on November 14, 2022, one week after the midterms, and before any other recent presidential candidates; Jimmy Carter had done so on December 13, 1974.
>
> Trump threw his hat in the ring early for several reasons: he had promised to do so on that date and did not want to disappoint his followers or look weak; he desired to put his own spin on the 2022 midterm elections in which an expected red wave did not materialize and most of his endorsed Republican candidates nominees lost; he wished to keep his support base energized and money flowing into his Super PAC; and he wanted to delay or end, if possible, federal court proceedings against him and his company.
>
> Trump's announcement differed in tone and content from his previous declarations of candidacy. Sounding subdued, reading from a teleprompter, addressing policy issues, such as immigration, crime, trade, and "Biden's failed left-wing policies," the ex-president downplayed the results of the 2022 midterm elections, did not engage in personal ridicule and continued to talk about American greatness, past and future. Only about one hundred people attended his announcement ceremony; his son, Donald Trump Jr., and daughter, Ivanka, were not present.
>
> Nor did Trump's announcement generate a large donation response. The campaign received less than $10 million, mostly in small contributions, by the end of 2022. A low-budget campaign was planned with the use of free media supplementing radio, television, and social media advertising. The strategy and structure of the 2024 campaign was to be similar to his 2016 quest with a fluid advisory sys-

BOX 5.1 ★ The Start of the 2024 Race for Party Nominations *continued*

tem and no designated campaign manager. The candidate would be his own chief of staff and make the campaign's major strategic and tactical decisions himself.

If he won the nomination, Trump intended to have the Republican National Committee manage field operations and finance with right-leaning Super PACs helping out with the advertising. However, in a major disappointment to Trump, the Super PAC organized by libertarians Charles and David Koch announced that it would not contribute to presidential primary candidates in 2024.

A team of experienced campaign operatives who had worked for Trump in the past were tasked with overseeing the principal operational and advisory functions. The headquarters was to be in Mar-a-Lago, Florida, not at Trump Towers in New York.

Trump began to hit the road in January 2023, going to New Hampshire and South Carolina, the two first primary states. He spoke to small groups of invited Republicans not to big campaign rallies as in his previous nomination quests. He received endorsements but mostly from GOP members of the House of Representatives. In short, the campaign got off to a slow start, but Trump was still ahead in pre-election polls of Republicans for the nomination in the spring of 2023.

Nikki Haley, daughter of Indian immigrants, former UN Ambassador (during Trump's presidency) and governor of South Carolina, was the second Republican to announce her candidacy for the 2024 GOP nomination. She did not criticize Trump in doing so, but said it was time for a new generation of leadership. Haley then visited the early primary states. Her campaign raised $11 million in the first six weeks after her announcement.

About the same time, Senator Tim Scott (SC), the only African American Republican Senator began a listening campaign in preparation for a presidential run. Scott was in a good financial position to do, with $22 million left over from his previous Senate campaign. He had also endorsed and contributed to many Republican candidates in the 2022 midterm primaries and general elections. A conservative Reagan Republican, Scott advocated a new beginning for America, criticized the "grievance politics of the left," and Biden's Washington-based policies and politics.

Ron DeSantis, the governor of Florida, was also preparing to seek the GOP nomination DeSantis, term-limited under state law, had received much attention for his anti-mask and anti-immigrant policy positions, and for his outspoken opposition to the teaching of new critical race theory in Florida public schools. After the Florida legislature completed its 2023 session in the late spring, DeSantis was expected to officially declare his candidacy.

The fifth Republican to enter the race was Asa Hutchinson, former governor of Arkansas, who announced that he would seek the GOP nomination in April.

There were also other Republicans considering running. Most were going around the country to the early primary states, speaking to groups, contacting party strategists, pollsters, and state organizers, and raising money. These potential candidates included former vice president Mike Pence, former secretary of state Mike Pompeo, New Hampshire governor Chris Sununu, South Dakota governor Kristi Noem, Virginia governor Glenn Youngkin, former New Jersey governor Chirs Christie, and businessman Vivek Ramaswamy.

BOX 5.1 ★ The Start of the 2024 Race for Party Nominations *continued*

A very competitive contest for the nomination was anticipated. The Republican National Committee, which was planning to sponsor debates among the candidates beginning in late summer of 2023, contacted top executives of news networks interested in hosting the debates. The RNC chair, Ronna McDaniel, announced that the first debate would be scheduled in August 2023 in Milwaukee, Wisconsin, the site of the 2024 Republican nominating convention. She also proposed that the candidates take a loyalty oath to support the eventual nominee as a condition for participating in the debates. By the end of February, one year before the primaries were scheduled, the GOP contest was underway.

On the Democratic side, President Biden had been active in raising money and supporting Democratic candidates in 2022, was also gearing up for reelection in 2024. Since the 2022 midterm elections, his political advisors had been planning for his campaign. The probability of another Trump candidacy encouraged their efforts; Biden had defeated Trump by 7 million popular and 74 electoral votes in 2020. He believed he could win again against him or another Republican nominee despite the president's low job approval ratings for most of his presidency, ratings that were in the low to mid-forties, but rising after his trip to Ukraine. In February 2023. External conditions were improving. COVID infections were declining with fewer hospitalizations and deaths. The economy remained resilient, unemployment reached new lows, but inflation continued to be a problem. The United States and its NATO allies were still unified in support of Ukraine; Americans also backed the president's Ukrainian policy, but Biden did not receive much credit for the domestic legislative policy initiatives that were enacted by Congress in his first two years in office.

Despite the Democrats' loss of control of the House of Representatives in the 2022 midterm elections, the party's losses were much less than expected. The president was credited by Democrats for his vigorous campaigning and fundraising. The Democrats appeared more unified than the Republicans. Moreover, Biden had been successful in getting his party to change its nomination calendar, pending approval by individual states, some of which were controlled by Republicans.

The new schedule, predicated on giving minorities within the party a greater voice in the selection of the nominee, favored Biden. The first primary would be in South Carolina, a state that had given Biden a lead in the 2020 Democratic nomination contest, a lead that he never relinquished. Even though early pre-election polls indicated that a plurality of Democrats did not want him to seek reelection, there was no consensus on another nominee. Biden had received a clean bill of health from his doctors in February 2023, taken a trip to Ukraine on the first anniversary of the Russian invasion which demonstrated the president's resolve, courage, and leadership, and to some extent, undercut the age factor that received so much media attention. Only two minor candidates—Marianne Williamson and Robert F. Kennedy Jr., an anti-vaccine advocate—announced their candidacies; no debates were planned; Biden was off and running for reelection.

Concentrate Efforts in the Early Contests

Doing well in the initial caucuses and primaries, raising money, gaining endorsements and public recognition in the news, organizing the campaign, and staffing it with political professionals are the principal tasks most candidates face. The early contests are particularly important for lesser-known aspirants, less for the number of delegates they can win than for the publicity they can gain, the supporters they can mobilize, and the momentum they can build. That momentum in turn generates donations and political endorsements.

For most candidates, visiting the states that have the early caucus and primaries, even staying for extended visits is essential. In the run-up to the 2020 nominating conventions, Democrats made 163 visits to Iowa. Four years earlier, New Hampshire received 492 visits from Republicans and 136 from Democrats.[3]

Although doing well in the early contests is good news; losing in them can be fatal, especially for a non-front-runner. It may not be fatal for a front-runner, however, who has the resources and reputation to run in other early states as Republicans Ronald Reagan (1980), George H. W. Bush (1988), Robert Dole (1996), Ted Cruz (2016), and Joe Biden (2020) can attest.

New Hampshire has traditionally been the first state to hold a primary in which the state's entire electorate can participate. Candidates who do surprisingly well in this primary have benefited enormously. Eugene McCarthy (1968), George McGovern (1972), Jimmy Carter (1976), Bill Clinton (1992), John McCain (2000 and 2008), Mitt Romney (2012), and Donald Trump (2016) all gained visibility, credibility, and confidence from their New Hampshire performances, although none received a majority of the vote. Bill Clinton came in second with 25 percent of the Democratic vote in 1992, 8 percent less than former Massachusetts Senator, Paul Tsongas. Clinton's relatively strong showing, however, in the light of allegations of marital infidelity and draft dodging made his performance impressive in the eyes of the news media, more so than Tsongas's expected win in a neighboring state. Similarly, John McCain's impressive victory in 2000 over front-runner George W. Bush (by 18 percent) elevated him overnight from just another candidate to a serious contender. His victory in that state, though smaller in 2008, revived his campaign for which the press had already written a premature obituary. Neighboring elected officials, such as Bernie Sanders in 2016 and 2020 and Elizabeth Warren in 2020, can mute the importance of a New Hampshire victory if they win or cast doubts about their viability if they lose. Iowa and New Hampshire and the other first-month caucuses and primaries usually receive disproportionate attention from the news media.

During presidential nomination cycles, the coverage begins early. It is focused primarily on the candidates and their standing in the horse race. In 2016, Donald Trump dominated coverage for the Republicans and Hillary Clinton for the Democrats; in 2020, Trump continued to receive the most coverage as did Biden after he won the South Carolina primary and his principal opponents bowed out.[4]

The states that hold the early contests also gain from disproportionate spending from the candidates and their supporters. Their residents see the candidates up close. Many of them can communicate with the candidates directly. Extensive news coverage, campaign spending, and personal contact are the principal reasons that "go-first" states benefit.

Raise and Spend Big Bucks

Having a solid resource base at the outset of the nomination process provides a significant strategic advantage. The ability to raise relatively large amounts during the year before the caucuses and primaries gives a candidate an edge in getting political endorsements. Money tends to flow toward the likely winner. It also attracts the attention of the news media. The press evaluates candidates in the year before the election based on how much money they can raise and from how many people they can raise it. Trump's fundraising ahead of the 2020 Republican nomination and Bernie Sanders's in 2016 and 2020 made headlines. Dollars portend votes, the reason why the press calls the year before the election "the invisible primary."

The candidates who raise and spend the most during the competitive phase of the nomination process tend to do better, although they do not always win. Mitt Romney in 2008 and Jeb Bush in 2016 had the largest war chests but did not win their party's nomination nor did Michael Bloomberg in 2020.

Gain Media Attention

What can non-front-runners do to gain more press coverage? They can stage events, release a stream of seemingly endless faxes, emails, tweets, and videos to local media and place them on popular internet sites, leak unfavorable information about their opponents, solicit invitations to appear on talk/entertainment programs on radio and television, and participate in debates if invited to do so.

Trump gained disproportionate news coverage from his rallies, tweets, and politically incorrect rhetoric. That coverage overwhelmed the news and visibility of the other Republican candidates, creating a headwind that Bush's money, Cruz's ideology, and other candidates could not overcome in 2016.

Debates

Nomination debates are important, more so than in the general election. They give lesser-known candidates a chance to be seen and heard and compared on the same stage as their front-running opponents. Trump, especially, benefited from the comparison in 2015 and early 2016 Republican debates, but Bloomberg did not in 2020. His abrupt manner, facial grimaces, and unemotional rhetoric damaged his leadership imagery.

During the 2007–2008 nomination campaign, there were twenty-one debates among the Democratic contenders and sixteen among the Republicans; in 2012, the Republicans held twenty debates. During subsequent election cycles there have been fewer—twelve among the Republicans and nine among the Democrats, in 2015–2016 and twelve for the 2019–2020 cycle.

The scheduling of debates became a contentious issue for the Democrats in 2015–2016. Bernie Sanders and others accused the DNC of designing a schedule that benefited front-runner Hillary Clinton. The debates took place on Saturday nights; consequently, the number of people viewing or listening to them was much smaller than for the Republican debates.[5]

Nonetheless, almost two-thirds of the population watched at least part of the debates, thereby increasing public interest in the presidential nomination process.[6]

At the outset of the 2016 Republican nomination campaign, there were sixteen candidates, forcing the news networks that sponsored the debates to divide the number of candidates into two groups, one scheduled for prime time and the other earlier. The division, based on the candidates' standing in public opinion polls, gave the front-runners an advantage. The Democrats faced a similar problem four years later. To give all the principal candidates an opportunity to share the initial spotlight, the party required only two relatively easy-to-achieve criteria to qualify for participation in the first two debates scheduled on back-to back weeknights in June and July 2019: receive donations of at least $65,000 from two hundred contributors living in twenty states and obtain at least 1 percent support in three preapproved, pre-debate public opinion polls. The two-night debates were scheduled at the same time and random selection determined the participants in each.

News Coverage

In general, there has been a decline in the amount of time given to election news on the "broadcast" networks and even a larger decline in stories about the candidates on their evening news shows. On the other hand, the 24/7 cable news channels have increased their coverage, as have the websites of the major news networks and other online sites.

Donald Trump dominated press coverage for the Republicans from the moment he entered the race in each of his presidential campaigns. His celebrity status, unconventional rhetoric, and assertive personal style captivated news media attention, as did his antitraditional media campaign.[7] It is estimated that if Trump had to pay for the news coverage he received, it would have cost him billions.[8]

The success of Trump's approach benefitted from the public's distrust of the traditional news media, a distrust that has been increasing among Republicans and Republican-leaning voters. The more he criticized the press, the more coverage he received from them, and the more money the news networks made.[9]

Advertising

Advertising remains one of the most effective ways to reach and inform potential voters. Studies have shown that people tend to retain more information from repetitive candidate commercials than they do from viewing a single news story,[10] a reason why campaigns spend much of their revenues on the design, airing, and targeting of political commercials. Figure 5.2 traces advertising in 2012, 2016, and 2020 during the competitive phase of those presidential nominations.

FIGURE 5.2 ★ Presidential race ads by week and year.

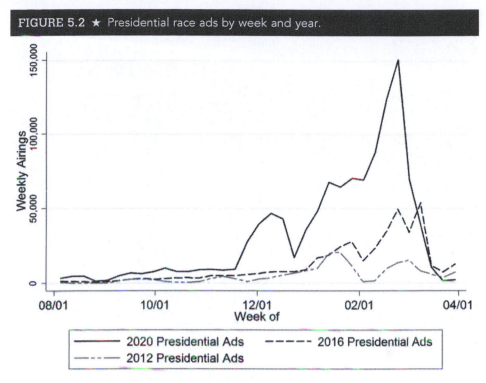

Source: "Presidential, House Ads Slow to Trickle," Kantar/CMAG, with analysis by the Wesleyan Media Project, April 9, 2020.

How effective ads are in promoting the candidates and groups that sponsored them is another matter. In general, lesser-known candidates gain recognition, which they need to establish their viability; the better-known candidates use them to maintain theirs.

Develop an Organization

The major task of any campaign is to mobilize voters and build electoral coalitions among core partisan-oriented groups. Having an organization in the field is deemed especially important in caucus states to get supporters and sympathizers to the precinct meetings; the starting time and location of these meetings are less well known to voters than the places at which they cast their primary and general election ballots. The increasing use of the internet to identify, inform, and mobilize voters must still be buttressed by an on-the-ground organization that includes rallies, field offices, paid staff, and hundreds of volunteers. Face-to-face contacts are considered the most effective way to turn out the vote. Super PACs, which raise and spend extensive amounts, usually do not mount extensive field operations; labor unions, chambers of commerce, and active ideological groups, often do. Field organizations tend to be concentrated in the early primary states.

Monitor Public Opinion

With intentions clear, money in hand, events planned and scheduled, and an organization in place, it is necessary to monitor public sentiment and try to manipulate it to one's political advantage. To achieve these goals, polls and focus groups are used to one's political advantage.

Republican Thomas Dewey was the first candidate to have private polling data available to him when he tried unsuccessfully to gain the Republican nomination in 1940. John Kennedy was the first Democrat to engage a pollster in his quest for the nomination. Preconvention surveys conducted for Kennedy in 1960 indicated that Hubert Humphrey, Kennedy's principal rival, was potentially vulnerable in West Virginia and Wisconsin. Based on this information, Kennedy decided to concentrate time, effort, and money in these predominantly Protestant states. Victories in both helped demonstrate his broad appeal, thereby improving his chances for the nomination.

Today, all major presidential candidates commission their own polls. If candidates lack the financial resources to do so, they must depend on public polls conducted by national and state-based news organizations or academic institutions. Surveys provide critical information about the perceptions, attitudes, and opinions of voters as well as the kinds of appeals to which they are likely to be most receptive. Focus groups engage people in conversation and have become an increasingly valuable tool for speechwriters and media consultants. Almost all campaign advertising is pretested by such groups to gauge likely reactions to it. Adjustments, if necessary, are made before the ad is aired; a negative response by the focus group may kill the ad entirely.[11] Experiments and analytics are also important components of campaign research and messaging.

Although polls and focus groups affect strategy, tactics, and fundraising, their impact on the general public is less direct. Despite the fears expressed by politicians, there are few empirical data to suggest that poll results, spotlighted in the news, generate a "bandwagon effect" among the general public; polls are more likely to affect the attentive public, people who follow the campaign more closely. Standing in the polls improves a candidate's ability to attract contributors, volunteers, and news coverage.

During the 2015–2016 election cycle, Jeb Bush initially led Republicans in the preelection polls until Trump took the lead in July 2015. Trump never relinquished it as the debates and primaries victories boosted his popularity among Republicans. In 2019, Elizabeth Warren was the early leader among the Democratic candidates; in 2020, Pete Buttigieg took the lead. After the South Carolina primary, Biden was ahead. His last opponent, Bernie Sanders, dropped out in April.

Design and Target a Distinctive Image and Message

The information obtained from polls, focus groups, and other analyses is used to create and sharpen leadership images and campaign appeals and target them to sympathetic audiences. Candidates first must establish their credentials, then articulate their general themes, and finally present specific policy positions.

Designing a distinctive leadership image and policy appeal that falls within the mainstream of partisan views is difficult, especially when there are a lot of candidates competing for the nomination. Obama and Clinton emphasized change, Clinton and Biden experience, Republican McCain stressed his independence, Romney his conservatism, and Trump his leadership skills.

People tend to gain greater awareness and information about the candidates and their positions as the nomination advances, particularly in states in which candidates actively campaign, but there are significant knowledge gaps on the issues within the general public. Endorsements and attacks can also inform voters and, in some cases, do influence voting, but many people are not aware of endorsements and, when they are, deny that they affect the way they vote. In the 2016 nominations, endorsements reinforced Clinton's support among Democratic partisans, but the Republican establishment's opposition to Trump seemed to have little impact on his. In 2020, they helped Biden.

Make Effective Use of Communication Technologies

One of the distinctive aspects of nomination campaigns since the beginning of the 1990s has been the propensity of candidates to circumvent the national news for less expensive local media and online social networking. Candidates now try to reach voters directly, rather than going through the traditional news media to do so. Social media have become the most popular online sources of campaign news, more so than candidate websites and emails. In 2020 and 2024, the candidates targeted their messages to groups on Facebook in addition to traditional television, radio, and social media advertising.[12]

Trump's tweets received considerable news coverage, especially his ridicule of his Republican opponents. Trump was also the most searched for of all the candidates on the online search engines.

Campaigning on the internet is not without its problems, however. Squatters have registered web addresses of potential candidates long before they declare their candidacy and then demand large sums of money to give them up. Parody sites and linkages have mushroomed. Unsubstantiated rumors circulate widely and rapidly. Videos and tapes recorded long ago can be accessed and widely circulated. Security has also become a problem. In 2016, WikiLeaks posted hacked emails from the DNC and Clinton's campaign chair, John Podesta; an off-the-record recording of Trump's derogatory comments about women in 2005 was aired on television and YouTube in 2016.

The news media give considerable coverage to the nomination campaign because elections generate public interest, which in turn produces revenue for news outlets. In short, it is in their journalistic interests to prolong the contest for as long as possible.

Coordinating Strategy with Candidacy Status

Timing, finance, organization, and communications affect the quest for delegates. They help shape the candidates' strategies and tactics for the nomination. Generally speaking, there have been two successful strategic approaches, one for front-runners and another for lesser-known challengers.

Campaigning as Front-Runner

Front-runners begin with greater reputations, more resources, and better-known national credentials. What they need to do is stay in the lead. The strategy is straight-forward—take advantage of their resources: recognition as the potential nominee, the political influence that recognition conveys, a larger war chest, more staff, endorsements, press coverage, volunteers, and the ability to wage a multistate campaign.

A front-runner's advantages are most potent at the beginning of the nomination process when the perceived gap with the other candidates is the widest. The front-loading of the primaries provides an additional benefit because it makes it more difficult for the lesser-known competitors to parlay an early, unexpected victory into other quick wins. Proportional voting requirements in party primaries, however, make an early knockout less likely than in the past, especially for the Democrats.

As the nomination campaign progresses, most front-runners have to combat the inevitable "anyone but them" campaign that will be waged by their opponents and the news media to keep the race competitive for as long as possible. When Trump became the Republican front-runner in 2016, Republicans and Super PACs opposing his candidacy spent millions to prevent him from winning the GOP nomination.

Ronald Reagan's preconvention campaign in 1980 is a good example of a front-runner approach. Reagan raised and spent much of his money in the early primaries and caucuses. His tightly run, top-down campaign, built in-depth organizations in key states, obtained the support of many party leaders, and benefited from a large staff of professionals and volunteers. George W. Bush and Al Gore followed similar strategies in 2000 as did Hillary Clinton in 2008 and 2016 (although unsuccessfully in 2008), and Mitt Romney in 2012 (textbox 5.2).

BOX 5.2 ★ Successful Front-Runner Campaigns

Republican John McCain (2008)
In 2000, John McCain challenged George W. Bush and other Republicans for that party's nomination and lost. He began his campaign too late, raised insufficient funds, received few endorsements from Republican leaders, and was unable to generate a genuine grassroots movement in states in which only Republicans could participate. His reputation for independence, so appealing to the general public, worried GOP partisans; his emphasis on national security issues raised questions about his priorities, particularly among social conservatives. Clearly, McCain needed to refashion his conservative image and strengthen his appeal among Republican leaders if he was going to run again, and he did.

As the 2007–2008 campaign got underway, McCain stayed in the public eye, touted his experience, and proclaimed his loyalty to basic conservative principles

BOX 5.2 ★ Successful Front-Runner Campaigns *continued*

of his party. Recognized and respected by most Republicans, he began as the party's front-runner. He also adjusted his campaign strategy accordingly, from renegade in 2000 to that of the Republican leader in 2008.

The 2006 midterm elections and a slowing economy marred his fundraising and partisan mobilization efforts. Moreover, his history of independence, his support of immigration reform, and his de-emphasis of social issues also continued to generate concerns among conservative Republicans. The financial and political support he anticipated did not materialize. By summer 2007, the press was reporting that his campaign was suffering from internal divisions, insufficient revenue, and an incoherent strategic plan. Top aides were dismissed, and money had to be borrowed to keep the campaign afloat. Failing as the logical and consensus nominee, McCain was forced to change his strategy and adopt one that was more consistent with his personal character and political style. He decided to skip the Iowa caucus, a state with a large number of social conservatives, and concentrated instead on New Hampshire, a state, he had won in 2000 against George W. Bush. He did so again in 2008, receiving 37.1 percent of the vote, less than he got in 2000, but more than any of his opponents received.

McCain lost the next primary to Romney in Michigan, a state in which Romney's father had served as governor, but when the campaign shifted to South Carolina, McCain won the popular vote and most of the state's convention delegates with support from that state's party leaders.

Florida, the next big Republican primary, provided the opportunity for McCain to break out from the pack, and he did. Although he won 36 percent of the popular vote, he received all the delegates in this winner-take-all state. As importantly, the victory gave him momentum going into the Super Tuesday primaries and caucuses. Winning all the big states that allocated most of their delegates to the popular-vote winner, he added a large number of delegates to the lead he already had built. By the beginning of the next month, he had a majority. The race was essentially over.

Republican Mitt Romney (2012)

In 2008, Mitt Romney had floundered despite spending the most money. However, he gained national recognition. In the years that followed, he mended his ties with party leaders, received substantial contributions from partisans, and became the candidate to beat as the 2011–2012 nomination cycle got underway.

Romney's strategy, much like other front-runners, was to play it safe and campaign as if he were the nominee. He purposely maintained a low public profile. His campaign staged fewer media events and aired fewer commercials than it had four years earlier. Aides limited press access to him; they structured the interviews he had with reporters and kept him on script. He was cautioned not to ad-lib.

Romney made only eleven visits to Iowa prior to its caucus. Only after polls revealed him running into electoral difficulty when Governor Rick Perry (Texas) entered the race in summer 2011, did Romney redirect his attention to his partisan opponents and unleash a negative advertising campaign against them. By doing so, he took some of the heat off his own personal and policy vulnerabilities, particularly his support for Massachusetts health care as governor, and his profit-oriented decisions as head of Bain Capital.

BOX 5.2 ★ Successful Front-Runner Campaigns *continued*

His strategy was successful. After tying his social conservative opponent Rick Santorum in Iowa, Romney won the New Hampshire primary. A loss to Newt Gingrich in South Carolina was followed by wins in Florida, Arizona, and Michigan, which extended his delegate lead. His superior organizational and financial resources that exceeded those of his GOP opponents combined made it difficult for them to close the delegate gap or the perception that Romney was the most electable Republican candidate. One by one, his challengers dropped out; the last to do so was Rick Santorum who ended his candidacy on April 10. The front-runner had won easily against a small number of relatively weak challengers.

Democrat Hillary Clinton (2016)
Even before the first caucuses and primaries were held, the Clinton campaign, with the help from the DNC, had the deck stacked in her favor. The DNC had scheduled three of the first four Democratic debates on weekend evenings when fewer people were likely to watch them; the party had signed a fundraising and revenue-distribution agreement with the Clinton campaign in which Clinton would solicit donations for the party, which in turn, would redistribute most of the money back to the Clinton's Victory Fund. A large number of super delegates endorsed her candidacy.

Clinton had learned from her 2008 loss to Obama to focus on gaining delegates more than obtaining huge popular vote victories, a strategy that made sense in the light of the Democrats' proportional voting system. Concentrating her campaign in the big states' delegate-rich, urban precincts, she won most of them as well as close-in suburbs, areas that have large numbers of minority voters.[15] Exit polls indicated that she won 78 percent of African American vote and 60 percent of the Hispanic vote. Most of the larger states held their Democratic primaries in March on the first and second Tuesdays of the month. Part of the Clinton strategy was to maximize the front-runner's advantage. Her goal was to set up a firewall in South Carolina, the second primary, and then in the Super Tuesday states just in case she did not do well in the Iowa caucus or the New Hampshire primary. She won Iowa barely but was soundly defeated in New Hampshire by Bernie Sanders.

Her strategy proved to be successful. She won most of the large state primaries that were held during this period, enhanced her large delegate lead, and reinforced the perception among Democratic partisans, donors, and journalists that she would be her party's nominee. By the time the Sanders campaign picked up steam with victories in later primaries and caucuses, Clinton was too far ahead of him in pledged and unpledged delegates for Sanders to claim persuasively that he could catch up. The perception of Clinton's likely nomination magnified the amount and tone of news coverage she received. Beginning her quest as the strong front-runner, Clinton adopted centrist policy positions. Initially, she ignored her Democratic opponents and directed her fire toward what she termed "failed" Republican policies that led to the Great Recession and the war in Iraq. She appealed to mainstream Democratic voters with centrist issue positions, consistent with most of the domestic policy pursued by the Obama administration.

In her style and campaign rhetoric, Clinton played it cautiously. Most of her messages were pretested. She thoroughly prepared for her speeches, interviews, and debates and made few tactical errors, although her remark, "we're going

BOX 5.2 ★ Successful Front-Runner Campaigns *continued*

to put a lot of coal miners and coal companies out of business," did generate a backlash in West Virginia and forced her to apologize to voters in that and other coal-producing states.

Her "play-it-safe" approach, however, did not generate the enthusiasm nor project the authenticity of her principal opponent, Bernie Sanders. Clinton was not as rousing a motivational speaker as Sanders; she preferred small meetings with groups of citizens in which she could listen to their views, address their concerns, and demonstrate her knowledge.

Her nomination victory did not boost her general election candidacy. Clinton's popularity declined over the course of her quest to be the party's standard-bearer. She was hounded by her use of a private internet server as secretary of state, an incident in which four US diplomats were killed in Benghazi, Libya, and Republican criticism directed toward her rather than toward Sanders or President Obama. Nonetheless, she went into the general election with a large lead in the preelection polls over Republican Donald Trump.

Campaigning as a Non-Front-Runner

Candidates who are less well-known, staffed, and funded have fewer options. They have to adopt an "exceeding-expectations" strategy. Jimmy Carter is a good example. When he began his quest for the Democratic presidential nomination in 1974, few people had heard of him. Hamilton Jordan, Carter's campaign manager, designed a basic game plan to achieve surprising and newsworthy victories. He explained:

A crowded field enhances the possibility of several inconclusive primaries with four or five candidates separated by only a few percentage points. Such a muddled picture will not continue for long as the press will begin to make "winners" of some and "losers" of others. The intense press coverage, which naturally focuses on the early primaries, plus the decent time intervals, which separate the March and mid-April primaries [in 1976], dictate a serious effort in all of the first five primaries. Our "public" strategy would probably be that. New Hampshire would just be a warm-up. In fact, a strong, surprise showing in New Hampshire should be our goal which would have tremendous impact on successive primaries.[13]

Jordan's plan worked. Carter won the Iowa caucus and the New Hampshire primary. He defeated George Wallace in Florida, overcoming a disappointing fourth place in Massachusetts a week earlier. The Carter effort in 1976 became the model for George H. W. Bush in 1980, Gary Hart in 1984, John McCain in 2000, and most of the Democratic non-front-runners since then.

Barack Obama faced a similar hurdle in 2008. Although he received a substantial number of contributions, he needed a victory to demonstrate his viability as a potential nominee. He also had to show he could win in states with a relatively small African American population. His victory in Iowa demonstrated that he could do so. Although he lost the popular vote in New Hampshire, he received half the state's convention delegates and then secured a large electoral victory in South Carolina. These early wins changed the dynamics of the 2008 Democratic nomination; they raised questions about Hillary Clinton's inevitability as the party's standard-bearer, helped solidify Obama's support among African American women, and generated a new round of donations. By doing well early in the calendar, he had quickly made the nomination into a two-person contest.

Most non-front-runners are not as successful as were Carter in 1976, Obama in 2008, and Trump in 2016 (textbox 5.3). It is hard to run uphill. The number of primaries; their concentration at the beginning of the process; the difficulty of building, training, and sustaining volunteers; and the disparities in financial resources, especially during the media-heavy phase of the nominations, make it more difficult for non-front-runners to win.

BOX 5.3 ★ Successful Non-Front-Runner Campaigns

Democrat Barack Obama (2008)

Preliminary planning for Obama's presidential campaign began in 2006 after the midterm elections; more intensive planning started in January 2007 after he decided he would run. The initial task was to create a lean organization, focused on the campaign's critical needs: hiring personnel, raising money, mobilizing supporters, scheduling and advancing events, and setting up field and digital operations. Winning the Iowa caucus was the campaign's initial goal. Iowa was important for three reasons: to demonstrate that Obama, of mixed race but identifying himself as African American, could win in a predominantly white state; to show that Hillary Clinton's nomination was not inevitable; and to prove that an army of volunteers could be identified, organized, and mobilized from the internet for the campaign. Because Clinton began with the endorsements of many prominent state and national party leaders, labor union officials, and the sympathy of much of the Democrats' rank-and-file voters, Obama concluded that the only way he could win Iowa was to enlarge the base of caucus attendees by attracting new voters and appealing to independent-leaning Democrats.

With the caucus a year away, the campaign literally set up shop in Iowa along with those of most of the other Democratic candidates, except for Clinton. During his visits to Iowa, Obama held up to six events a day while campaign volunteers went to every high school, college, and university in the state to inform and recruit students to help them reach and excite voters about Obama's candidacy. At major events, email addresses, cell phone numbers, and zip codes were collected and used to stay in touch, generate new "friends," and register new voters. Training sessions were held to convert these volunteers into a viable grassroots organization. The work paid off. Twice as many people turned out for the caucus than four years earlier. Obama won 37.6 percent of the vote compared with John Edwards's 29.7 percent and Hillary Clinton's 29.5 percent.

As a result of his victory in Iowa, Obama's candidacy gained national attention, fundraising increased, but so did public expectations of future performance in the contests that followed, notably the New Hampshire primary scheduled five days after Iowa. Clinton had a stronger ground operation in that state and the support of most of the state's party leaders, labor unions, and many interest groups, including Emily's List, a support group for women candidates. Moreover, Obama had to

BOX 5.3 ★ Successful Non-Front-Runner Campaigns *continued*

compete with John McCain for the support of Independent voters. His campaign could not overcome these hurdles.

Clinton won 3 percent more of the popular vote in New Hampshire, but they divided the delegates evenly, moderating the significance of her popular vote victory. Although Clinton also won the Nevada caucus, the next contest, the pledged delegates were again divided evenly. The last early contest before Super Tuesday was South Carolina, a state in which Clinton was expected to do well. Obama succeeded in mobilizing the African American community that constituted more than half that state's Democratic electorate. As a consequence, he won 55 percent of the popular vote and twenty-five of the state's forty-five delegates and took a small delegate lead into Super Tuesday. His revenue flow and funds on hand at that point exceeded Clinton's. Obama used his financial advantage to advertise extensively in the large Super Tuesday states; he also competed in all the smaller caucus states whereas Clinton did not; she contested only one of them. Obama's strategy proved successful in terms of the pledged delegates he won. Although he lost the large states to Clinton, he won the smaller ones and received a total of fifteen more delegates than she did. He had survived Super Tuesday and extended his delegate lead during the rest of the month.

The press's campaign narrative began to change. Instead of emphasizing the popular vote, news coverage began to turn to the pledged delegate vote in which Obama was ahead. Even though Clinton won several large states in the days that followed, she was able to reduce Obama's pledged delegate lead marginally.

The most significant obstacle that stood in the way of Obama's nomination was the unpledged super delegates that constituted 19 percent of the Democratic convention, most of whom had previously endorsed Clinton. The Obama campaign then proceeded to wage a public and private battle for them, convincing these delegates that they should reflect the popular will of their states. To Democratic politicians, sympathetic to party rules, this was a compelling argument. The "supers" from states that supported Obama began to join his camp.

Although the Democratic contest continued until all the primaries and caucuses had concluded, Obama never relinquished his delegate lead. His campaign had designed and executed a successful, delegate-oriented strategy that not only won him the nomination but also the resources and organization to advantage his candidacy in the general election.

Republican Donald Trump (2016)

Donald Trump did not begin as the Republican front-runner but quickly became the most popular GOP candidate by mid-July 2015. He remained that way throughout the nomination campaign. Trump announced his candidacy at Trump Towers on June 16, 2015. He did so in a way that attracted and maintained public attention. Bemoaning domestic job losses that he blamed on unfair trade agreements, stressing illegal immigration on the southern border, and the threat of Islamic terrorism at home and abroad, he appealed to fears and discontent of Republicans who had lost faith in the country's political leaders, suffered economically from Great Recession, and were upset by the rapid transformation of the United States into a multicultural society.

Trump also bragged about his personal wealth, said "he couldn't be bought, and would self-finance his own campaign." A billionaire, he bridged the gap between

BOX 5.3 ★ Successful Non-Front-Runner Campaigns *continued*

his wealth and lifestyle and that of the people to whom he wanted to reach with language that his base understood and used in their everyday lives. He ate fast foods, rallied against political correctness, and promised straight talk. He used insult, outrage, and innuendo to gain attention, excite his audiences, and evoke emotions of his supporters, such as his statement about Mexican immigrants:

> When Mexico sends its people, they're not sending their best. They're sending people that have lots of problems, and they're bringing those problems with us. They're bringing drugs. They're bringing crime. They're rapists. And some, I assume, are good people.[14]

Trump's comments naturally attracted extensive news coverage. He increased the amount of coverage he received by repeatedly using reporters and news organizations as foils, a tactic that resonated with Republicans in particular.

The increasing proliferation of ideologically oriented news sources on cable and online provided him with a coterie of conservative media outlets that magnified and justified his rhetoric and convictions. With the exception of Fox, the traditional news networks became targets of opportunity for Trump. He alleged them biased and accused them of reporting "fake news." They, in turn, highlighted his factual inaccuracies. Truth itself had become a contentious issue in the campaign.

During the first year of the election cycle, the news media gave more coverage to the nomination campaign than it did in most preelection years, the exception being 2007. Republicans received twice as much coverage as the Democrats with Donald Trump getting the most. Of the 857 minutes that ABC, CBS, and NBC evening news shows devoted to the presidential selection process through November 30, 2015, Trump received a total of 234 minutes (27 percent of total coverage) compared with Clinton's 113 minutes, Bush's 56, Carson's 54, Rubio's 22, Sanders's 10, and Cruz's 7.[15]

Trump's rallies were also newsworthy events, not only for what he said and how he said it but also because rallies generated protests and violence. The news coverage fired up Trump's appeal among his supporters and reduced his need for paid advertising to reach them. It also increased the amount of news coverage he received.

Trump ridiculed and negatively stereotyped his political opponents, both Republican and Democratic. The stereotypes, repeated in news accounts and the Republican debates, stuck in the public's mind. They also helped distinguish his candidacy from that of his opponents.

In the early caucuses and primaries, Trump did well. In the same manner of other non-front-runners, Trump concentrated his efforts in Iowa, New Hampshire, and South Carolina. Although he lost Iowa by a small margin (3 percent) to Ted Cruz, he won the New Hampshire and South Carolina primaries, getting about one-third of the popular vote and most of the delegates. By the end of February, he had twice as many pledged delegates as his Republican opponents.

The Super Tuesday primaries and caucuses extended Trump's lead. He won seven of the ten Republican primaries. Had he not lost Texas, Cruz's home state, he would have doubled the number of delegates that his opponents won that day. By mid-March, Trump led by almost three hundred delegates; he had more than half the number he needed to win the nomination.

In April, Trump extended his lead, winning New York and the other states in the Northwest and forcing Cruz to adopt a desperation tactic. In some states,

BOX 5.3 ★ Successful Non-Front-Runner Campaigns *continued*

the actual delegates were chosen after the state voted in its primary or caucus. Cruz tried to influence the selection of those delegates who might support him on the second and subsequent ballots if Trump did not win a majority on the first. About 80 percent of the delegates had to vote as their state did in the initial convention ballot.

By the end of May, the race was effectively over despite continued efforts by some elected Republicans, large donors, and Super PACs to deny Trump the nomination. He ended up with almost 1,600 delegates compared to Cruz's 559; a lead he extended with popular vote victories in Florida, Illinois, and Ohio in mid-March.

Donald Trump (2020)

President Trump did not face a major challenge for the Republican nomination in 2020. He had a huge war chest, minimal opposition, and extensive media coverage. Initially only three other Republicans declared their candidacy or intention to run. Only one, former Massachusetts governor and 2016 Libertarian Party vice presidential nominee, William Weld, was still campaigning in 2020. With little money, recognition, and news coverage, he fared badly even in his home state. Trump ignored him. The race was over by mid-March.

Democrat Joe Biden (2020)

Former vice president, Joe Biden began his campaign in April 2019, later than most of the other Democratic contenders. Well-known and well-liked, he did not need the time that others did to gain recognition. But starting late was a disadvantage in fundraising and organization. With most of the major Democratic consultants hired by other candidates, Biden turned to people he knew and had worked for him for the top strategic, financial, and legal positions.

Fundraising went slowly, but Biden ran ahead in the preelection polls on the basis of his reputation and recognition by the Democratic electorate. Bernie Sanders emerged as his principal challenger with a large base of supporters, staffers, and donors from his 2016 campaign. He also gained considerable news coverage because, like Trump, he energized his base with fiery speeches and a distinctive ideological orientation that focused on democratic socialism. He did well in the first three early Democratic nomination contests with frightened Democratic moderates who feared that he would be a weak candidate and would hurt other Democratic candidates running for office.

Biden was popular with minority voters, particularly African Americans, the majority of the Democratic electorate in South Carolina; he was also endorsed by Representative James Clyburn, a popular Black leader in that state. Although Biden campaigned less and spent less in South Carolina than did most of his principal rivals, he won an overwhelming victory, much larger than expected. His challengers who had competed vigorously in the other early states had depleted most of their resources, divided elected delegates and with the exception of Michael Bloomberg, suspended or ended their campaigns. Most importantly, they all began to endorse Biden whom they considered the most electable Democrat. Sanders stayed in the race until April 10 when it became clear that Biden would win a first ballot victory at the Democratic National Convention, and then, he too gave his backing to Biden to unify the party against Trump. In short, Biden had won by default.

Campaigning as a Pulpit Candidate

If using the public podium is a primary goal and winning the nomination is un-realistic, then non-front-runners can last longer and achieve more limited objec-tives, such as promoting their distinctive ideological views, policy positions, or gaining recognition for a future run.

Pulpit candidates cannot afford large staffs, high-priced consultants, or much, if any, paid media. They depend on volunteers, news coverage, and special events (especially debates) if they are invited to participate. In 2004, former Illinois senator Carol Moseley-Braun ran for the Democratic nomination because she did not want her party to take its large female constituency for granted. Campaigning on the theme of gender equality, her biggest applause line was "Take the men-only sign off the White House door." But she could not afford to campaign for long. Unable to raise sufficient funds, even among women, she was forced to drop out before the first primary was held.

Rev. Al Sharpton had greater name recognition than Moseley-Braun when he ran in 2004. He had been at the forefront of various social protests, giving voice to many of the concerns of those at the lower end of the socioeconomic scale. A critic of the war in Iraq and the George W. Bush administration's probusiness economic and social policies, he presented the "other" side, often with great wit. Although his campaign helped energize the African American community and bring attention to racial and social issues, he was unable to expand his base of support or the perception that he could not win the party's nomination or the general election.

Initially, Congressman Ron Paul (Texas) did not want to run for president in 2008. He did not like government and couldn't imagine himself as head of it. Persuaded by aides who wanted to promote a libertarian policy agenda, Paul en-tered the contest to attract Republicans dissatisfied with the Bush administration and libertarians who had made few inroads into that party's nomination process. Although he raised enough money and gained enough support to keep his can-didacy alive, he was unable to attract mainstream Republican voters. Similarly, in 2012, he remained visible but not competitive for the nomination. His son, Senator Rand Paul (Kentucky), ran in 2016 as a libertarian Republican but was unable to generate support among a large cross section of the Republican voters.

Bernie Sanders began his 2016 campaign for the Democratic presidential nomination primarily to promote his socialistic agenda. Initially, he did not believe he could defeat Hillary Clinton. However, after his rallies generated en-thusiasm, campaign dollars, public attention, and political support, his strategy changed to winning nomination.

When Sanders intended to use the campaign as a pulpit to criticize the coun-try's widening income inequality, what he termed "massive corporate welfare," and inattention to the dangers of climate change, he limited his campaigning to extended weekends, not wanting to neglect his Senate duties. As his candidacy picked up steam in the winter of 2015–2016, he began to campaign full-time. His delay in full-time campaigning and organizing was costly, however, as Jeff Weaver, his campaign manager, notes:

We would have had a more robust staff earlier in the process if we had known we were going to have the resources we had. We also might have been tempted to have been drawn onto television when the Clintons went on television. We resisted then because we were trying to conserve money.[16]

When Sanders adopted a non-front-running strategy, his goals were similar to Obama's in 2008. Win Iowa and New Hampshire to establish viability as a candidate, gain attention from the news media that had questioned the inevitability of Clinton's nomination, and generate a flow of revenue from excited supporters who now had reason to believe that Sanders could win. Despite his late start, Sanders did attract a few experienced staff aides to help him recruit volunteers, especially for those areas in which renting and staffing field offices or holding large rallies would have been impractical and inefficient. Young techies, using telephone and digital technologies, also aided him in identifying potential supporters, collecting and programing voting data, and generating a steady stream of money to maintain and expand his campaign. Coming within 1 percent of Clinton in Iowa and handily winning the New Hampshire primary, Sanders achieved his first strategic goal but had difficulty matching Clinton's head start in South Carolina and the thirteen states that held their primaries on Super Tuesday in March. Although he raised sufficient funds to advertise in many of these states, he was not competitive on the ground, winning only Colorado, Oklahoma, and his home state of Vermont. In 2020, it was different, although he had to drop out after Biden took a commanding lead.

Summary

In running for their party's nomination, candidates must make a number of important strategic decisions. These include when to begin, how to organize, where to concentrate their early efforts, how to raise money and on what to spend it, how to gain the necessary news media coverage, monitor public opinion, and design and target distinctive personal and policy appeals and simultaneously create an authentic leadership image.

Decisions on mobilizing and allocating sufficient resources to build and maintain delegate support depend on the particular status and circumstances of individual candidates, the environment in which the nomination occurs, and the time frame needed to implement a strategic plan. The new communications technologies of the late twentieth and early twenty-first centuries figure prominently in this effort. They have extended the reach but shortened the campaign's reaction time. Public opinion polls and focus groups are now used to design, test, and track political advertising; targeted personalized appeals are calibrated to arouse particular emotions in selective political communities; and interactive campaigning online is now standard fare. In general, there have been two successful prototypes for winning the nomination: "the out-front, big-bucks, challenge-me-if-you-dare approach" of the leading candidates and "the come-from-the-pack approach" of the non-front-runners.

Front-runners have to maintain their position as likely nominees. That position brings recognition, revenue, and political endorsements. These resources, in turn, provide flexibility and allow candidates to wage multistate campaigns, but they also have higher expectations to meet to maintain their leading-candidate status. The concentration of caucuses and primaries at the beginning of the nomination calendar and, usually, the requirement for proportional voting, adds to the front-runner's advantage.

In contrast, non-front-runners need stepping-stones to the nomination. Their initial goal must be to establish their viability as candidates. At the outset, the key is recognition. Over the long haul, it is momentum. Recognition is bestowed by the news media on those who do well in the early caucuses and primaries; momentum is achieved by winning a series of nomination contests. Together, recognition and momentum compensate for what the non-front-runners lack in reputation and popular appeal. That is why non-front-runners concentrate their time, efforts, and resources on the first few caucuses and primaries. They have no choice: Winning will enhance their status; losing will confirm it. It is an uphill struggle that few non-front-runners have successfully overcome, Carter, Obama, and Trump being the principal contemporary exceptions.

In the end, the ability to generate a popular appeal among the party's electoral base is likely to be decisive. Only one person in each party can amass a majority of the delegates, and that is the individual who can build a broad-based coalition. Although specific groups may be targeted, if the overall constituency is too narrow, the nomination cannot be won.

In 2016, Hillary Clinton ran a traditional front-runner's campaign. She appealed to partisan Democrats and was helped by the large number of endorsements she received from party leaders and elected officials, the large amounts of money that flowed into her war chest, the arrangements her campaign committee had made with the DNC, and the news coverage that exceeded that of her principal opponent. The perception that she would win contributed to her victory, but her public support declined over the course of the nomination process.

For Donald Trump, it was a different story. He did not begin as front-runner in 2016 but quickly emerged as the most popular of the multiple Republican candidates. His appeal stemmed from his nationalist and populist policy positions, controversial campaign rhetoric, and extensive news media coverage. Trump directed his remarks to angry Republicans, discontent with the country's direction and political leadership. During the nomination process, he won more popular voters than any other Republican candidate had received. Trump's appeal to his GOP supporters did not extend to the country as a whole. Expanding it was the challenge he faced in the general election.

Exercises

1. Check the official and unofficial websites of the candidates running for their party's nomination in 2024. Use the information from these websites to compare and contrast their positions on the most controversial issues in the campaign. Then compare the personal images that they have tried to project. On the basis of these comparisons, which of the candidates do you think has positioned themselves best for their party's nomination and why?

2. Follow the news of the nomination campaign from different news media sources: a major news organization, local television station, and a print or online magazine. How does their coverage differ? From which source did you learn the most about the candidates and their campaigns?

3. Provide reports on the campaign from one liberal, moderate, and conservative news source. How do these sources differ on the news they highlighted, the facts they emphasized, and the evaluations they provided for Republican and Democratic candidates? On the basis of your analysis, do you believe campaign news can be objective, accurate, or fair and balanced?

4. Analyze the nomination campaign on the candidates' basic strategic approaches, policy appeals, and personal images. Use internet sources from the candidates, the news media, and public interest groups to obtain the information you need for your analysis.

Selected Readings

Aldrich, John. "The Invisible Primary and Its Effects on Democratic Choice." *PS: Political Science and Politics* 42 (January 2009): 33–38.

Bitecover, Rachel. *The Unprecedented 2016 Presidential Election.* Cham, Switzerland: Palgrave/Macmillan, 2018.

Ceaser, James W., Andrew E. Busch, and John J. Pitney Jr. *Defying the Odds: The 2016 Elections and American Politics.* Lanham, MD: Rowman & Littlefield, 2017.

Clinton, Hillary Rodham. *What Happened.* New York, NY: Simon & Schuster, 2017.

Costa, Robert. "Donald Trump and a GOP Primary Race Like No Other." In Larry J. Sabato, Kyle Kondik, and Geoffrey Skelley, eds., *Trumped: The 2016 Election That Broke All the Rules.* Lanham, MD: Rowman & Littlefield, 2017.

Doherty, Brendan J. *The Rise of the President's Permanent Campaign.* Lawrence: University of Kansas Press, 2012.

Kamarck, Elaine C. *Primary Politics: Everything You Need to Know about How America Nominates Its Presidential Candidates*, 3rd ed. Washington, DC: The Brookings Institution, 2016.

Kennedy Institute of Politics. *Campaign for President: The Managers Look at 2020.* Lanham, MD: Rowman & Littlefield, 2021.

Mayer, William G. "The Nominations: The Road to a Much-Disliked General Election." In Michael Nelson, ed., *The Elections of 2016.* Los Angeles, CA: Sage/ CQ Press, 2018.

Plouffe, David. *The Audacity to Win.* New York, NY: Viking, 2009.

Rapoport, Ronald B., and Walter J. Stone. "The Sources of Trump's Support." In Larry J. Sabato, Kyle Kondik, and Geoffrey Skelley, eds., *Trumped: The 2016 Election That Broke All the Rules.* Lanham, MD: Rowman & Littlefield, 2017.

Sargent, Greg. "Feel the Bern." In Larry J. Sabato, Kyle Kondik, and Geoffrey Skelley, eds., *Trumped: The 2016 Election That Broke All the Rules.* Lanham, MD: Rowman & Littlefield, 2017.

Sides, John, and Lynn Vaverck. *The Gamble: Choice and Chance in 2012 Presidential Election.* Princeton, NJ: Princeton University Press, 2013.

Notes

1. Clinton never formally announced his candidacy to convey the impression that his decisions and actions as president were motivated by the country's needs and not by his desire for reelection.

2. In his first three years in office, Bush took 40 percent of his domestic trips from the White House to states he won or lost by 6 percent of the vote or less. Kathryn Dunn Tenpass and Anthony Corrado, "Permanent Campaign Brushes Tradition," *Arizona Daily Star*, March 30, 2004. See also Brendan J. Doherty, *The Rise of the President's Permanent Campaign* (Lawrence: University of Kansas Press, 2012).

3. "Iowa and New Hampshire," *Democracy in Action*.

4. Thomas Patterson, "News Coverage of the 2016 Presidential Primaries," Shorenstein Center on Media, Politics and Policy.

5. "Debates Help Fuel Strong Interest in 2016 Campaign," *Pew Research Center*, December 14, 2015.

6. Jeffrey Gottfried, Michael Barthel, Elisa Shearer, and Amy Mitchell, "The 2016 Presidential Campaign—a News Event That's Hard to Miss," Pew Research Center, February 4, 2016.

7. Jeffrey Gottfried and Eliza Shearer, "Contentious Republican Debates Lure Many Democrats to Tune in," *Pew Research Center*, January 28, 2016.

8. Nicholas Confessore and Karen Yourish, "$2 Billion Worth of Free Media for Trump," *New York Times*, March 16, 2016.

9. Jeff Zucker, *Campaign for President: The Managers Look at 2016* (Lanham, MD: Rowman & Littlefield, 2017), 64.

10. Thomas E. Patterson and Robert D. McClure, *The Unseeing Eye* (New York, NY: Putnam, 1976), 58.

11. "Super PACs Dominate Airwaves," *Wesleyan Media Project*, December 15, 2015.

12. Kenneth T. Walsh, "The News Campaign," *U.S. News and World Report*, December 31, 2015.

13. Hamilton Jordan, "Memorandum to Jimmy Carter, August 4, 1974," in Martin Schram, ed., *Running for President 1976* (New York, NY: Stein & Day, 1977), 379–80.

14. Donald Trump, as quoted in the *Washington Post*, July 8, 2015.

15. Kenneth T. Walsh, "The News Campaign," *U.S. News and World Report*, December 31, 2015.

16. Jeff Weaver, *Campaign for President: The Managers Look at 2016* (Lanham, MD: Rowman & Littlefield, 2017), 93.

The Post-Primary Campaign

Introduction

Caucuses and primaries start early in the year, and recent nominating conventions occur in mid- to late summer, leaving a period of months from the time a nominee has been effectively determined to the time that the nominee is officially "crowned" as the party's standard-bearer. This interregnum is an important recovery and reconsolidation period for the candidate who has won a highly competitive nomination as well as for the party in which that nomination contest has occurred.

The successful nominees need to repair any damage that the process inflicted on their electoral coalition, policy stands, and leadership images. They also need to replenish their war chests, restructure and expand their organization, stay in the news, shift their criticisms to their partisan opponent, design a broader-based appeal to the entire electorate, and present a winning campaign narrative—a lot to be done in a short period of time.

After a divisive nomination, the parties also have to reunify and reenergize its base, raise money for its election committees, and promote its candidates for the general election. During this period, they need to remain in their presidential mode in public while strengthening their campaign organization, behind the scenes.

The Noncompetitive Preconvention Phase

Healing Partisan Discord

After a competitive nomination has occurred, it is necessary for the winning candidate to consolidate the party, appealing to partisans who supported other candidates. The sooner such an effort is undertaken the better because the news media will continue to highlight rifts within the party as potential problems for the campaign. Egos must be soothed, losing candidates invited to participate in the convention, and the electoral base has to be expanded.

In 2008, both candidates faced unification issues with their partisan core. McCain's maverick appeal did not sit well with Republican activists who desired a candidate who advocated and prioritized their values and beliefs. His choice of Sarah Palin as his running mate did, however. Her nomination as vice presidential candidate energized the Republican partisans, so much so that McCain began to appear at her rallies.

Although Obama did not face the financial constraints that confront most winners after a divisive nomination in 2008, he did have to gain the support of Clinton voters, particularly women and organized labor, and do so in a much shorter period, only ten weeks from the end of the Democratic primaries in June to the beginning of its convention at the end of August. To accomplish this goal, Obama met secretly with Clinton, two days after the last primaries were held, to begin the healing process. To encourage Clinton's volunteers and donors to work for him in the general election, he promised her and her husband a major role at the Democratic convention and agreed to help pay off some of her campaign's debt. The Clintons' conventions prime-time speeches and subsequent campaigning for Obama ended the bitterness and brought her supporters quickly into the Democratic fold. In 2012, Romney had little difficulty coalescing the Republicans. The strength of their partisan loyalties, their negative evaluation of President Obama, and Romney's selection of economic conservative Paul Ryan as his running mate contributed to the strong backing he received from fellow Republicans, even those that did not support him initially in the 2012 caucuses and primaries. He was generally well liked, adequately conservative, and perceived as the most electable of all the GOP candidates.[1]

Hillary Clinton began her unifying efforts after she won enough delegates early in June 2016 to gain a first ballot convention victory. Initially, her principal opponent, Bernie Sanders, said he would continue his quest for the party's nomination to its national convention, but by mid-July, under pressure from party and interest group leaders, he announced his support of Clinton about two weeks before the convention convened and urged his backers to do so as well. At a joint rally, Clinton praised Sanders' efforts and directed her criticism to Trump's controversial policy stands.

Trump was not nearly as successful in 2016 in initially coalescing Republicans. Instead of appealing to party leaders and partisans who had not supported his candidacy, he continued to reiterate his preconvention anti-immigrant, anti-trade, and anti-Washington rhetoric. His promise to drain the swamp in Washington did not endear himself to many nationally elected Republican officials who were offended by his criticism of them, including former presidents George H. W. Bush and George W. Bush, former presidential candidate Mitt Romney, several of his nomination challengers, and prominent GOP senators. Others, such as House Speaker Paul Ryan, gave him only tepid support. Several prominent Republican senators and governors did not even attend the GOP convention in Ohio, including the state's governor, John Kasich.

In 2020, both parties' cohesion was not a problem. Trump maintained his Republican support despite the opposition of a small number of anti-Trump

Republicans. Sanders backed Biden after Biden became the presumptive Democratic nominee.

Repositioning and Reprioritizing the Issues

In addition to unifying the party, the winning candidates also must reposition their campaign war chests and usually reshape and reprioritize their campaign agendas. After moving toward their party's ideological core during the contested phase of the nomination process by emphasizing issues important to partisan activists, nominees usually have to soften and broaden their appeals, move toward the political center, and reposition their issue stands for the general electorate. They also may restructure their campaign narrative.

Repositioning and reprioritizing can be tricky business; however, because the news media and opposition party are sure to point out the policy inconsistencies, strident oratory, and the most controversial stands, candidates have taken and reiterated throughout the contested stage of the nominations, raising questions about their credibility and dependability to follow through on their campaign promises if elected.

George W. Bush adopted the move-to-the-middle strategy in 2000. Forced to appeal to the conservative Republicans to win the GOP nomination, Bush then accentuated the positive, stressed his compassion, and focused on issues that had special appeal to Democrats, and especially to women voters. By taking moderate stands on social issues, Bush was following the same strategy that Bill Clinton used in 1995–1996 when he emphasized the Republican ideological policy agenda but took more centrist positions than did their congressional leadership.[2]

In 2004, however, Bush campaigned for president as if he were running for the Republican nomination. His conservative orientation was consistent with the policies of his administration, although he did place greater emphasis on domestic issues in the 2004 campaign than he was able to do as president after the terrorist attacks of September 11, 2001.

Bush's conservative policy emphasis in 2004 was a response to the highly polarized political climate in the United States. In that election, Republican strategists operated on three assumptions: that the country was evenly divided between Republicans and Democrats; that most partisans have already made up their minds for whom to vote by the time of the national conventions; and that the proportion of independent or swing voters had shrunk to a very small percentage of the electorate. Bush's advisers believed that they stood a better chance of winning by motivating their base than persuading the relatively few undecided voters to support him.[3]

In 2008, with public dissatisfaction rising, the issue was change and the presidential leadership needed to achieve it. McCain stressed his independence and experience; he also pointed to his family values and voiced support for continuing the Bush tax cuts, which he had opposed as a senator. In contrast, Obama drew a sharp distinction between the economic policies of the Bush administration and his Democratic policies, which he said would bring greater benefit to the middle class.

In 2012, the Obama campaign had a choice: paint Romney as a flip-flopper, given the moderate policies he pursued as governor of Massachusetts, including the support of a state health care program similar to the Affordable Care Act, or describe him as an ideological conservative, given the positions he had taken to win the Republican nomination. The campaign decided to do both but in different stages. During 2011, when the news media's narrative focused on Romney's policy inconsistencies, the Obama campaign took the position that Romney lacked core beliefs, that he would say and do anything that worked to his political advantage. Later, Obama emphasized the conservative policy stands Romney had taken to win the Republican nomination.[4]

The task for Romney after winning a majority of the delegates in early April 2012 was to turn the focus toward Obama and his economic and social policies. With the country still mired in the residue of the Great Recession, with high unemployment, tight credit, decreased real estate values, and general economic pessimism, the Romney campaign presented the election as a referendum on the president and the failure of his policies to turn the economy around. The Republican narrative emphasized its candidate's successful business career as evidence that he had the vision, experience, and knowledge to improve economic conditions.[5]

Hillary Clinton had a short preconvention campaign in 2016, less than two months. During it, she tried to heal the rife created by Sanders's candidacy by adopting a new slogan, "stronger together," placing greater emphasis on economic mobility, income inequality, and climate change, and pointing to her historic victory as the first woman to be nominated for president by a major political party.

In contrast, Donald Trump stuck to his guns in 2016 and again in 2020. He appealed to congressional Republicans on his own terms. He did not modify the controversial policy stands and promises he made during his successful nomination campaign in 2016 nor did he apologize for ridiculing Republican challengers and some elected Republican officials. In fact, he dismissed their criticism, saying he had the support of a "silent majority," a term that Richard Nixon used in 1968, a majority that would elect him president.

Repairing Leadership Images

In a fiercely competitive nomination, the more negative the campaign, the more likely that the eventual nominee's personal image will have been tarnished, policy positions criticized, and divisions within the party widened. Each of these election-oriented problems requires attention and a private and public campaign to overcome them. Candidates may have to reintroduce themselves to the voters to regain the electorate's attention and to remove or at least reduce the negative stereotypes by which their partisan opponents, news media commentators, and late-night talk show hosts characterized them. Biographical ads, public testimonials, and convention speeches given by distinguished public officials and party leaders can help alter a less-than-flattering public image.

Bill Clinton faced this problem after winning the Democratic nomination in 1992. Savaged first by press allegations of womanizing, draft dodging, and smoking marijuana, and later by criticism of his centrist policy positions by his opponent, former California governor Jerry Brown, Clinton needed to reconstruct his presidential image. To do so, his campaign designed a series of commercials that detailed the hardships and struggles that this poor boy from Arkansas encountered growing up and ultimately surmounted in his rise to political prominence. The ads, combined with talk-show appearances in which the candidate reminisced about his upbringing, gradually clouded aspects of Clinton's self-serving personal behavior that had marred his leadership image.

Al Gore and George W. Bush faced a different type of problem in spring 2000. They needed to establish their own presidential credentials by moving out of a president's shadow, in Bush's case, his father's and in Gore's, Bill Clinton's. The primaries had not enabled them to do so fully, in part because they won easily and early. To gain stature, Bush needed to highlight his tenure as a popular, twice-elected, governor of Texas. Gore had to either stand on his own or be credited with some of the economic successes of the Clinton administration. He chose to be his own man, asserting his independence, distancing himself from the president, and thereby making it harder for him to claim credit for the administration's accomplishments.

Obama faced a different challenge in 2008, demonstrating that his lack of experience was not a liability but an asset, that he had the knowledge, judgment, and stature to be a successful president. He displayed his knowledge in detailed policy discussions with the press, hundreds of one-on-one interviews, and candidate debates as well as in a book he had written, *The Audacity of Hope*,[6] published prior to his presidential campaign. He also took the ritual trip abroad to raise his international stature.

The attention Obama received from his trip abroad was substantially greater than that which McCain received from his international travels and literally left McCain in the dark and out of the news.[7] McCain had no alternative but to stress his independence in 2008, given the unpopularity of the Republican incumbent, George W. Bush. The plan, according to campaign manager, Rick Davis, was for McCain to visit the White House the day after he had won a majority of the delegates and not go near it again.[8] The country's financial crisis in September, however, forced McCain to return to Washington to participate in the emergency meetings with President Obama and members of Congress.

Both Hillary Clinton and Donald Trump had to overcome negative perceptions that increased over the course of their 2016 nomination campaigns. Clinton's problems stemmed from her long years in the public spotlight and the criticism she received as First Lady, senator, and secretary of state: her failed health care initiative during her husband's presidency, her vote to allow President Bush to resort to military force in Iraq, her use of a private internet server, and her evasiveness on an incident that occurred in Libya, when she was secretary of state.

Trump's unconventional rhetoric, controversial policy stands, and factual inaccuracies were also highlighted negatively by the traditional news media and his political opponents in 2016 and again in 2020. Biden was not perceived negatively by Democrats and Independents. Trump was viewed positively by most Republicans.

Gaining the Stature of an Incumbent

The image problems that challengers face are magnified when running against an incumbent. Less well-known to the country, less experienced in higher office, and with fewer major accomplishments associated with their public career, challengers have to present and enhance their leadership credentials at the same time they are raising money, unifying their party, refocusing their criticism, and restructuring their campaign. Nor do they have as loud a pulpit to do so as the incumbent president has until their party's convention and the presidential debates.

Few challengers emerge from contested nominations with a sizable war chest to match the incumbent's. Lack of money is a major strategic disadvantage during this period. Romney's manager, Matt Rhoades, described his candidate's predicament in 2012:

> we had spent $87 million to secure the nomination and become the presumptive nominee. And we were not going to take matching funds so that we could be more competitive down the stretch. So that meant that we were being outspent over the summer, and we always understood that was going to be one of the bigger challenges that we had, even to the point where we did take out a loan at the end of the primary process going into the convention.[9]

The 2004 and 2012 interregnum periods between the primaries and the convention illustrate the challenger's dilemma. After John Kerry had effectively secured the Democratic nomination in March 2004, the first objective of Bush and the Republicans' reelection advertising was to reduce his stature. Almost immediately, the Bush campaign aired negative Kerry commercials that presented the Massachusetts senator as a flip-flopper who regularly voted on both sides of controversial issues. The Kerry campaign that needed time to reorganize itself, raise money, and tailor a biographical portrait of its candidate chose not to reply to the various allegations that Republicans were directing at him. By not confronting the flip-flopper accusation, however, Kerry inadvertently let the charges stick in the public's mind. His personal negatives increased; his standing in the polls declined; and he lost much of the luster that he had gained by winning the Democratic nomination.

The same thing happened to Romney in 2012. The Obama campaign front-loaded its advertising to frame the election as quickly as possible to its advantage. David Axelrod, the campaign's senior political strategist, reflected on the strategy:

> My reading of history was that there was no ad that ran after the convention that ever in the modern era won a presidential race; paid media becomes largely irrelevant in the general election after the conventions because the debates take over for better or worse. We did that [front-loaded the advertising] because we thought the combined forces of the Super PACs and [Republican] spending were going to be great, but also because we knew that we had to define the race before the conventions.[10]

Because none of the 2016 nominees were running against an incumbent, their personal images were contrasted with conventional beliefs about desirable presidential traits, and neither of them fared well in that comparison. Trump's aggressive style, super-charged rhetoric, limited information on complex policy matters, and his factual inaccuracies contributed to his unpresidential stature as did Clinton's negatives. The imagery of both candidates was influenced by partisan leanings in 2020 with Republicans and Democrats perceiving their presidential candidates positively and their opponents' candidates negatively.

Picking the Vice Presidential Nominee

Considerable planning and much hype go into the convention buildup. Media attention turns to the vice presidential selection, usually the only unknown left before the big show. The decision of whom to choose as running mate has traditionally been given to the presidential standard-bearers The last time that a convention actually selected the vice presidential nominee rather than ratified the choice of the winning presidential candidate was in 1956 when Adlai Stevenson, the Democratic candidate, professed no choice between Senators John F. Kennedy and Estes Kefauver, both of whom were vying for the vice presidential nomination. The convention chose Kefauver.

The selection of the vice presidential nominee is one of the most important decisions that the prospective nominee must make. It is a character judgment that reflects directly on the presidential nominee. Picking an experienced, well-respected person who could become president usually suggests a willingness to delegate power as well as share some decisional responsibility.

Another factor is the political benefit that the vice presidential nominee brings to the ticket. In the past, the vice presidential nominee has been selected in part to provide geographic or ideological balance. Occasionally, demographic variables, such as gender, race, and age, have also been factors.

Bill Clinton broke with tradition in 1992 when he chose a fellow southerner and moderate, Al Gore, to reinforce the "new" Democrat image that Clinton wanted to project. George W. Bush's selection of Dick Cheney—a former White House chief of staff, representative from Wyoming, member of the Republican House leadership, and defense secretary in his father's administration—brought experience, particularly in national security affairs, expertise that Bush lacked as a state governor. The choice of a governing mate more than a running mate also broke with tradition and foreshadowed an enhanced vice presidential role in the Bush administration.

There had been speculation and even a campaign launched by Hillary Clinton's supporters to urge Obama to choose her for the number-two spot in 2008. Such a choice would have quickly unified the party, but it would also have put a person who had been highly critical of Obama on the same ticket, and if successful, another Clinton and potential presidential rival in the White House. Obama did not want to encourage the kind of press coverage that focuses on internal rivalry between the president and the vice president, nor did he want the former president in or near the White House.[11] Instead, he chose Joe Biden. As chair of the Senate foreign relations committee, Biden had the experience in foreign affairs. He was also popular with rank-and-file Democrats, many of whom had supported Hillary Clinton.

McCain chose Sarah Palin as his running mate in 2008 because he needed a "game changer."[12] He also wanted to appeal to women. With her reputation as a reform governor, Palin complemented McCain's record of independence and his opposition to special interest politics.

Romney established three criteria for his selection of a running mate in 2012: be qualified to be president from day 1, be compatible ideologically and personally with him, and be unlikely to detract attention from the themes and messages of his campaign. Before making his selection, Romney made a point of campaigning with each of his potential vice presidential choices; he and his staff reviewed their appearances on news shows and in interviews, evaluating their partisan and public support and how their staffs interacted with senior campaign advisers in his campaign organization. Paul Ryan's relative youth, economic conservatism, knowledge of budgetary matters, and his Midwest background, particularly coming from a battleground state, Wisconsin, were seen as pluses.

Trump's choice of Mike Pence in 2016 followed disinterest expressed by other governors and senators on his short list. He wanted a person with political and managerial experience. Pence had been a member of the House of Representatives for twelve years, governor of Indiana, and had conservative credentials that appealed to mainstream Republicans, especially social conservatives.

Hillary Clinton pursued her "play-it-safe" strategy with her selection of Senator Tim Kaine, although she waited until the weekend before the Democratic convention to do it. Kaine, son of a welder, had working-class credentials, spoke fluent Spanish, was Roman Catholic, and came from a pivotal state, Virginia, whose governor, a Democrat, would have picked his successor in the Senate (prior to a special election) had the Democratic ticket been successful.

Because so much media attention is directed toward the vice presidential selection, nominees and their advisers try to keep their decisions secret for as long as they can. The preoccupation with surprise, however, has often precluded adequate screening of the candidates for fear that the news media will reveal the identity of the prospective choice before the presidential candidate announces it. The worst-case scenario of this charade occurred in 1972 when George McGovern selected Thomas Eagleton, a senator from Missouri, as his running mate. Although McGovern had spoken with the Democratic governor of that state, the senator himself, and the Missouri press, he had not been informed of Eagleton's hospitalization for depression and the electric shock treatments he received for it at the Mayo Clinic.[13] When this information became public, McGovern was caught in a dilemma; he could admit he made a mistake and drop Eagleton from the ticket, looking weak and perhaps mean-spirited in the process, or he could indicate that it was not a mistake and stick with him. Initially, McGovern chose to do the latter. However, when medical authorities suggested that the malady was serious and too risky for a person who might become president, McGovern was forced to drop him and select another person.

George H. W. Bush faced a similar dilemma in 1988. Although he had chosen Dan Quayle, a senator from Indiana, in part because he wanted a person who could appeal to the next generation of voters, Bush was unaware of Quayle's mediocre record as a university student or his family's help in getting him an appointment in the Indiana National Guard, which lessened the possibility of active-duty service in Vietnam during the war. Bush, who had been accused of being a "wimp," felt he could not back off when the going got tough, so he stayed with Quayle.

In the case of Sarah Palin, the problem she encountered after her selection and rousing convention speech was knowledge lapses that negatively reflected on her intellectual abilities. Palin had not been adequately briefed by McCain's policy aides and showed it in her responses to interviewers' questions. She did not seem to know the Bush doctrine in foreign affairs and became confused over the bailout of Wall Street investment firms, large banks, and the insurance giant AIG. Pundits questioned her understanding of world affairs while comedians mocked her intelligence.

Neither of the vice presidential picks in 2012, 2016, and 2020 incurred much criticism or detracted from the attention and support the presidential candidate received, although as the first woman of color to be chosen, Kamala Harris, did increase the coverage, especially in publications geared to minorities. She had run for the party's nomination, but her campaign was unsuccessful, marred by organizational and financial difficulties.

Planning for the Convention

In addition to the vice presidential selection, the prospective nominee also must oversee planning for the national nominating convention. One objective is to avoid any problems, especially factional divisions that carry over from the primaries or are generated by a dispute over policy or rules. A unified convention is viewed as the most successful way to launch a presidential campaign, energize the party, and frame the issues for the forthcoming general election.

Candidates and their handlers go to great lengths to orchestrate public events leading up to the convention. Nothing is left to chance. In 2000, George W. Bush let it be known that he opposed changes to the traditional positions the party took in its platform. He did not want to alienate any group in the Republicans' core constituency. Obama and McCain had similar objectives in 2008. They wanted to minimize internal dissent, a major reason that Hillary Clinton was given a prominent convention role and made the motion to make Obama's nomination unanimous. On the Republican side that year, McCain's senior aides nixed his desire to pick his close friend and former Democratic vice presidential candidate Joe Lieberman as his running mate because they feared that such a choice would have divided the convention, resulted in considerable internal opposition, and could have been defeated.[14] Harmony is the name of the game for contemporary nominating conventions.

Donald Trump faced another problem in his campaign's preparation for the 2016 Republican Convention. He was gaining the votes necessary for a first-ballot victory but had no staffer with experience to run the convention. In March, he hired Paul Manafort, a long-time Republican operative, to do so. Manafort's influence increased when Trump fired his campaign manager, Corey Lewandowski. Although the convention proceeded as planned, Manafort's business dealings with people in Ukraine and Russia led to his forced resignation after the convention and subsequent convictions for bank fraud, tax evasion, witness tampering, and perjury. Trump later granted him clemency.

The pandemic was a problem that both parties had to consider in 2020. Democrats planned for a virtual convention, whereas Republicans initially planned for a traditional one, but they too had to change to a virtual format. Some delegates attended the Republican meeting, but the president delivered his address from the White House. The Democratic convention was staged and conducted virtually (box 6.1).

BOX 6.1 ★ Convention Controversies in Historical Perspective

National nominating conventions were at one time important decision-making bodies. They were used to decide on the party's nominees, platforms, and rules and procedures, as well as to provide a podium for launching presidential campaigns. They also became an arena for settling internal party disputes, unifying the delegates, reiterating the themes, and introducing the nominees for the general election. Today, however, they are not nearly as important and certainly not as newsworthy. They are theater orchestrated for television. Conventions are designed to present a picture of a cohesive and energized party that enthusiastically supports its nominees and its platform and optimistically launches its presidential campaign. Nineteenth- and twentieth-century conventions (until the 1970s) were brokered by party leaders who exercised considerable influence over the selection and actions of their state delegations. The leaders debated among themselves, formed coalitions, and fought for particular candidates and over credentials, rules, and the platform. Many of these internal disputes occurred within committees and then led to floor debates and votes.

Twice in the twentieth century, Republican conventions were the scene of major credential challenges that ultimately determined the winning nominee. William Howard Taft's victory over Theodore Roosevelt in 1912 and Dwight Eisenhower's victory over Robert Taft in 1952 followed from convention decisions to seat certain delegates and reject others. Rules fights have also been surrogate disputes over the selection of the nominees. Until 1936, the Democrats operated under a rule that required a two-thirds vote for winning the nomination. James K. Polk's selection in 1844 was a consequence of Martin Van Buren's failure to obtain the support of two-thirds of the convention, although Van Buren had a majority. The two-thirds rule in effect permitted a minority of the delegates to veto a person they opposed.

Today most convention rules are accepted without dispute. The most recent rules controversy that potentially could have affected the outcome of a major party nomination occurred in 1980 at the Democratic convention. At issue was a proposed requirement that delegates vote for the candidate to whom they were publicly pledged at the time they were chosen. Trailing Jimmy Carter by about six hundred delegates, Ted Kennedy, who had previously supported this requirement, urged an open convention in which delegates could vote their consciences rather than merely exercise their commitments. Naturally, the Carter organization favored the pledged delegate rule and lobbied strenuously and successfully for it. Subsequently, the Democrats modified the rule to allow delegates to reflect in good conscience the sentiments of those who elected them and the candidates to whom they were pledged.

The Democrats had a major policy dispute in 1948 that led to a walkout of delegates from several southern states. At issue was the party's stance on a civil rights plank. When they were unable to get the convention to change its position, several of the southern delegations left and backed the states' rights candidacy of Senator Strom Thurmond for president. In 1964, Republican delegates fought over proposed amendments opposing extremism and favoring a stronger position on civil rights, amendments that delegates supporting Barry Goldwater defeated. The 1968 Democratic convention witnessed an emotional four-hour debate on US policy in Vietnam. Although the convention voted to sustain the majority's position, which had the approval of President Johnson, the discussion, carried on television, reinforced the image of a divided party to millions of home viewers.

Before the choice of the nominee was dictated by the results of the caucuses and primaries, the delegates had to make that decision themselves by voting on the convention floor. Sometimes agreeing on a nominee took several votes. In 1924, Democratic delegates cast 103 ballots before they agreed on John W. Davis and Charles W. Bryan as their nominees; in 1932, they took four roll calls before obtaining the two-thirds vote needed to nominate Franklin Roosevelt. After the two-thirds rule was changed to a simple majority, the Democratic conventions had much less difficulty agreeing on its nominees. In fact, the only other Democratic convention that took more than one ballot was in 1952 when it took three votes to nominate Adlai Stevenson. In 1940, Republican Wendell Willkie was selected on the eighth ballot, breaking a deadlock among Thomas Dewey, Arthur Vandenberg, and Willkie himself. Eight years later, Dewey was nominated on the third ballot.

Since 1980, a first-ballot nomination has been preordained by the results of the caucuses and primaries. Few disputes make it to the convention floor because the winning candidate controls a majority of the delegates and wants to project a unified party.

Contemporary Conventions: Composition, Content, Communications, and Impact

In past conventions, there used to be a keynote address, which occurred early in the convention and was intended to unify the delegates, smoothing over any divisions that may have emerged during the preconvention campaign, and arouse the delegates, partisans, and the general public for the forthcoming election. In 1988, a folksy and humorous address at the 1988 Democratic convention, Ann Richards, then treasurer of Texas, ridiculed George H.W. Bush for being aloof, insensitive, and uncaring, she concluded sarcastically, "He can't help it. He was born with a silver foot in his mouth."[15] Richards's comment so irritated his son, George W. Bush, who was sitting with his mother watching the Democratic convention on television that he resolved to run against her for governor, a race that he won, and later for president. In 2004, it was Barack Obama's well-received keynote address that gave him national recognition and initiated blogs encouraging him to run for the nation's highest elective office. Former president Bill Clinton energized Democratic delegates and partisans in 2012 with his comparison of the achievements of the Obama administration with the failures of the George W. Bush administration; in 2016, he spoke about his wife as a "change-maker."

In recent conventions, the vice presidential candidate is nominated and gives an acceptance address on the third night, a practice that both parties followed in 2008, but the Republicans had to modify in 2012 to avoid a conflict with the televising of the first regular season game of the National Football League. The vice presidential candidate's speech recounts the positive images and deeds of the party and its presidential nominee and attacks the opposing presidential candidate.

The custom of giving an acceptance speech began in 1932 with Franklin Roosevelt. Before that time, conventions designated committees to inform the presidential and vice presidential nominees of their selection. Journeying to the standard-bearers' homes, the committees would announce the choice in a public setting. The presidential nominee in turn would accept by giving a speech indicating his position on the major issues. The last major party candidate to be told of his nomination in this manner was Wendell Willkie in 1940. Since then, acceptance speeches have become a call to the faithful and an address to the nation.

Today, acceptance speeches are both a call to the faithful and an address to the country. They articulate the principal themes for the general election and the priorities that the nominee attaches to them. Harry Truman's address to the 1948 Democratic Convention is frequently cited as one that fired up the party. Truman chided the Republicans for obstructing and ultimately rejecting his legislative proposals and not living up to their convention promises. He called a special session of Congress to enact those proposals. When the Republican did not do so in the special session, Truman pinned on them a "do-nothing" label and made that label the basic theme of his successful presidential campaign.

In 1984, Democratic candidate Walter Mondale made a mammoth political blunder in his acceptance speech. Warning the delegates about the US budget deficit that had increased dramatically during Reagan's first term, Democrat Mondale said that he would do something about it if he were elected president: "Let's tell the truth. Mr. Reagan will raise taxes, and so will I. He won't tell you. I just did." Democratic delegates cheered his candor, directness, and boldness; the public did not. Mondale and his party were saddled with the tax issue throughout the entire campaign.

One of the most notable acceptance speeches was Barack Obama's in 2008. Desiring to highlight their candidate's rhetorical skills and inspirational oratory, the Democrats moved his speech from the convention hall to a football stadium that could accommodate 75,000 people. The speech in which Obama pledged to transform policy and politics received an enthusiastic response, media plaudits, and ignited Democrats in their forthcoming campaign. In 2012, Obama toned down his transformational rhetoric, admitting that his goals needed more time to be achieved.

Hillary Clinton, after articulating traditional Democratic values and goals in 2016, directed attention to the negative attributes of her Republican opponent. To Democratic delegates and people who were watching the convention, she said:

Do you really think Donald Trump has the temperament to be commander-in-chief? Donald Trump can't even handle the rough and tumble of a presidential campaign. He loses his cool at the slightest provocation, when he's gotten a tough question from a reporter, when he's challenged in a debate, when he sees a protester at a rally. Imagine, if you dare, imagine, imagine him in the Oval Office facing a real crisis. A man you can bait with a tweet is not a man we can trust with nuclear weapons![16]

In 2008, the Republicans, fearful that John McCain's acceptance speech would be anticlimactic after the enthusiasm that greeted Sarah Palin the night before, convention planners tinkered with the setting in which McCain would address the delegates. They moved him closer to the audience, recreating the town meeting environment in which he was familiar and did well. McCain personalized his remarks, referring to himself as a maverick, contrasting his positions to Obama's, emphasizing his experience in foreign affairs, and ending with the story about his own mistreatment and forced confession as a prisoner of war in Vietnam:

I was in solitary confinement when my captors offered to release me. I knew why. If I went home, they would use it as propaganda to demoralize my fellow prisoners. Our code said we could only go home in the order of our capture, and there were men who had been shot down before me. I thought about it . . . But I turned it down. After I turned down their offer, they worked me over harder than they ever had before. For a long time. And they broke me.

When they brought me back to my cell, I was hurt and ashamed, and I didn't know how I could face my fellow prisoners. The good man in the cell next door, my friend, Bob Craner, saved me. Through taps on a wall he told me I had fought as hard as I could. No man can always stand alone. And then he told me to get back up and fight again for our country and for the men I had the honor to serve with. Because every day they fought for me.[17]

Mitt Romney, not a great orator, also had to distinguish himself, present his credentials, and at the same time, reiterate the themes articulated at the convention that were to guide his presidential campaign. He highlighted his personal and professional accomplishments.

Donald Trump's acceptance speech, an hour and fifteen minutes long, reiterated his campaign theme of law and order to combat the dangers Americans face from domestic terrorism, illegal immigration, and crime in the streets. He spoke about lost jobs and lost opportunities, criticized Hillary Clinton's domestic and foreign policies, and promised to bring jobs back, lower taxes, rebuild the nation's infrastructure, enhance the military, and abolish costly government regulations that burden businesses, including the health care law that was enacted during the Obama administration. He said:

I have a different vision for our workers. It begins with a new, fair-trade policy that protects our jobs and stands up to countries that cheat, of which there are many. With these new economic policies, trillions of dollars will start flowing into our country. . . . I have made billions of dollars in business making deals—now I'm going to make our country rich again. We Will Make America Great Again.[18]

In 2020, he gave the speech remotely, from the White House, the first Republican to do so since Alf Landon in 1936. His speech contrasted his version of America with that of his partisan opponents:

> This election will decide whether we SAVE the American Dream, or whether we allow a socialist agenda to DEMOLISH our cherished destiny.
>   It will decide whether we rapidly create millions of high paying jobs, or whether we crush our industries and send millions of these jobs overseas, as has foolishly been done for many decades.
>   Your vote will decide whether we protect law abiding Americans, or whether we give free reign to violent anarchists, agitators, and criminals who threaten our citizens.
>   And this election will decide whether we will defend the American Way of Life, or whether we allow a radical movement to completely dismantle and destroy it.[19]

Biden painted a different and disturbing picture of Trump's America:

> Too much anger, too much fear, too much division. Here and now I give you my word. If you entrust me with the presidency, I will draw on the best of us, not the worst. I will be an ally of the light, not the darkness. It is time for us, for we, the people, to come together. And make no mistake, united we can and will overcome this season of darkness in America.[20]

The acceptance address comes on the final night. It is usually preceded by a biographical video, which lauds the nominee's extraordinary qualifications. It has also become the custom for their spouses to testify to the more human qualities of their partners: their sincerity, thoughtfulness, honesty, integrity, and empathy, telling stories about them with which Americans can identify. The acceptance speech by the party's presidential candidate nominee marks the beginning of the general election campaign.

Platform

In addition to the speeches, conventions must approve the party's platform, which is a statement of the party's principal positions and agenda for the fall campaign. Contrary to popular belief, platforms are important even though few people read them in their entirety or know what is in them. They are important because they help shape the agenda for the government if the party is successful. The news media also refer to them during and after the campaign, especially when candidates and newly elected presidents achieve or deviate from them.

Political scientists have found that government officials of both parties have a relatively good record of redeeming their campaign promises and platform planks. Although party platforms contain high-sounding rhetoric and lofty goals, they also have fairly specific policy pledges. Of these, the majority have been proposed as laws or implemented as executive actions if the party wins control of government. Elected officials follow through on their platform's promises because they believe in them personally, want to demonstrate their partisan loyalty, and need to maintain the support of their electoral coalition as well as their own credibility.

Democratic and Republican platforms differ from each other in substance and style, more so now than in the past.

Contemporary platforms have become more detailed, policy specific, and philosophically divergent. The ideological distinctiveness began to emerge clearly in the 1980s when the Republicans articulated economic and social policies significantly different from those of the Democrats. These differences have become distinct doctrinal differences since then.

Box 6.2 contrasts the 2020 Republican and Democratic Party platforms on several of the most salient contemporary issues of that election year.

BOX 6.2 ★ Contrasting the 2020 Democratic and Republican Party Platforms

	Republican	Democratic
Human Life	The unborn child has a fundamental right to life which cannot be infringed	Democrats will oppose and fight to overturn national and state laws that create barriers to reproductive health and rights
Planned Parenthood	We oppose the use of public funds to perform or promote abortion or to fund organizations, like Planned Parenthood	We will restore federal funding for Planned Parenthood
Judges	We support the appointment of judges who respect traditional family values and the sanctity of innocent life	We will appoint judges who are committed to the rule of law and will respect and enforce foundational precedents, including *Brown v. Board of Education* and *Roe v. Wade*
Education	We support options for learning including home-schooling, career and technical education, private or parochial schools, and magnet schools, charter schools, online learning and early-college high schools	Democrats oppose private school vouchers and other policies that divert tax-funded resources away from the public school system

Source: 2020 Republican and Democratic Party Platforms.

News Media Coverage

Political conventions used to be major newsworthy events. Radio began covering national conventions in 1924 and television in 1956. Because conventions in the 1950s were interesting, unpredictable events in which important political decisions were made, they attracted a large audience, one that increased rapidly as the number of households having television sets expanded. During the 1950s and 1960s, about 25 percent of the potential viewers watched the conventions, with the numbers swelling to 50 percent during the most significant part of the meetings, especially during the acceptance speeches of the presidential standard-bearers. The sizable audience made conventions important for fledgling television news organizations, which were beginning to rival newspapers for news reporting. Initially, the three major television networks (ABC, CBS, and NBC) provided almost gavel-to-gavel coverage. They focused on the official events, that is, what went on at the podium. Commentary was kept to a minimum. The changes in the delegate selection process that began in the 1970s had a major impact on the amount and type of television coverage as well as the size of the viewing audience. As the decision-making capabilities of conventions declined, their newsworthiness decreased, as did the proportion of households that tuned in and the amount of time spent watching them.

With the exception of the public broadcasting system (PBS) and the major 24/7 networks, broadcast networks reduced their coverage beginning in 1992. In 2020, the national news networks provided full evening coverage and C-SPAN gavel-to-gavel coverage, but the broadcast networks limited their coverage to about one hour.

Although coverage on the major broadcast networks has declined, the reporting on cable news, public television, and the websites of major news organizations has picked up the slack. The audience for 2008 was larger than in 2012 and 2016. According to the Nielsen company, which monitors the size of the viewing audience, 38.9 million watched John McCain's acceptance speech in 2008 and 38.4 million saw Obama's; the figures were 30.5 million for Romney and 35.7 million for Obama in 2012; and 34.9 million for Trump and 33.7 million for Clinton in 2016.[21] In general, Trump received a greater amount of coverage than Clinton with the bulk of the reporting focusing on the horserace, not policy issues or leadership qualifications.[22] The tone of the coverage was primarily negative for both candidates.

Viewership varies with partisanship. Partisans watch their party's convention more than do Independents and people who identify with other political parties. The viewing audience is also disproportionately older and more educated than the population as a whole.

Because conventions are less newsworthy, reporters who cover them have to search for engaging news. Television cameras constantly scan the floor for dramatic events and human-interest stories. Delegates are pictured talking, eating, sleeping, parading, and even watching television. Interviews with prominent party leaders and elected officials, rank-and-file delegates, and family and friends of the candidate are interspersed with the speeches, convention videos, and the breaks for advertising. To provide a balanced presentation, supporters and opponents are frequently juxtaposed. To maintain the audience's attention, the interviews are kept short, usually highlighting delegates' reactions to actual or potential political problems. There are also endless commentaries, prognoses, and forecasts of how the convention is likely to affect the electorate and their voting decisions.

Coverage inside the convention is supplemented by coverage outside of it. Knowing this, groups come to the convention city to protest. The most violent of these political demonstrations occurred in 1968 in Chicago, the city in which the Democratic Party was meeting. Thousands of people, many of them students, marched through the streets and parks expressing their anger with US military involvement in the Vietnam War. Under the orders of Chicago's mayor, Richard Daley, police set up barricades, blocking, beating, and arresting many of the protestors. Claiming that these events were newsworthy, the broadcast networks broke away from their convention coverage to report on these activities and show tapes of the bloody confrontations between police and protestors. Critics charged that the presence of television cameras incited the demonstrators and that coverage was disproportional and distracted viewers from the convention proceedings. The news networks denied that the coverage was too great. Protests have occurred during subsequent conventions, but they have not received much attention from the mainstream press.

The news media's orientation, which highlights conflict, drama, and human interest, obviously clashes with the party leadership's desire to present a united and enthusiastic front to launch its presidential campaigns. The clash between these two conflicting aims has resulted in a classic struggle for control between TV reporters and commentators and convention planners. That the managers have been more successful in orchestrating their meetings to achieve their objectives than the news media is a principal reason for the decline in the amount of coverage and the size and attentiveness of the audience watching it.

When the conventions are over, however, they are rarely mentioned in the reporting of the campaign, although clips of their highlights, especially from the acceptance speeches of the nominees, reappear in candidate advertising. Nonetheless, the national party conventions still receive a bigger audience than any other election event except for the debates between the major party's presidential and vice presidential candidates.

Although the Republican and Democratic conventions get limited news coverage, minor party conventions do not, even on 24/7 cable news. The absence of competition within most of these parties combined with the improbability of their candidates winning the election or even affecting its outcome explains the minimum coverage given to these events. The one exception was the Reform Party's conventions in 1996 and 2000, which received some attention from the cable news and public affairs networks. The broadcast networks covered them only as items on their news shows. H. Ross Perot, the party's founder and financial backer, had much to do with getting coverage in 1996, whereas the attraction in 2000 was the battle between supporters and opponents of Pat Buchanan, the former Republican who left that party to run as the Reform candidate.

Assessing the Conventions' Impact on the Electorate

Do national nominating conventions have an impact on the election? Most observers believe that they do. Why else would the major parties devote so much time, money, and effort to these events? Why else would party leaders and academics concerned with civic education bemoan the reduction of convention coverage by the broadcast networks? Why else would the parties conduct focus groups, consult poll data, tally hits on their convention websites, and monitor blogs, email, and social media platforms, especially Google, Facebook, and Twitter, continuously? And why else would people watch them when they know the identity of the nominees, have a general sense of the parties' political stands, and probably have heard portions of the successful nominees' campaign speeches during the nomination process?

Political scientists also believe that conventions matter. They have hypothesized that there is a relationship between convention unity and electoral success. Convention planners believe this hypothesis as well and do everything they can to promote unity, energy, and public interest during them.

In the short run, conventions almost always boost the popularity of their nominees and decrease that of their general election opponents. This boost is referred to as the convention "bounce," which tends to average about a 5–6 percent gain in the public opinion polls. The only recent nominees who did not get a bounce from their conventions were George McGovern in 1972, John Kerry in 2004, and Mitt Romney in 2012. Table 6.1 indicates the bounces that nominating conventions since 1960 have given their party's nominees. These bounces can be short-lived, however.

The long-term impact is more difficult to measure. Nonetheless, there seem to be three major effects of conventions on voters:

- they heighten interest, thereby increasing turnout;
- they arouse latent feelings, thereby raising partisan awareness;
- they color perceptions, thereby affecting personal judgments of the candidates and their stands on issues.

Conventions, however, increased public interest and knowledge as does the news about them. Convention watchers also tend to make their voting decisions earlier in the campaign. Whether they make those decisions because they watch the convention or whether they watch the convention because they are more partisan and politically aware and have made or are making their voting decisions is unclear.

In brief, conventions can have a powerful psychological impact on those who watch them for extended periods of time. They make viewers more inclined to follow the campaign after the convention is over and vote for their party's candidates. They energize partisans. They can also have an organizational effect, fostering cooperation among the different and frequently competing groups within the party, encouraging them to submerge their differences and work toward a common goal.

TABLE 6.1 ★ Convention Bounces, 1964–2020				
Year	Democratic Candidate	Bounce	Republican Candidate	Bounce
1964	Johnson	3	Goldwater	5
1968	Humphrey	2	Nixon	5
1972	McGovern	0	Nixon	7
1976	Carter	9	Ford	5
1980	Carter	10	Reagan	8
1984	Mondale	9	Reagan	4
1988	Dukakis	7	G. H. W. Bush	6
1992	Clinton	16	G. H. W. Bush	5
1996	Clinton	5	Dole	3
2000	Gore	8	G. W. Bush	8
2004	Kerry	−1	G. W. Bush	2
2008	Obama	4	McCain	6
2012	Obama	2	Romney	1
2016	H. Clinton	2	Trump	3
2020	Biden	0	Trump	0

Source: Gallup Polls of registered voters, 1964–2016; 2020 data comes from a CNN poll conducted from August 25–September 6, 2020.

Characteristics of the Nominees

In theory, many are qualified to be nominated for the presidency. The Constitution prescribes only three formal criteria: a minimum age of thirty-five, a fourteen-year residence in the United States, and native-born status. Naturalized citizens are not eligible for the office.

In practice, several informal qualifications have limited the pool of potential candidates. Successful nominees have usually been well-known and active in politics and have held high government positions. Of all the positions from which to seek the presidential nomination, the presidency is clearly the best. Only six incumbent presidents (three of whom were vice presidents who became president through the normal succession process) have failed in their quest for the nomination.

Over the years, there have been a variety of paths to the White House. When the congressional caucus system was in operation, the position of secretary of state was regarded as a stepping-stone to the nomination if the incumbent chose not to seek another term. When brokered national conventions replaced the congressional caucus, the Senate became the incubator for most successful presidential candidates. After the Civil War, governors emerged as the most likely contenders, particularly for the party that did not control the White House. Governors possess a political base and a prestigious executive position. They also are *not* forced to take stands on as many controversial national issues as members of Congress must do during their terms in office and do not get as much critical coverage in the national news media as do Washington-based politicians. The vice presidency is also seen as a stepping-stone to the presidential nomination.

There are other informal criteria, although they have less to do with qualifications for office than with public attitudes about religion, race, ethnicity, and gender. Prior to John F. Kennedy's election in 1960, no Catholic had been elected, although in 1928, the Democrats nominated Governor Alfred E. Smith of New York, a Catholic, who did not win. Prior to Joseph Lieberman's selection as Al Gore's running mate in 2000, no Jewish American had been nominated for that position. The selection of Barack Obama as the Democratic standard-bearer in 2008 marked the first time a candidate who identified himself as African American had been chosen to lead his party, and Hillary Clinton was the first woman to do so in 2016.

Public attitudes have changed, although contemporary surveys still indicate that some still face barriers to nomination and election. Health is still relevant. Age has also become a factor. After Alabama governor George Wallace was disabled by a would-be assassin's bullet in 1972, even his own supporters began to question his ability to cope with the rigors of the office. As noted previously, Senator Thomas Eagleton was forced to withdraw as the Democratic vice presidential nominee in 1972 when his past psychological illness became known. Before George W. Bush announced Dick Cheney's selection as his running mate, he had his father, former president George H. W. Bush, inquire about Cheney's medical condition. Cheney had suffered three heart attacks in the 1980s, but his Houston doctors described his health as excellent. Republicans rumored about health issues concerning Hillary Clinton when she had to be aided by staff leaving a campaign event. Donald Trump questioned her stamina during one of the presidential debates. With an incumbent president, Joe Biden, in his eighties, the energy and mental agility of the elderly have also become relevant issues. The Constitution sets a minimum age limit but not a maximum one. Now people are asking whether there should be one.

Family ties have also affected nominations and elections, as the father-son relationships of the Adams and the Bushes and the marriage between Bill and Hillary Clinton demonstrate. Only two bachelors have been elected president, James Buchanan and Grover Cleveland. During the 1884 campaign, Cleveland was accused of fathering an illegitimate child and was taunted by his opponents with the jingle, "ma, ma, Where's my Pa? Gone to the White House, ha! ha! ha!" Cleveland admitted responsibility for the child, even though he could not be certain he was the biological father.[23]

Until 1980, no person who was divorced had ever been elected. Andrew Jackson, however, married a divorced woman, or at least a woman he thought was divorced. As it turned out, she had not been granted the final court papers legally dissolving her marriage. When this information became public during the

1828 campaign, Jackson's opponents asked rhetorically, "do we want a whore in the White House?"[24] Jackson and Cleveland both won. That a candidate has been divorced and remarried several times seems to have little impact or even gain much notoriety today. Trump was married three times before getting elected.

Adultery may be another matter. Senator Edward Kennedy's marital problems and his driving accident on Chappaquiddick Island, off the coast of Massachusetts, in which a young woman riding with the senator was drowned, were serious impediments to his presidential candidacy in 1980. Gary Hart's alleged "womanizing" forced his withdrawal in 1988 and made his reentry into Democratic presidential politics problematic. On the other hand, Bill Clinton and Donald Trump were elected despite persistent allegations of sexual improprieties.

Summary

With the end of the competitive stage of the caucuses and primaries coming months before the nominating conventions, victorious candidates have to continue campaigning even though their nomination as their party's standard-bearer seems to be a certainty. During this interregnum, which can last several months, depending on when the competitive phase of the nomination is over and the conventions are scheduled, the would-be nominees must consolidate and expand their base, unify their party, and gain the support and endorsements of their political opponents. In addition, if they were in a competitive campaign, they will have to raise money for themselves and their parties. They also have to design their election strategy, developing and testing the themes they plan to emphasize, the policy stands they take, and the personal images they try to project. Moreover, they must stay in the news, avoid mistakes, and build their campaign organization. There is little rest for the weary.

As the nomination process now preordains the party's presidential candidate and control of the committees that set the rules, review the credentials, and draft the platform, the national nominating conventions have become more scripted than spontaneous, more glamorous than substantive, and more entertaining than newsworthy. They have become theater designed to energize the delegates, attract viewers, emphasize certain policies, create or reinforce leadership images, and launch the presidential campaign.

The parties still see their conventions as important events that generate publicity, enthusiasm, and solidify partisan support. The press sees them differently. Not oblivious to their public service function, journalists still need to present them as newsworthy and entertaining. That's tough to do with the deliberations, debate, and decision about the nominee usually determined in advance. The commercial broadcast networks seem to be giving up this task, leaving most of the coverage to public broadcasting, cable news networks, and niche news media outlets.

Although contemporary conventions are more theatrics than politics and more rhetoric than action, they continue to attract public attention, although a smaller proportion of the electorate sees or hears them today and does so for much less time than they did three or four decades ago. For those who watch them, inadvertently or deliberately, conventions increase awareness and shape perceptions of the candidates, parties, and their respective issue positions.

The impact of conventions varies with the attitudes and predispositions of those who watch, listen, or read about them. For partisans, conventions reinforce allegiances, making party identifiers more likely to vote and work for their party's nominees. For those less oriented toward a particular party, conventions may deepen interest in the campaign and knowledge about the candidates, which enables them to make a more informed voting decision. But Independents and those less interested in politics spend less time and devote less attention to the "goings-on" at the national party conventions.

The changes in the nominating process have also enlarged the field of candidates. Times have changed; the electorate, reflecting the mores of the society, has become more accepting of candidates who mirror the country's diversity rather than reflecting majority demographic characteristics.

Exercises

1. Compare the most recent Democratic and Republican conventions based on their schedules, the tenor of their televised speeches, and their in-house video presentations. Which did you find more interesting and why?

2. Compare the acceptance speeches of the major party candidates for the presidential and vice presidential nominations. On the basis of your comparison, to what extent did these speeches preview the principal appeals of the candidates in the general election?

3. To what extent do the major party platforms today reflect the increasing ideological content of contemporary politics? Are there any major areas in which the major parties take similar stands or use similar rhetoric today?

4. Contrast the major party platforms with those of two minor parties, one on the left of the political spectrum and one on the right. Would you categorize the major parties as more centrist than the minor ones? Are the Democratic and Republican platforms still within the mainstream of American public opinion today? You can answer this question by examining poll data on the primary issues emphasized in the platforms and the campaign.

5. Looking at the previous presidential campaign, indicate which parts of the winning party's platform and promises of the winning candidate became public policy and which ones did not. (You can get help on this exercise by going to Politifact.com.) Were there any promises or platform planks that the winners seemed to ignore?

6. Examine the inauguration address of the newly elected president and any other major addresses made by the president within the first one hundred days in office to see which of the party's platform positions were highlighted and which were not. Based on your analysis, do you think that platforms are important agenda setters for the new administration?

Selected Readings

Adler, Wendy Zeligson. "The Conventions on Prime Time." In Martha Fitzsimon, and Edward C. Pease, eds., *The Homestretch: New Politics* (pp. 55–57). New York: The Freedom Forum Media Studies Center, 1992.

Atkinson, Matthew D, et al. "(Where) Do Campaigns Matter? The Impact of National Party Convention Location," *The Journal of Politics* 7 (October 2014), 1045–58.

Brown, Gwen. "Change in Communication Demands of Spouses in the 2012 Nomination Conventions." In Robert E. Denton, Jr., ed., *The 2012 Presidential Campaign: A Communication Perspective* (pp. 23–44). Lanham, MD: Rowman & Littlefield, 2014.

Cera, Joseph, and Aaron C. Weinschenk. "The Individual-Level Effects of Presidential Conventions on Candidate Evaluations." *American Politics Research* 40 (2012): 3–28.

Coleman, Kevin J. "The Presidential Nominating Process and the National Party Conventions, 2016: Frequently Asked Questions." *Congressional Research Service* (December 30, 2015).

Heaney, Michael T. "Polarized Networks: The Organizational Affiliations of National Party Convention Delegates." *American Behavioral Scientist* (October 19, 2012): 1–23.

Holloway, Rachel L. "The 2012 Presidential Nominating Conventions and the American Dream: Narrative Unity and Political Division." In Robert E. Denton, Jr., ed., *The 2012 Presidential Campaign: A Communication Perspective* (pp. 1–22). Lanham, MD: Rowman & Littlefield, 2014.

Jordan, Soren, Clayton McLaughlin Webb, and B. Dan Wood. "The President, Polarization and the Party Platforms, 1944–2012," *The Forum: A Journal of Applied Research in Contemporary Politics* 13 (April 2014).

Patterson, Thomas E. "News Coverage of the 2016 National Conventions: Negative News, Lacking Context." Shorenstein Center for Media, Politics and Public Policy, Harvard University.

Panagopoulos, Costas, ed. *Rewiring Politics: Presidential Nominating Conventions in the Media Age.* Baton Rouge: Louisiana State University Press, 2007.

Shafer, Byron E. *Bifurcated Politics: Evolution and Reform in the National Party Convention.* Cambridge, MA: Harvard University Press, 1988.

Simas, Elizabeth, and Kevin Evans "Linking Party Platforms to Perceptions of Presidential Candidates' Policy Positions, 1972–2000." *Political Research Quarterly* 64 (2011): 831–39.

Smith, Larry David, and Dan Nimmo. *Cordial Concurrence: Orchestrating National Party Conventions in the Telepolitical Age.* New York, NY: Praeger, 1991.

Notes

1. In their analysis of the 2012 electorate, political scientists John Sides and Lynn Vavreck argue that voters' perceptions of candidate electability were more highly correlated with their voting preferences than was their ideological proximity to the voters. In other words, Republican primary voters were more concerned with who was most likely to beat Obama than whose beliefs were closest to their own. John Sides and Lynn Vavreck, *The Gamble: Choice and Chance in the 2012 Presidential Election* (Princeton, NJ: Princeton University Press, 2013), 91.

2. Alison Mitchell, "Bush Strategy Recalls Clinton on the Trail in '96," *The New York Times* (April 18, 2000), A18.

3. Matthew Dowd, *Campaign for President: The Managers Look at 2004* (Lanham, MD: Rowman & Littlefield, 2005), 100.

4. According to David Axelrod, Obama's chief campaign strategist, "in the long run, flip-flopper was not a very good argument for us in the general election context because we didn't want to give people an out to say, Well yeah, his ideas seem kind of nutty, but he doesn't really mean them." David Axelrod, *Campaign for President: The Managers Look at 2012* (Lanham, MD: Rowman & Littlefield, 2013), 112.

5. Stuart Stevens, *Electing the President 2012: The Insiders' View*, edited by Kathleen Hall Jamieson (Philadelphia: University of Pennsylvania Press, 2013), 28–29.

6. Barack Obama, *The Audacity of Hope*. New York, NY: Crown/Three Rivers Press, 2006.

7. To counter their predicament, McCain's media consultants designed and aired a clever political commercial that compared the Democratic candidate's notoriety to that of singer Britney Spears and socialite Paris Hilton; the intent was to paint the Democratic candidate as a celebrity but at the same time question his leadership credentials.

8. Rick Davis, *Campaign for President: The Managers Look at 2008* (Lanham, MD: Rowman & Littlefield, 2009), 88.

9. Rhoades, *Campaign for President: The Managers Look at 2012*, 95.

10. Axelrod, *Electing the President 2012: The Insiders' View*, 38–39.

11. In 2011, with the economy in doldrums and the president's reelection uncertain, Obama's political advisers toyed with the idea of replacing Joe Biden on the 2012 ticket with Hillary Clinton. Polling results and focus group discussions, however, indicated little benefit from such a switch and the suggestion was quickly dropped. Jonathan Martin, "Book Details Obama Aides' Talks About Replacing Biden on 2012 Ticket," *New York Times*, October 31, 2013.

12. Plouffe, *Campaign for President: The Managers Look at 2008*, 155.

13. Nicole Wallace, *Electing the President 2008: The Insiders' View* (Philadelphia: University of Pennsylvania Press, 2009), 27.

14. George McGovern, conversation with author.

15. Ann Richards, "Address to the Democratic Convention in Atlanta, Georgia, on July 19, 1988," as quoted in *Congressional Quarterly* 46 (July 23, 1988): 2024.

16. Hillary Clinton, "Address to the 2016 Democratic National Convention," *New York Times*, July 28, 2016.

17. John McCain, "Acceptance Address at the Republican National Convention, Minneapolis, MN," September 4, 2008.

18. Donald Trump, "Address to the 2016 Republican Convention," *New York Times*, July 22, 2016.

19. Donald Trump, "Address to the 2020 Republican Convention," *New York Times*, August 27, 2020.

20. Joe Biden, "Address to the 2020 Democratic Convention," August 20, 2020.

21. The audience for the 2016 Republican convention averaged twenty-three million viewers and twenty-four million for the Democrats. Stephen Battaglio, "TV Viewership for Hillary Clinton's Acceptance Speech Is Smaller than Donald Trump's," *Los Angeles Times*, July 29, 2016.

22. Thomas E. Patterson, "News Coverage of the 2016 National Conventions: Negative News, Lacking Context," *Shorenstein Center for Media, Politics and Public Policy*.

23. Thomas A. Bailey, *Presidential Greatness* (New York, NY: Appleton-Century Crofts, 1966), 74.

24. Ibid.

PART THREE

The General Election Campaign

Strategy, Tactics, and Operations

Chapter 7

Introduction

Elections have been held in the United States since 1789; campaigning by parties for their nominees began soon thereafter. It was not until the end of the nineteenth century, however, that presidential candidates actively competed in the campaigns. Personal solicitation initially was viewed as demeaning and unbecoming of the dignity and stature of the presidency.

Distributed by the parties, election paraphernalia first appeared in the 1820s; by 1828, there was extensive public debate about the candidates. Andrew Jackson and, to a lesser extent, John Quincy Adams generated considerable commentary and controversy. Jackson's supporters lauded him as a hero, a man of the people, and "a new or second Washington"; his critics referred to him as "King Andrew the first," alleging that he was immoral, tyrannical, and brutal.[1] Adams was also subjected to personal attack. Much of this heated rhetoric appeared in the highly partisan press of the times.

The use of the campaign to reach, entertain, inform, and mobilize the general electorate began on a large scale in 1840. Festivals, parades, slogans, jingles, and testimonials were employed to energize voters. The campaign of 1840 is best remembered for the slogan "Tippecanoe and Tyler too"—promoting Whig candidates General William Henry Harrison, hero of the battle of Tippecanoe in the War of 1812, and John Tyler—and for its great jingles:

What Has Caused This Great Commotion?
(Sung to the tune of "LITTLE PIG'S TAIL")

What has caused this great commotion, motion, motion, our country through?
It is the ball a rolling on, on.

Chorus
For Tippecanoe and Tyler too—Tippecanoe and Tyler too,
And with them we'll beat little Van, Van, Van, [Martin Van Buren] Van is a used up man, and with them we'll beat little Van.[2]

The successful Whig campaign made it a prototype for subsequent presidential contests.

The Evolution of Presidential Campaigns

The election of 1840 was also the first in which a party nominee actually campaigned for himself. General William Henry Harrison made twenty-three speeches in his home state of Ohio.[3] He did not set a precedent that was quickly followed, however. It was twenty years before another presidential candidate took to the stump and then under the extraordinary conditions of the onset of the Civil War and the breakup of the Democratic Party.

Senator Stephen A. Douglas, Democratic candidate for president, spoke out on the slavery issue to try to heal the split that it had engendered within his party. In doing so, however, he denied his own personal ambitions. "I did not come here to solicit your votes," he told a Raleigh, North Carolina, audience. "I have nothing to say for myself or my claims personally. I am one of those who think it would not be a favor to me to be made President at this time."[4]

Abraham Lincoln, Douglas's Republican opponent, refused to reply, even though he had debated Douglas two years earlier in their contest for the Senate seat from Illinois, a contest Douglas won. Lincoln, who almost dropped out of public view when the campaign was underway, felt that it was not even proper for him to vote for himself.[5] He cut his own name from the Republican ballot before he cast votes for others running in the election.[6]

The Republicans mounted a massive campaign on Lincoln's behalf. They held what were called "Wide Awake" celebrations in which large numbers of people were brought together. An account of one of these celebrations reported:

> The Wide-Awake torch-light procession is undoubtedly the largest and most impos-
> ing thing of the kind ever witnessed in Chicago. Unprejudiced spectators estimate
> the number at 10,000. Throughout the whole length of the procession were scat-
> tered portraits of Abraham Lincoln. Banners and transparencies bearing Republican
> mottoes, and pictures of rail splitters, were also plentifully distributed. Forty-three
> bands of music were also in the procession.[7]

From Porch to Train

Presidential candidates remained on the sidelines until the 1880s. Republican James Garfield broke the tradition by receiving visitors at his Ohio home. Four years later in 1884, Republican James Blaine made hundreds of campaign speeches in an unsuccessful effort to deny public accusations that he profited from a fraudulent railroad deal. Benjamin Harrison, the Republican candidate in 1888, resumed the practice of seeing people at his home, a practice that has been referred to as front porch campaigning. Historian Keith Melder writes that Harrison met with 110 delegations consisting of almost 200,000 people in the course of the campaign.[8] William McKinley received even more visitors at his front porch campaign in 1896. He spoke to approximately 750,000 people who were recruited and, in some cases, transported to his Canton, Ohio, home by the Republican Party.[9]

McKinley's opponent in that election, William Jennings Bryan, traveled around the country making speeches at Democratic political rallies. By his own account, he logged more than eighteen thousand miles and made more than six hundred speeches. According to press estimates, he spoke to almost five million people, nearly collapsing from exhaustion at the end of the campaign.[10]

In 1900, Republican vice presidential candidate Theodore Roosevelt took on Bryan, "making 673 speeches, visiting 567 towns in 24 states, and traveling 21,209 miles."[11] Twelve years later, former President Theodore Roosevelt once again took to the hustings, only this time he was trying to defeat a fellow Republican president, William Howard Taft, for his party's nomination. Roosevelt won nine primaries, including one in Ohio, Taft's home state, but was denied the nomination by party leaders. He then launched an Independent candidacy in the general election, campaigning on the Progressive, or "Bull Moose," ticket. His Democratic opponent, Woodrow Wilson, was also an active campaigner. The Roosevelt and Wilson efforts ended the era of passive presidential campaigning. The last front porch presidential campaign was waged by Warren G. Harding in 1920.

From Rally to Radio and Television

Harding's campaign was distinguished in another way: He was the first to use radio to speak directly to voters. This new electronic medium and, followed thirty years later by television, radically changed presidential campaigns. Initially, candidates were slow to adjust their campaigns to these new techniques.[12] It was not until the candidacy of Franklin Delano Roosevelt in 1932 that radio was employed skillfully. Roosevelt also pioneered the "whistle-stop" campaign train, which stopped at railroad stations along the route to allow the candidate to address the crowds that came to see and hear him. In 1932, Roosevelt, who took a train to Chicago to accept his nomination, visited thirty-six states, traveling some thirteen thousand miles. His extensive travels, undertaken in part to dispel a whispering campaign about his health—he had polio as a young man, which left him unable to walk or even stand up unaided—forced President Herbert Hoover onto the campaign trail to defend his presidency and seek reelection.[13]

Instead of giving the small number of speeches he had originally planned, Hoover traveled more than ten thousand miles across much of the country. He was the first incumbent president to campaign actively for reelection. Thereafter, with the exception of Franklin Roosevelt during World War II, personal campaigning became standard for incumbents and nonincumbents alike.

Harry Truman took campaigning by an incumbent a step further. Perceived as the underdog in the 1948 election, Truman whistle-stopped the length and breadth of the United States, traveling thirty-two thousand miles and averaging ten speeches a day. In eight weeks, he spoke to an estimated six million people.[14] While Truman was rousing the faithful with his down-home comments and hard-hitting criticisms of the Republican-controlled Congress, his opponent, Thomas E. Dewey, was promising new leadership but providing few particulars. His sonorous speeches contrasted sharply and unfavorably with Truman's straightforward remarks.

The end of this era of presidential campaigning occurred in 1948. Within the next four years, television came into its own as a communications medium. The number of television viewers grew from less than half a million in 1948 to approximately nineteen million in 1952, a figure that was deemed sufficient in the minds of campaign planners to launch a major television effort. The Eisenhower presidential organization budgeted almost $2 million for television, and the Democrats promised to use both radio and television "in an exciting, dramatic way" in that election.[15]

The potential of television was evident from the outset. Republican vice presidential candidate Richard Nixon took to the airwaves in 1952 to reply to accusations that he had appropriated campaign funds for his personal use and had received money and other gifts from wealthy supporters, including a black-and-white cocker spaniel named Checkers. Nixon denied the charges but said that under no circumstances would he and his family give up the dog, which his children dearly loved. A huge outpouring of public sympathy for Nixon followed his television address, effectively ending the issue, keeping him on the ticket, and demonstrating the impact television could have on a political career and a presidential candidate. Ironically, it was the televised Senate hearings into the practices of Nixon's 1972 reelection committee that informed the public of the dirty tricks in which his campaign had engaged and the taping system in the White House that revealed the president's culpability in the Watergate cover-up.

Television not only made mass appeals easier but also created new obstacles for the candidates. Physical appearance became more important as did oratorical skills. Instead of just rousing a crowd, presidential aspirants had to convey a personal message and a compelling image to viewers. Television had other effects as well. It eventually supplemented the party as the principal link between its nominees and the voters. It decreased the incentive for holding so many public events because more people could be reached through this mass communications medium than at a rally, parade, or speech, but it also increased the need to participate in personal interviews, appear on news, talk, and eventually, entertainment shows, and hire campaign staff skilled in visual communications and marketing. The candidates became showbiz celebrities or already were ones: Reagan a former movie star and Trump who played a CEO in the television series, *The Apprentice*.

Campaign activities and events had to be carefully orchestrated and scripted, keeping in mind how they would appear on the screen and what images they would convey to voters. Off-handed comments and quips were discouraged because they invariably got candidates into trouble and diverted attention from the narrative that their campaigns wished to present to the American electorate.

The campaigns added public relations experts to apply mass-marketing techniques. Pollsters and media consultants supplemented and to some extent replaced old-style politicians in designing and executing campaign strategies. Even the candidates seemed a little different. With the possible exception of Lyndon Johnson and Gerald Ford, both of whom succeeded to the presidency through the death or resignation of their predecessors, incumbents and challengers alike reflected the grooming and schooling of the age of television. And when they did not, as in the cases of Walter Mondale, Michael Dukakis, and Robert Dole, they fared poorly.

From Art to Science: The Digital Revolution

The age of television campaigning is obviously not over, but the revolution in the news media from broadcast to cable to the internet and interactive digital communications, from search engines to apps to social networking, and from generic partisan appeals to the collection, integration, and analysis of large data sets of personal information has provided political campaign organizations with the means to discern and disaggregate public opinion and target individualized messages to specific groups of voters.

This chapter and the one that follows discuss these alternations in modern presidential campaigns. We begin by examining broad strategic components: basic appeals, leadership imagery, and Electoral College coalition building. We illustrate that discussion with a box outlining the major party candidates' strategies in recent presidential elections. We then turn to more specific tactical decisions: the staging, timing, and "war room" reactions to unexpected events, verbal miscues, and embarrassing situations that become public from time to time. Finally, we examine the complexities of organization and operations of presidential campaigns at their headquarters and in the field. We end our discussion by examining how the new technologies have benefited and hurt a democratic electoral process.

Strategic Planning

Designing a strategy starts early, well before the general election campaign gets underway. It is an ongoing process that guides tactical considerations. Strategies are built on past races. They consider the successes and failures of previous presidential candidates. They also must adjust to the resources potentially available to the campaign, the mood of the electorate, and the public perceptions of the candidates and their parties in the year of the election. As those variables change, the assumption on which the strategies are based must also be adjusted. Failure to do so can be fatal. However, there is also a danger of overreacting to unexpected events that may have short-term consequences.

There is another problem. Strategic changes that become evident during the campaign, often as a consequence of internal leaks, personnel departures, position shifts, or press speculation. If the original design is not working, a perception that the press highlights within the context of its horse race type of coverage, then adjustments must be made.

The first step in constructing a campaign strategy is fashioning a basic appeal. This appeal has two principal components: partisan imagery and policy beliefs often disaggregated into specific issue positions and priorities. The objective is to frame the electoral choice in as advantageous a manner as possible to as many people as possible as soon as possible and for as long as possible.

Partisanship

All things being equal, the candidates of the dominant party have an advantage that they try to maximize by emphasizing their partisan affiliation, lauding their political heroes, and making a blatant party appeal. When the Democrats were the majority from the 1930s through most of the 1960s, their candidates traditionally clothed themselves in partisan garb. During this period, the Republicans did not. Eisenhower, Nixon, and Ford downplayed their party affiliation, pointing instead to their personal qualifications and their policy preferences. As the partisan gap narrowed, Republican candidates adjusted and highlighted their political loyalties and ideologies. Today, both parties' nominees utilize their parties to identify themselves, energize their most intense supporters, and others whose values and beliefs would lead them in the same policy direction.

Since 2000, the major parties have been at or near parity with one another. In 2000, both major party candidates moved toward the political center after they had won their party's nomination to appeal to Independent voters and weak party identifiers. Since 2004, they have not done so. Rather they have tried to maximize their electoral base on the belief that most voters have a partisan orientation even when they identify themselves as Independents.

Regardless of how much emphasis is placed on partisanship, the popular images of the party still evoke strong feelings among voters. For the Democrats, common economic and, increasingly, social interests have been the most compelling cues for most of their supporters. Perceived as the party that got the country out of the Great Depression and Great Recession, the party of middle class and those that are less wealthy, Democratic candidates stress "bread-and-butter" issues and nondiscriminatory social policy. They contrast their concern for the plight of average Americans with the Republicans' ties to the rich, especially to big corporations, banks, and investment capitalists.

The downside to this perspective, however, is the Republican contention that Democratic policies discourage individual initiative, impede private enterprise, and create dependency on government programs. Since the days of the New Deal, the GOP has typecast Democratic presidential candidates as liberal, "tax and spend," big government advocates, and most recently socialists.

Bill Clinton sought to reassert his party's middle-class appeal in his two presidential campaigns. Calling himself a "New Democrat," Clinton took pains to distinguish his own moderate views from those of his more liberal Democratic predecessors and the conservative ideology of his Republican opponents. He presented himself as a change-oriented candidate in 1992 and as a builder of progress in 1996. In contrast, Al Gore and John Kerry took more populist stands, emphasizing their desire to help working families and those in need. Barack Obama and Joe Biden also targeted the middle class in their campaigns; they pointed to the plight Americans face in maintaining, much less improving, their standard of living and their opportunities for economic advancement.

Since the 1970s, Republican presidential candidates have focused on those matters on which the Democrats' electoral constituency has been divided. They have appealed to the fears and frustrations of older, conservative, male, and predominantly white voters. Republicans have lauded the benefits of individual initiative, religious freedom, smaller government, lower taxes, more vigorous law enforcement, and a robust national security apparatus.

When foreign policy and, more recently, homeland security have been salient, GOP candidates have traditionally done better. They have been viewed as stronger leaders in addressing national security concerns than their Democratic opponents. In 1952, Dwight Eisenhower campaigned on the theme "Communism, Corruption, and Korea," projecting himself as the candidate most qualified to end the Korean war. Richard Nixon took a similar tack in 1968, linking Humphrey to the Johnson administration and the war in Vietnam. Nixon and Ronald Reagan were considered "cold warriors."

Lacking his father's expertise in foreign affairs, George W. Bush did not stress foreign policy in his 2000 campaign but did point to the war on terrorism, which he declared after the terrorist attacks in New York and Washington, DC, on September 11, 2001. Foreign policy issues took a back seat to economic concerns in 2008 and 2012, thereby reducing the Republican advantage, particularly that of John McCain.

Donald Trump appealed to nationalism and weak presidential leadership abroad in his pro-America 2016 campaign rhetoric. He stressed strong leadership, patriotism, and law and order in 2020. Biden said he would repair international alliances with friendly countries and stand up to foes, especially China and Russia.

Democrats usually counter the perception that they are weaker in foreign and military affairs by talking tough on national security policy issues. In his 1976 campaign, Jimmy Carter vowed that an Arab oil embargo would be seen by his administration as an economic declaration of war. In 1984, Walter Mondale supported the buildup of US defenses, including Reagan's strategic defense initiative. In 1988, Michael Dukakis spoke about the need for America to be more competitive within the international economic arena, as did Bill Clinton in 1992. Al Gore and John Kerry emphasized the foreign policy expertise they gained in the Senate, their military service in Vietnam, and their support for a more vibrant and extensive American presence around the world. With the nation mired in two unpopular wars, Barack Obama emphasized the value of diplomacy and multistate coalitions in resolving international conflicts as did Hillary Clinton in 2016 and Biden in 2020.

Salient Issues

The electoral environment affects the priorities and substance of candidates' policy appeal. In 1992, the electorate was concerned about the economy, particularly the loss of American jobs at home and the growing federal government budget deficit. In 1996, with the economy strengthened, unemployment low, inflation in check, and a strong stock market, the electorate in general was more satisfied with the country's economic condition, a situation that favored the incumbent. The salient issues in 2000 were how to improve education, provide tax relief, and put Social Security and Medicare on a firmer financial foundation; in 2004, the war in Iraq was a primary concern, along with continuing budget deficits, unequal economic growth, the shift of manufacturing jobs overseas, and controversial social issues such as same-sex marriage. In 2008, the most important issue was the deep and broad economic recession, and four years later it was the nation's slow economic recovery rate and stagnant wages. In 2016, it was the desire for economic and social change and which candidate would be best able to achieve it. In 2020, it was the pandemic, the economy, and Trump's controversial words and actions as president.

In general, national economic problems tend to be the most important and recurrent ones in presidential elections. Ronald Reagan drove this home in 1980 with the question he posed at the end of his debate with President Carter, a question he directed at the American people: "Are you better off now than you were four years ago?" Similarly, James Carville, Clinton's chief strategist in the 1992 campaign, kept a sign over his desk that read, "It's the economy, stupid." He did not want anyone in the Clinton organization to forget that the poor economy was the campaign's primary selling point for a change in partisan control of the White House. From 2008 through 2020, perceptions of the economy, future opportunities for disaffected Americans, and the direction in which the country was heading drove the elections and influenced their outcomes. Multicultural issues were also a factor in 2016 and 2020, particularly immigration.

A strong economy helps the party in power but not to the extent that a weak one hurts it. The Great Recession that began during the presidency of George W. Bush adversely affected the chances of Republican John McCain; in 2008, the pace of the economic recovery was Romney's principal theme. Although the general economy declined in importance in the 2016 presidential election, specific economic problems such as job losses, wage growth, and income inequality divided the electorate with the candidates proposing different policy solutions to these problems as well as to divisive social issues. Four years later, the economy reemerged as one of the major problems because of the pandemic and supply chain shortages.

Leadership Imagery

Regardless of the partisan imagery and thematic emphases, candidates for the presidency must stress their own qualifications for the job and cast doubt on those of their opponents'. They must appear presidential, demonstrating those personal attributes and leadership qualities the voters consider essential and come to expect. In the words of David Axelrod, Obama's senior strategist in his two presidential campaigns:

> With very few exceptions, the history of presidential politics shows that public opinion and attitudes about who should next occupy the oval office are largely shaped by perceptions of the retiring incumbent. And rarely do the voters ask for a replica. Instead they generally choose a remedy, selecting a candidate who will address the deficiencies of the outgoing president.[16]

When incumbents are running for reelection, their experience in office usually works to their political advantage. They are seen as more knowledgeable than their opponents, as leaders who have stood the tests of time. Stability and predictability satisfy the public's psychological needs unless conditions are deemed unsatisfactory and presidential behavior unacceptable; the certainty of four more years with a known quantity is likely to be more appealing than the uncertainty of the next four years with an unknown one, provided the incumbent's job performance has been viewed as generally satisfactory.

Accentuating the Positive

A positive public image, of course, cannot be taken for granted. It must be created, or at least polished. Contemporary presidents are expected to be strong, assertive, and capable. If their policies are not seen as successful, they are criticized for the way in which they exercised power. During times of crisis and periods of social anxiety, these leadership attributes are considered essential. The strength that Franklin Roosevelt was able to convey by virtue of his bout with polio, Dwight Eisenhower by his military command in World War II, and Ronald Reagan by his tough talk, clear-cut solutions, and optimistic vision contrasted sharply with those of Adlai Stevenson in 1956, George McGovern in 1972, Jimmy Carter in 1980, and Walter Mondale in 1984 who were thought to be weak and indecisive.

For challengers, the task of seeming to be powerful, confident, and independent (of being one's own person) can best be imparted by a no-nonsense approach, a conviction that success is attainable, and clear, coherent, and consistent political beliefs that can be converted into specific policy solutions. John Kennedy's rhetorical emphasis on activity in 1960, Richard Nixon's tough talk in 1968, and Donald Trump's personal convictions, self-confidence, and business acumen helped them generate the impression of a take-charge personality. They were seen as strong leaders who knew what had to be done and would do it.

In addition to seeming tough enough to be president, it is also important to exhibit sufficient knowledge and skills for the job. One of the reasons that the Obama campaign wanted the first presidential debate with John McCain in 2008 to be on foreign policy was to demonstrate that Obama was as knowledgeable and thoughtful as his older and more seasoned opponent. Experience can also become an issue for candidates who have not held public office, less so when the view of government is unfavorable.

What many candidates without national experience do is run against Washington, pointing out that they are not part of the problem so they will be better able to fix it. Obviously, such a strategy works only if the public has a lot of grievances against those in power. This was the message Jimmy Carter presented after Watergate, Obama emphasized during the Great Recession, and Trump highlighted in an era of discontent with government in Washington. Trump said that he would "drain the swamp."

Empathy is also an important attribute. People want a president who can respond to their emotional needs, a person who understands what and how they feel. Roosevelt and Eisenhower radiated warmth. Carter, Clinton, and George W. Bush were particularly effective in generating the impression that they cared, whereas McGovern, Nixon, Dukakis, and Dole appeared cold, distant, and less personal.

Candor, integrity, and trust emerge periodically as important attributes in presidential image building. Most of the time these traits are taken for granted. Occasionally, however, a crisis of confidence, such as Watergate or the Clinton impeachment, dictates that political skills be downplayed, and these personal qualities stressed. Such crises preceded the elections of 1952, 1976, 2000, and 2008. In the first two of these elections, Eisenhower, a war hero, and Carter, who promised never to tell a lie, both benefited from the perception that they were honest, decent men. George W. Bush made much of the scandalous behavior in the Clinton administration with the phrase, "When I put my hand on the Bible, I will swear to not only uphold the laws of our land, I will swear to uphold the honor and dignity of the office to which I have been elected, so help me God."[17] Neither candidate scored high on the honesty and integrity scale in 2016. Clinton was viewed as evasive and, from the perspective of her opponents, dishonest; Trump was criticized for creating his own reality, being uninformed, and factually inaccurate in both 2016 and 2020. Republicans questioned Biden's age and stamina.

Character is important in elections when issues involving personal behavior are directed toward those in power. Character also tends to be more important when less is known about the candidates, particularly at the beginning of their presidential quest. It is less important for incumbents running for reelection because the electorate has had time to judge them.

Highlighting the Negative

Naturally, candidates can be expected to raise questions about their opponents. These questions assume particular importance if the public's initial impression of the candidates is fuzzy, as it may be with outsiders who win their party's nomination. When Republican polls and focus groups commissioned by the George H. W. Bush campaign in 1988 revealed that the image of his opponent, Michael Dukakis, was imprecise, Bush's campaign advisers devised a strategy to take advantage by discrediting him. The strategy was based on the premise that the higher the negatives of a candidate, the less likely that candidate would win.[18]

Both Hillary Clinton and Donald Trump campaigned on this premise in 2016. Clinton claimed that Trump was unfit to serve as president because he lacked the temperament, knowledge, and judgment essential for the job. Trump called Clinton "crooked . . . the most corrupt person ever to seek the presidency."[19] In its advertising, the Clinton campaign was more overtly negative than Trump's.[20] In 2020, both candidates used negativity in their ads, speeches, and social media.

Increased negativity in presidential elections has been fueled by the avalanche of ads by Super PACs and other groups, including those by the major parties. The ads of these groups have been overwhelmingly negative, more so than the ads of the presidential candidates.[21] The rule that nonparty groups cannot coordinate their election activities with the candidates' campaigns contributes to the attack and contrast ads that these groups sponsor.

In summary, candidates try to project images of themselves that are consistent with public expectations of the office and its occupant and images of their opponents that are inconsistent with those expectations. Traits such as inner strength, stamina, decisiveness, competence, and experience are considered essential for the presidency, as are empathy, sincerity, credibility, honesty, and integrity. Which of these traits are considered most important varies to some extent with the assessment of the strengths and weaknesses of the incumbent and the nature of the times. Challengers try to exploit an incumbent's vulnerabilities by emphasizing the very skills and qualities that the president is perceived to lack.

Dealing with Incumbency

Claiming a leadership image requires a different script for an incumbent. As noted previously, incumbents usually have an advantage in running for reelection. Between 1900 and 1972, thirteen incumbents sought reelection and eleven won; the two who lost, Taft in 1912 and Hoover in 1932, faced highly unusual circumstances. In Taft's case, he was challenged by former Republican president Theodore Roosevelt, splitting the GOP vote and enabling Democrat Woodrow Wilson to win. Hoover ran during the Great Depression, for which he received much of the blame. (Box 7.1 summarizes the advantages and disadvantages of incumbency in running for president.)

Since 1932, only four other incumbents have lost. Adverse political, economic, and social factors help explain their defeats.

BOX 7.1 ★ An Incumbency Balance Sheet

Incumbency can be a double-edged sword, strengthening or weakening a claim to leadership. Incumbents ritually point to their accomplishments, noting the work that remains and sounding a "stay-the-course" theme; challengers argue that it is time for a change and that they can do better.

Advantages of Incumbency
Being president is thought to help an incumbent in the quest for reelection more often than not. The advantages stem from the visibility of the office, the esteem it engenders, and the influence it provides.

The public's familiarity and comfort with incumbents permit presidents running for reelection to highlight their opponent's lack of experience, limited leadership qualities, and few public policy accomplishments and contrast these deficiencies with their own experience and record in office. Carter used a variation of this tactic in 1980 to no avail when he described the arduous job of the president and then compared his energy, knowledge, and intelligence with his thirteen-year older political opponent, Ronald Reagan. Clinton and Obama campaigned as candidates for the future, pointing to their opponents' failed policies. George W. Bush and his father both ran for reelection on their national security records. For George H. W. Bush, that record was not sufficient because of the economic recession in 1992; for George W. Bush in 2004, it was but barely. Public grievances must be sufficiently intense and broad based to oust an incumbent.

The ability of presidents to make news, to affect events, and to dispense the "spoils" of government can also work to their advantage. Presidents are in the

BOX 7.1 ★ An Incumbency Balance Sheet *continued*

limelight and can maneuver to remain there. Having a "bully pulpit" gives them an agenda-setting advantage. All recent presidents campaigning for reelection have utilized the status, perquisites, and ceremonial aspects of their office to enhance their personal image in seemingly nonpolitical roles. Obama was helped by Hurricane Sandy, which occurred a week before the 2012 election; the huge storm and the damage and distress it caused enabled him to act presidential by showing empathy and promising to help people whose houses and businesses were damaged or ruined.

Most presidents have another "trump" card. Presumably, their actions can influence events. They try to gear economic recoveries to election years. They also use their discretionary authority to distribute government resources such as grants, contracts, and emergency aid, being careful not to seem overtly partisan when doing so. The incumbency advantages extend to vice presidents seeking their party's presidential nomination but not nearly as much to their general election campaign. Of the five most recent vice presidents who tried to succeed to the presidency by election—Nixon (1960), Humphrey (1968), George H. W. Bush (1988), and Al Gore (2000), Joe Biden (2020)—only Bush and Biden were successful.

The difficulty that incumbent vice presidents face is that they cannot demonstrate leadership from a position of followership. To establish their leadership credentials, vice presidents need to get out of their president's shadow; they have to separate themselves. If they do so, however, it becomes much more difficult for them to claim and share the administration's successes. George H. W. Bush dealt with this problem by stating that he would pursue Reagan's agenda but do so in a kinder and gentler way. Al Gore, on the other hand, articulated a populist appeal in contrast to the Clinton administration's more moderate, mainstream approach.

Disadvantages of Incumbency

Incumbents face a leadership problem that can work against them. In their campaigns for office, presidential candidates hype themselves, make promises, and create expectations difficult to meet. Once in office they find these expectations difficult to meet in a constitutional system that divides authority, a political system that that decentralizes power, and a representative democracy in which public opinion is often ambiguous, can vary, and may be inconsistent all of which produces a gap between promise and performance. Persistent criticism by the news media contributes to these difficulties. With radio and television emphasizing controversy and engaging in investigatory reporting, incumbents are criticized for the country's problems, whether or not they are to blame for them. Under the circumstances, it may be difficult for presidents to maintain a favorable leadership image, although Reagan and Clinton were able to do so. George W. Bush and Barack Obama had mixed approved ratings in the low fifties. Trump's ratings started low and ended even lower. Biden received positive approval ratings for his first six months and negative ones through 2022.

In summary, incumbents are helped or hurt by their perceived performance in office. Having a good record contributes to a president's reelection potential just as a poor record detracts from it. Bad times almost always hurt an incumbent. A crisis, however, helps, at least in the short run. Rightly or wrongly, the public places more responsibility for domestic economic conditions, internal social relations, and

BOX 7.1 ★ An Incumbency Balance Sheet *continued*

foreign policy on the president than anyone else in government; that a president exercises little control over some of these external factors seems less relevant to the electorate than do negative conditions, which they blame on the president.

Personal favorability ratings appear to be less important. Both Carter and George H. W. Bush had favorable personal ratings, yet both were defeated in their reelection attempts. Clinton's favorability evaluation was much less positive, yet he was easily reelected in 1996. However, his highly negative ratings in 2000 may have hurt Gore, or so Gore feared when he designed a strategy to separate himself from Clinton. Obama was viewed more positively at the end of his term than either Trump or Clinton were in 2016 and Biden more favorably than Trump in 2020.

Building a Winning Electoral College Coalition

In addition to designing a general appeal and addressing leadership and related incumbency issues, assembling a winning geographic coalition is also a critical priority. Since the election is decided in the Electoral College, the primary objective must always be to win a majority of the college and not necessarily a majority of the popular vote.

In building their Electoral College coalitions, candidates start with their base—areas that have been traditionally favorable to their party's nominees. Following the Civil War, the Democrats could depend on the "Solid South," while Republicans were stronger in the Northeast. Beginning in the 1960s, these areas began to shift their partisan allegiances. By the mid-1990s, the South had become solidly Republican, and the Northeast was becoming more Democratic. With the Rocky Mountain region strongly Republican, except for Colorado in recent years, and the mid-Atlantic and Pacific Coast states Democratic, the focus of presidential campaigns in the twenty-first century has been on the relatively small number of competitive states, about twenty at the beginning of the campaign and less than eight by the end.

Electoral College strategies almost always require candidates to campaign in the most competitive states, giving priority to those with the most electoral votes. These states are the most important in an Electoral College system because of the winner-take-all method by which state votes are allocated in all but two, Maine and Nebraska.

One criterion for assessing the level of competition, at least at the beginning of the election cycle, is how the state voted in past presidential elections. Was the popular vote difference that the presidential candidates received in the state 5 percent or less? If it was, the state is potentially competitive; if not, it probably is not unless there has been a major economic, social, or political upheaval, such as that which occurred in the South after the enactment of civil rights laws in the 1960s, or a large influx or exodus of new residents, such as the growth of Hispanics in the Southwest and exodus of African Americans from Louisiana following Hurricane Katrina in 2005.

A second criterion is the number of electoral votes that each party needs to win, a number that can change after the census. At the very least, candidates need to rely on the states their party carried and those in which preelection polls suggest are becoming more competitive.

A third strategic factor that can influence resource allocation is the existence of a third-party or Independent candidate such as H. Ross Perot in the 1992 and 1996 and Ralph Nader in 2000 and 2004. Nader's vote in Florida substantially exceeded the margin of Bush's 2000 victory in that state, yet the Gore campaign prematurely decreased its advertising in Florida, unaware that the Nader vote could be the difference between victory and defeat. The Kerry campaign, determined not to make the same mistake four years later, worked hard at limiting Nader's ballot access and his popular vote in competitive states. There have not been any major third-party or Independent campaigns since then, although former New York City mayor Michael Bloomberg contemplated such a run in 2012, 2016, and 2020 but concluded that partisan orientation of the country and its Electoral College voting system raised the hurdles too high, even for a billionaire willing to spend his own money.

The enlargement of the Democratic electorate by the Obama campaigns in 2008 and 2012 seemed to enhance the chances of the Democratic presidential candidate in the Electoral College. Some said that the Democrats had a near-lock on it. That contention proved to be a false assumption that contributed to Hillary Clinton's Electoral College defeat in 2016.

The Clinton campaign concentrated on the competitive states she wanted to win, Florida, North Carolina, Iowa, New Hampshire, and initially, Ohio and Virginia and not the states she needed to win to maintain her party's recent Electoral College advantage. Her strategists assumed that Michigan, Wisconsin, and Pennsylvania with their forty-six electoral votes would go Democratic as they had in the last six presidential elections.

Trump, on the other hand, focused his efforts in fewer states but ones he had to carry to win in the Electoral College. These included Florida, North Carolina, Pennsylvania, Colorado, and Ohio. He won all of them except for Colorado.

Trump had little choice; he had no other road to victory. Clinton did but wanted to extend her lead in the polls and gain a larger mandate for governing. Consequently, she held fewer campaign events and ran less advertising in the traditional blue states. She made no public appearances in Wisconsin and only one in Michigan as the race tightened in its final days. In 2020, Biden focused on suburban areas for Independent and Republican votes in addition to the large cities, while Trump continued his drive to get more rural residents out to vote.

The confluence of geography and demographics matter in the way in which the Electoral College voting system works. Campaign strategy needs to take that confluence into account, especially as the election nears its conclusion.

Box 7.2 outlines and evaluates the basic strategies of the major party candidates in the last five presidential elections. These strategies did not necessarily dictate the outcome, but they did affect turnout and voting behavior, particularly in the key battleground states, the expectations of voters following the election, and the political clout of the newly elected or reelected president.

BOX 7.2 ★ Presidential Campaign Strategies: 2004–2020

2004

George W. Bush: A Strategy for Staying in Place

The components of Bush's 2004 reelection strategy were derived from the political environment in which the country found itself at the beginning of the twenty-first century, the character strengths George W. Bush demonstrated as president following the terrorist attacks on September 11, 2001, John Kerry's perceived policy inconsistencies, and the incumbency advantages, particularly when national security issues are salient.

The principal goal of Bush's reelection strategy, to expand the Republican electorate, assumed that most voters had already made up their minds and were strongly inclined to cast ballots in accordance with their partisan loyalties. Karl Rove, Bush's campaign manager, believed that there were not many undecided voters in 2004. This election strategy grew out of the failure of Bush's 2000 election campaign to win the popular vote. Republican planners chided themselves for not maximizing their base vote in that election and were determined not to repeat this failure. Republican efforts to improve partisan turnout began immediately after the 2000 presidential campaign. Fifty million dollars were spent in 2002 alone, developing and testing "victory-type" programs.[22] Convinced that the old-style turnout efforts were no longer sufficient, Republican political strategists decided on a multifaceted approach to identify and contact people with Republican leanings.

The plan required well-trained and committed partisans who could be counted on to initiate and maintain personal contacts with potential GOP supporters. In the past, both parties had turned to paid organizers, party professionals, labor unions, nonparty groups, and even profit-making firms to do so. The Republican plan deviated from these past grassroots efforts by depending primarily on community-based volunteers and taking advantage of the intensity of their partisan's supporters for President Bush. Democrats did not display the same level of enthusiasm for their candidate, John Kerry.

The Republicans also used social issues to their advantage. Eleven state ballot initiatives against same-sex marriage, the president's repeated reference to a constitutional amendment defining marriage as a union between man and woman, and his frequently stated beliefs about God and the sanctity of human life all contributed to the success of these get-out-the-vote efforts.

Bush's reelection campaign emphasized his leadership after 9/11. This emphasis highlighted his attributes of strength, conviction, determination, and purpose of his war on terrorism. The message: "Bush had passed the leadership test, and Kerry had not."

John Kerry: "Anything You Can Do, I Can Do Better"

With the electorate divided along partisan lines and Kerry's leadership qualities disputed, the Democratic challenger did not have an obvious or easy road to the White House. In fact, he began with several disadvantages. There was a five-week period following the Democratic convention and before the Republican one. Kerry, who was using federal funds for his campaign expenses, did not want to spend this limited amount of money during this period so he did not respond to allegations by

BOX 7.2 ★ Presidential Campaign Strategies: 2004–2020 *continued*

the Swift Boat Veterans for Truth that criticized his Vietnam War record and antiwar activities after he left the military. Consequently, their criticism stuck.

A second problem for Kerry concerned the president's personal favorability ratings that precluded a campaign to demonize him. Kerry went after Bush's policies with some success among Democrats but not among Republicans. Nor were voters that considered themselves Independents angry enough for Kerry to gain a decisive edge.

Advocating leadership change in times of crisis is difficult for challengers unless they can demonstrate that the incumbent's policies or actions were responsible for the crisis and that the challenger had superior leadership qualities to deal with it. The Kerry campaign did not try to tag Bush with the responsibility for 9/11, only with a failed policy in Iraq. In the end, that was not sufficient to convince voters for a change in leadership.

2008

Barack Obama: Empowering the People for Change

Obama's campaign message in 2008 was political and policy change. He appealed for unity in a country deeply divided by partisanship and ideology and gave hope and conveyed optimism to a public increasingly nervous about the depressed and deteriorating economy.

The emotion Obama generated provided his campaign with several strategic opportunities that his opponent lacked—a large war chest capable of expanding even further, virtual and actual on-the-ground operations, and an ability to alter the traditional red–blue make-up of the Electoral College map. "Our goal was to force them to defend Bush states," wrote David Plouffe, Obama's campaign manager. "We saw little to no evidence that they could add to the Bush Electoral College margin."[23]

The rejection of federal funds was critical to Obama's success. Not only did it give him a significant resource advantage, but it also enabled his campaign to control its own advertising and field operations without depending on the Democratic Party and outside groups to do so.

Initially, the message was about the need for change and who could best achieve it. Over time, the narrative turned increasingly to the depressed economy and the candidate and the party best able to fix it. After the mid-September financial meltdown, when McCain said, "The fundamentals of our economy are strong," the Obama campaign pointed to McCain's ill-chosen words and his erratic behavior.[24] In the end, there was little that McCain could say or do to improve the economy or shift the blame from Republican George W. Bush.

John McCain: An Experienced Maverick

Although John McCain wrapped up the Republican nomination early in March, he was not able to generate much enthusiasm for his candidacy. His choice of Sarah Palin not only helped solidify his partisan base but also gave the press and his Democratic opponent a target of opportunity to raise questions about Palin's competence and suitability as vice president, much less as president. Late-night comedians had a field day.

Because McCain began the general election with a significant financial disadvantage, his campaign was forced to depend on the Republican National Committee to supplement the $84.1 million he received from the federal treasury's

BOX 7.2 ★ Presidential Campaign Strategies: 2004–2020 *continued*

election fund. His plan to launch a coordinated advertising campaign with the Republic National Committee required that the combined ads promote congressional Republican candidates as well as himself. "In half our ads, it looked like we were running against Harry Reid, [the Democratic Senate leader]" said Sarah Simmons, McCain's director of strategy.[25] Moreover, the bulk of these "hybrid" ads had to be negative because of the low esteem in which Congress was held by the American people. Negative ads appeal more to partisans than to Independents; they did not help McCain expand his base.

By October, the people who advised McCain concluded that they needed a new campaign narrative if he was going to win. That narrative took the form of "Joe the Plumber," a person who challenged Obama's proposed economic policies at one of his campaign rallies. Joe became a symbol for middle-class workers who had lost their jobs and were angry about legislation that bailed out the large financial firms that caused the problem but not average Americans who lost their jobs. Joe rallied Republicans but did not change the dynamics of the race. With the economy dominating the news, domestic terrorism less salient, and an agreement with the government of Iraq to withdraw American forces, there was little McCain could do to reverse the negative national political environment for his candidacy. His defeat was almost inevitable.

2012

Barack Obama: Continue the Progress

Obama's reelection strategy was fashioned by the political consequences of the 2010 midterm elections and the nation's tepid recovery from the Great Recession. The victory of the Tea Party candidates during the 2010 congressional elections moved the GOP to the right, deadlocked policy making in Washington, and turned the economic focus to deficit spending, the growing national debt, and the pending expiration of the Bush tax cuts. It provided Obama with an opportunity to claim the middle ground much as Bill Clinton had done in his reelection campaign.

Obama described the electorate in terms of the haves and have-nots, asking voters to reflect on which parties would be likely to help them in the future. The president's appeal shifted attention from the present to the years ahead. It allowed him to point to the country's upward economic trajectory during his first term and mute criticism that his policies were not working.

Defining his opponent early in the election cycle was also part of Obama's strategy. No sooner than the Republican nomination had been settled early in April, the Democrats launched advertising portraying Romney as a wealthy venture capitalist, more successful at making profits for his company, Bain Capital, than keeping jobs for American workers.

Obama also used his symbolic and discretionary powers effectively as president. Helped by Hurricane Sandy, which hit the mid-Atlantic region a week before the election, he went to the distressed areas, empathized with those who suffered, and promised federal relief. People approved his handling of the disaster.

Mitt Romney: Turning the Economy Around

Every incumbent's reelection campaign is a referendum on the president's first term. The Republican strategy in the 2012 campaign emphasized the tepid economy and the inability of the Obama administration to turn it around in four years.

BOX 7.2 ★ Presidential Campaign Strategies: 2004–2020 *continued*

Romney promised change, claiming that his economic policy based on private sector performance would create 6 million more jobs. He criticized the expansive federal role, arguing that health care, education, and other social issues should be decided on a state-by-state basis. He did not emphasize Obamacare to which Republicans were strongly opposed because he had supported a similar health care initiative in Massachusetts when he was governor.

The Republican candidate also had to overcome the fuzzy image that many challengers face. To do so, his campaign had to learn what type of information voters wanted to know about him. What would he do as president? To answer this question, the campaign initiated a "day one" advertising effort but had funds to run the ads in only four states; in fact, $20 million had to be borrowed just to stay on the air before the Republican Convention. Super PACs that backed Romney did advertise during this period, but, unable to coordinate their advertising with Romney's, they ran negative Obama ads and not positive Romney ones. Consequently, Romney was not able to counter the negative image that his opponents portrayed of him throughout spring and summer 2012.

Although Romney's personal image improved a little, he still trailed Obama in likeability by twenty-three points before the Republican Convention and twelve points on election day. That Romney was unable to bridge the character gap worked to the president's political advantage. Voters simply liked Barack Obama more.

2016

Donald Trump: I Know What Is Wrong, and I Can Fix It

Donald Trump's general election strategy mirrored the one he used in his successful nomination campaign. He emphasized the same issues, directed his message to the same disaffected voters, and ridiculed his political opponent. His style, words, and modes of communication were also similar, however, the geography of the Electoral College dictated where he held rallies; it influenced his expenditure of resources, on air and online advertising, and social media outreach.

Trump had a narrow road to an Electoral College victory. He had to retain all the states that Romney won in 2012. He had to win the large, competitive states of Florida and Ohio. He also had to retake some of the smaller competitive ones (Colorado, Iowa, New Hampshire, North Carolina, and Virginia) as well as a few of the larger blue states that traditionally voted Democratic (Michigan, Pennsylvania, and Wisconsin).

Within the competitive and Democratic-leaning states, he targeted areas that suffered the most and recovered the least from the 2008 recession, areas that had lost manufacturing jobs, poorer rural communities, and the more distant suburbs of their major cities. He directed his appeal toward white blue-collar workers, social conservatives, particularly people who identified themselves as fundamental or evangelical Christians, and of course, to Republicans, unhappy with eight years of Democratic control of the White House.

His message with these disaffected voters was simple and direct. He would change the direction in which the country was heading back to its basic roots and values and "Make America Great Again." By great again, he was referring to the period during and after World War II, when the middle class grew and prospered. This was an era in which men were the principal wage earners; most

BOX 7.2 ★ Presidential Campaign Strategies: 2004–2020 *continued*

people professed a belief in God and were affiliated with religious institutions; and Americans believed in their own exceptionalism at home and abroad. Trump said that he would achieve this turnaround by curbing illegal immigration, reversing unfair and unwise international agreements, reducing government interference in the private sector, protecting religious liberties, and strengthening the military to defeat terrorists and promote national security. His appeal was nativist, nationalistic, and populist.

Trump communicated his message in three ways: conducting large enthusiastic rallies that received extensive coverage in the news media; tweeting his opinions online that in turn were reinforced by pro-Trump supporters and the attention given to them by the traditional press corps; and reaching voters via social media primarily on Facebook. In the words of Brad Parscale, Trump's media guru:

> We knew the 14 million people we needed to win 270. We targeted those in over 1,000 different universes with exactly the things that they mattered to them. We didn't let the media go to them. We went straight to them. And we spent money on digital to do that because we couldn't compete with them on TV. We won exactly where we laid our money other than one state [Colorado], Wisconsin, Michigan, Pennsylvania, Ohio. We pulled out of Virginia.[26]

Trump also took advantage of the proliferation of news sources and the growth of conservative outlets that his base frequented by distinguishing their reporting of events from the "fake news" of the traditional news networks. In doing so, he provided an alternate truth to them.

He adopted a harsh leadership style much like the one he portrayed in the television series, *The Apprentice*, in which he was an abrasive and dominant CEO. He campaigned as a celebrity rather than as a politician. His use of politically incorrect language further distinguished his candidacy from others who had run or were running for the presidency. His reference to Washington, DC, as a swamp, his boast that he could not be bought because he was so rich; the quick and instinctive judgments he expressed gave him authenticity in the eyes of disaffected voters and contributed to their hope and belief that he was the leader they were craving. The Trump campaign relied on a turnout model based on the 2014 midterm elections. It depended on a field organization that the Republican Party had expanded and computerized after Romney's defeat in 2012. Many of the same GOP operatives continued to work in the same communities, giving Trump the field organization and personal contacts that his campaign lacked during the nomination process. Unforeseen events also benefited Trump. On October 28, eleven days before election day, FBI Director, James Comey, stated that new emails that potentially revealed additional information about Hillary Clinton's use of a private internet server had been found and were being examined by the FBI. Eight days later, Comey stated that these emails contained no new information, but the damage had been done. The episode gave Trump the opportunity to reassert his charge about Clinton's corrupt behavior. In her book about her campaign, *What Happened*, Clinton expressed the belief that Comey's revelations cost her the election.[27]

Trump's campaign strategy proved to be effective. It had marshalled his resources and messages and targeted them to the most receptive voters. The

BOX 7.2 ★ Presidential Campaign Strategies: 2004–2020 *continued*

strategy was implemented in an efficient manner. The election result surprised the public and the press covering the campaign. It was seen as a remarkable, unexpected victory.

Hillary Clinton: Partisan Unity, Continuity with Change, and Proven Leadership

Clinton began her general election campaign with three strategic goals: unify the party after a divisive nomination process, continue the successful policies of the Obama administration and address those that remained, and demonstrate superior leadership qualifications for the presidency. To achieve these objectives, she needed to obtain the support of Sanders's supporters. His endorsement of her candidacy prior to the Democratic convention and his speeches on her behalf during the campaign helped return liberal Democrats who backed him for the nomination to their partisan roots and inclinations. Change-oriented Independents who supported his policy agenda were less enthusiastic.

To attract people who voted for Sanders, Clinton embraced his goals but not his revolutionary fervor, suggesting that her more moderate proposals were more likely to be enacted into law. Clinton's dilemma was reconciling her support for most of Obama's policies, particularly those in which she had a hand in framing as secretary of state, with new policies she was proposing that would address the general dissatisfaction of the electorate. Her expansive and detailed policy agenda, more inclusive than focused, appealed to her partisan base but not to disenchanted voters. In other words, she solidified her Democratic base but did not sufficiently expand it. Nonetheless, she won a popular vote victory.

The leadership issue dominated Clinton's message and clouded and overwhelmed her policy appeals. Her speeches, advertising, and campaign communications emphasized her opponent's unsuitability for the presidency: Trump's erratic temperament, instinctive judgments, governing experience, and his factual inaccuracies and knowledge gaps that characterized his public utterances. Trump would be a risky president, she argued.

In addition to crowding out the positive reasons for supporting her, Clinton's anti-Trump rhetoric was undercut by her own negatives: allegations that she was dishonest and evasive, that she refused to admit to the seriousness of using a private internet server as secretary of state, and her populist appeal that seemed hypocritical in the light of the money she received for her speeches and donations given to the Clinton Foundation from foreigners she interacted with in government. Clinton's unfavorable public image reduced the impact of the personality claims that she and fellow Democrats were making against Trump. By election day, voters had unfavorable perceptions of both candidates.

Clinton's penchant to demonstrate her knowledge with detailed policy analyses, her tendency to play it safe, to stick to a pretested script, take the middle ground, her inability to fire up her supporters, and to generate emotional intensity that Trump had achieved adversely affected her campaign. It lowered the anticipated turnout of Democratically oriented minorities and the support she received from Independents.

There was also a disconnect between her campaign's strategic goals and their implementation. The Clinton campaign was driven by a sophisticated data model that identified and targeted sympathetic voters, primarily Democrats, in "tipping

BOX 7.2 ★ Presidential Campaign Strategies: 2004–2020 *continued*

point" states, the ones that the campaign initially targeted. The model, reinforced by polls that showed Clinton in the lead, contributed to her campaign advisers' perception that she would win and that their strategy was working.

In the last week, the polls indicated that the race was tightening although Clinton was still ahead. Her advisors attributed the tightening to the pull of Republican partisanship as well as the desire of the press to highlight the closeness of the race. Thus, the Clinton campaign failed to respond quickly enough to late shifts in voter sentiment in the key battleground states. Clinton went to bed on election night thinking she would win.

2020

Trump: Keep America Great

The president continued his law-and-order appeal, claiming that anarchy and violence would increase if Biden gained power. He blamed Democratic governors and mayors for not protecting property and for letting protests get out of control. In addition to reasserting that outside agitators incited the violence, Trump also cited a conspiracy theory group, QAnon, which held that a group of Satan-worshipping pedophiles engaged in sexually oriented child trafficking and was responsible for the unrest and were plotting to remove him from office.

Throughout his campaign, he tried to keep his base energized. He appealed to the fears of his conservative supporters: an "alien" invasion of immigrants, threats to America's culture heritage, and fraudulent voting and a rigged election outcome.

In mid-September, the campaign designed a new series of ads that promoted Trump's economic record. The new ads were based on Republican polls that indicated that the economy was more important to the people than the racial issue. The economy was the only issue in which Trump received a higher public evaluation than Biden. The ads contrasted Trump's economic record to that of the Obama-Biden administration's and the merits of the capitalistic system to the Democrat's "socialistic" policies. Job growth, stock market strength, and a quick economic recovery once the pandemic receded were the principal selling points of the advertising campaign.

Although Trump did not emphasize foreign policy, he continued to claim that he would be tough on China, tough on trade, and tough on immigration. He also pointed to his efforts to promote the security of Israel by encouraging a preach process with its Arab neighbors.

Trump rarely mentioned the pandemic in his campaign. He also avoided discussing environmental issues, but as president he was forced to acknowledge the natural disasters in the South, Midwest, and West Cost, although he never changed his belief that climate change was a hoax. Trump blamed the fires in Washington, Oregon, and California on poor forest management and the hurricanes and floods on cyclical weather patterns.

Biden: Return to Normalcy

The thrust of Biden's campaign strategy was to highlight the link between the pandemic and the recessed economy. "You can't deal with the economic crisis until you beat the pandemic," he said.[28] The strategy was based on several assumptions based on preelection polling:

BOX 7.2 ★ Presidential Campaign Strategies: 2004–2020 *continued*

- The pandemic remained the country's most important problem.
- Biden's steady lead in the polls indicated that his anti-Trump message was working.
- Most voters had made up their minds for which party and candidate to vote. Only a small percentage of the electorate was undecided.
- Trump's job approval rating continued to be more negative than positive by a substantial margin.
- Biden preached unity and an end to discord that divided Americans.

In the final two months before the election, Biden had to provide substance to his policy stands. He announced the names of experts with whom he had consulted, detailed plans to deal with these problems on his website, and announced what his first actions would be as president.

The Democratic candidate also had to deal with the law-and-order issue fueled by the protests. Giving a balanced response, Biden supported the right of protest, the prevention of violence, and the need for more humane policing. He vigorously denied Trump's allegation that he wanted to defund the police.

The rash of hurricanes in the South, floods in the Midwest, and fires on the West Coast elevated climate change as an election issue. Biden warned that Trump's denial of climate change and his antienvironmental policies posed significant dangers for the country. Biden favored investing in clean energy but did not endorse the Green New Deal that progressive Democrats advocated.

In addition to its general appeal to a cross-section of Democrats, the Biden campaign made a special effort to attract younger voters, particularly Hispanics and African Americans. As the youngest man ever elected to the Senate at the age of twenty-nine and the oldest to be nominated by a major party for president at seventy-seven, the Democratic candidate addressed the major concerns of younger voters: student debt, racial justice, climate change, and the pandemic's impact on their job opportunities. He also engaged celebrities to talk about these concerns to their online followers. One of Kamala Harris's principal tasks was to energize young African Americans and get them out to vote in the light of Hillary Clinton's failure to do so four years earlier. PACs reach reached out to mobilize their supporters. Ads in Spanish were targeted to Hispanic voters.

Strategic Execution

Running a campaign is a complex, time-consuming, nerve-racking venture. Constant emergencies and unanticipated events must be dealt with as well as the numerous personal issues, heightened by the pace of work, the hours spent at it, and egos of the ambitious, mostly young people who get involved.

Until the 1970s, the Democrats had stronger state parties and a weaker national base and, thus, tended to rely on the state parties to turn out the vote. In recent years, Republican presidential candidates have had to rely more on their party's local and state organizations to identify, contact, and turnout voters.

Sometimes, candidates circumvent their party's national committee entirely when they do not trust establishment leaders to support their nominees enthusiastically. In 1964, Barry Goldwater's backers were very leery of the backing they would receive from East Coast Republicans. Therefore, they built their own army of ideological supporters from whom they solicited funds and voluntary campaign efforts.[29]

The same desire for control and for circumventing the party was evident in Richard Nixon's reelection campaign in 1972. Completely separate from the national party, even in title, the Committee to Reelect the President (known as CREEP by its critics) raised its own money, conducted its own public relations (including polling and campaign advertising), scheduled its own events, and even had its own security division. It was this division, operating independently from the Republican Party's national organization, which harassed the Democratic campaign of George McGovern, heckling his speeches, spreading false rumors, and perpetrating other illegal acts, including the attempted bugging of the DNC headquarters at its Watergate offices. The excesses perpetuated by individuals in this group illustrate both the difficulty of overseeing all the aspects of a large presidential campaign and the risk of placing nonprofessionals in key positions of responsibility. Had the more experienced Republican National Committee exercised greater influence over the president's reelection, there might have been less deviation from accepted standards of behavior.

With the enactment of campaign finance legislation in the 1970s, separate presidential campaign organizations, distinct from the national party, must be established to receive federal funds, file quarterly financial reports, and abide by the contributions and spending limits.

The George W. Bush campaign organizations of 2000 and 2004, Obama's of 2008 and 2012, and Biden's of 2020 are prototypes of well-run, well-coordinated operations. Each had highly experienced managers, pollsters, fundraisers, and communications consultants. Each was hierarchical at the top and decentralized at the bottom. Each used the latest technologies to identify and persuade voters with each campaign more sophisticated than the previous one. Each campaign saw personal contact as the key to successful persuasion.

Organization

Presidential campaigns have become large and complex entities. They take months, even years, to design, structure, staff, and run. The organizational components of campaigning have enlarged over the years. The principal area of growth is the use of data-based computer models to design and drive campaign strategy. The models are predicted on electoral trends based on historic voting patterns, demographic shifts in the electorate, and the changing moods of voters, moods that are reflected in preelection polls and early voting calculations.

Mathematicians, statisticians, and experts in data collection, integration, and analysis regularly supplement the political pros, communication advisors, researchers, speechwriters, news spinners, and field organizers who comprise modern campaigns. Legal advisers, accountants, policy experts, plus a host of others who plan, advance, and implement the candidate's day-to-day activities are also involved. The large organization requires a headquarters, daily communications

FIGURE 7.1 ★ Contemporary presidential campaign organizations.

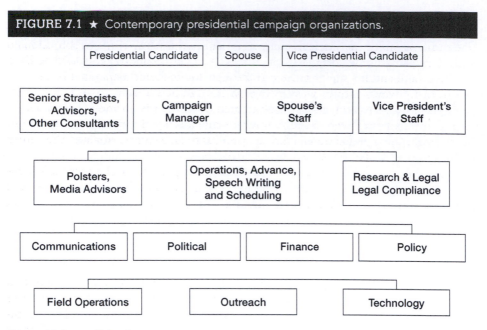

Source: AP Images/Julio Cortez

among top personnel, and a hierarchical structure that coordinates and facilitates decision-making. Figure 7.1 lists the principal units in a presidential campaign.

In 2016, Hillary Clinton had more paid workers, greater staff stability, and spent more resources on them and to support her campaign than did Donald Trump. Her campaign chair, John Podesta, had worked in the Clinton White House and on previous Bill and Hillary Clinton campaigns. Robby Mook, her day-to-day manager, also had extensive Democratic campaign experience but not at the presidential level. Chief strategist Joel Benenson had done polling for Obama's reelection campaign and headed a political consulting group. Clinton's organization also had a special analytic unit, run by Elan Kriegel who played a major role in the campaign's strategic decisions. Working behind the scene, Huma Abedin, a long-time aide to Hillary Clinton, traveled with the candidate. Abedin's close relationship to the candidate proved to be a problem when the FBI investigated her estranged husband's email correspondence during the latter stages of the campaign.

Trump's campaign staff was smaller than Clinton's and less experienced. It also had more turnover at the senior level. Nonetheless, Trump's campaign operatives performed most of the same functions that Clinton's did. There were political, communications, and policy directors, a less visible but highly success-ful digital operation, a field staff, reinforced by experienced operatives working for the Republican National Committee, plus the usual personal aides, lawyers, accountant, and fundraisers.

In 2020, Trump changed campaign managers but had the same basic orga-nizational structure as he had in his previous campaign. He had three different campaign managers, one during the caucuses and primaries (Corey Lewandowski), one before and during the Republican Convention (Paul Manafort), and one during the general election campaign (Kellyanne Conway). His son, Donald Trump Jr.; son-in-law, Jared Kushner; and daughter, Ivanka Trump also advised the candidate and his senior aides on strategic, tactical, and personnel issues.

In many ways, Trump was his own CEO. He had a hand in all major campaign decisions. Running his operation much as he ran his business, he needed to be in control and involved in the campaign's major strategic and tactical decisions. Both within the organization and in the public arena, Trump remained the center of attention, the dominant boss.

Biden also had a large staffed composed of experienced Democratic operatives and volunteers. His campaign manager was Jen O'Malley Dillon. Biden did not assume the role of CEO in directing his campaign but did participate with in meetings with Dillon and other senior advisers on strategy and tactics.

The Public Dimension

Orchestrating a campaign is not easy. There must be considerable work in advance. The appearance of the stage, the timing of the event, the dignitaries invited and their seating positions, the recruitment and composition of the audience, the facilities for press coverage, the videotaping by professionals and other attendees, and, of course, the candidate's appearance, speech (with the sound bites written into it), and interaction with those present must be planned in detail and well ahead of the event. Nothing is left to chance.

Speeches, Rallies, and Events

All campaigns have rallies, events that attract large audiences, the news media, and often protestors. Campaigns take steps to ensure friendly crowds and no hecklers, if possible, by distributing tickets to partisans, donors, volunteers, and other supporters. Their own camera crews record the events and distribute video film clips to local, cable, and regional media as well as post them on their websites and YouTube. Communication staff constantly tweet news about the event, the candidate's message, and the crowd's reaction to it. Knowing that their opponents and the press will focus on inconsistencies and slipups, candidates are warned to stick to a prepared and tested script. Frequently, speechwriters will insert code words to generate a reaction from a particular group.

In 2016, Trump depended on such events to excite and extend his base. In doing so, he demonstrated his ability to evoke strong emotions. His criticism tied Hillary Clinton to Obama's "failed" leadership. Trump also alleged that his opponent was dishonest, "the most corrupt candidate in history." At one debate, he questioned her stamina for the presidency. His message resonated with Americans unhappy with the direction of the country, the government in Washington, and current policy. They wanted change.

In 2020 he took the same tact, criticizing Biden's domestic policies, his internationalism, and his stamina and mental agility at the age of seventy-seven. Biden focused on the pandemic, the economy, the environment, and Trump's rhetoric, behavior, and actions as president.

Slip-Ups! Damage Control

Slip-ups do occur but not usually in carefully researched and written speeches. They result more often than not from ad-libbed remarks that candidates make.

Opposition research is a major source of negative news for political reporters. Remarks given privately to supportive groups, secretly recorded or reported by participants at the meeting, are another. Take Romney's comments at a private gathering of some of his political donors:

> There are 47 percent of the people who will vote for the president no matter what. All right, there are 47 percent who are with him, who are dependent upon government, who believe that they are victims, who believe the government has a responsibility to care for them, who believe that they are entitled to health care, to food, to housing, to you-name-it—that that's an entitlement. And the government should give it to them. And they will vote for this president no matter what. . . . These are people who pay no income tax [M]y job is not to worry about those people. I'll never convince them they should take personal responsibility and care for their lives.[30]

Unknown to the candidate and the aides that accompanied him, a person in attendance recorded his comments, leaked them to the press, and they went viral, reinforcing the "wealthy, uncaring" image by which his opponents had stereotyped him.

Hillary Clinton's description of half of Donald Trump's supporters as "a basket of deplorables" characterized by "racist, sexist, homophobic, xenophobic, Islamophobic" views was another unfortunate statement.[31]

Denials are difficult in the face of evidence to the contrary. Explanations such as "I was quoted out of context" or "that's not what I meant" are weak responses. Romney defended the substance of his remarks but acknowledged that they were not "eloquently" stated. Clinton apologized for being "grossly generalistic" by using the word "half."

The internet is a great source for revealing past statements or behavior that violate current norms. Old interviews are another. Off-the-record remarks that are recorded can also be embarrassing. During the 2016 campaign, the video of a conversation that Donald Trump had with Billy Bush of *Access Hollywood* on a bus going to do a segment on a show titled *Days of Our Lives* were obtained by the *Washington Post*. In the video, Trump is heard saying:

> You know I'm automatically attracted to beautiful—I just start kissing them. It's like a magnet. Just kiss. I don't even wait.
> And when you're a star, they let you do it. You can do anything. Grab them by the p****. You can do anything.[32]

Trump described his language as men's locker room talk, but many prominent public officials, both Republican and Democrat, believed the candidate's words were inappropriate and offensive. The video reinforced claims by several women of Trump's unwanted sexual advances and liaisons and of being paid to keep quiet about them.

Campaigns establish war rooms to respond quickly to such accusations and embarrassing remarks. They advise candidates how to react and do so quickly. The absence of a response is often deemed to be an admission of guilt. However, an overreaction can also be harmful if it keeps the item in the news.

There are times, however, that ad-libbed comments can work to a candidate's advantage. When Republican vice presidential nominee Dan Quayle compared his Senate experience with John F. Kennedy's in a debate with his Democratic counterpart, Senator Lloyd Bentsen, Bentsen shot back, "I served with Jack Kennedy; I knew Jack Kennedy; Jack Kennedy was a friend of mine. Senator, you are no Jack Kennedy."[33] Quayle, shaken by Bentsen's blunt reply, remained on the defensive for the remainder of the debate.

Field Offices

Modern campaigns mount extensive field operations to achieve their voter contact, mobilization, and turnout goals. They emphasize personal contacts between their volunteers and potential voters. Karl Rove, who oversaw George W. Bush's gubernatorial campaigns, masterminded the Republican grassroots effort. He was disappointed that Bush failed to achieve a popular vote victory in that election. Therefore, Rove moved from the older-style turnout instruments of mass market advertising, robocalls, and direct mail and initiated a new style, on-the-ground, data-driven, and field-based operation aimed at maximizing the Republican base vote.

To build their list of party leaners, Rove and other Republican leaders assembled a large databank from conservative magazine subscribers, regular churchgoers, listeners and viewers of certain radio and television stations and shows, and people living in heavily Republican areas. The plan was simple: to identify "lazy Republicans," determine if they were registered to vote, contact them repeatedly during the campaign, and once they made their voting decision, get them to vote as soon as state laws permitted.

In 2008 and 2012, Obama mounted an even more sophisticated effort in the field and online. He had about eight hundred storefront offices in 2012, at least one per state, with most concentrated in the key battleground areas. In addition, his campaign set up multiple staging areas (in homes of supporters) where canvassers would assemble, get their marching orders, and be directed to the locations they would be canvassing. Volunteers could also get their assignments through apps on their cell phones.

In contrast Romney's ground organization was smaller, less technologically advanced, and more dependent on local and state Republican party organizations. His campaign had only three hundred field offices, mainly in the most competitive states, and most of them promoted other GOP candidates as well as Romney. In contrast, almost all of Obama's offices were primarily devoted to his reelection. The gap was greatest in Ohio, Florida, and Virginia, all states that Obama carried in the general election.

In 2016 and 2020, it was more of the same partisan imbalance at the presidential level between the two principal candidates. Clinton and Biden had more than twice as many field offices as Trump. Do field operations make a difference? Most political observers and campaign operatives believe that they do.[34] In 2016, Clinton's larger field operation, however, was matched by the greater intensity of Trump supporters and the higher turnout rate of Trump voters in the key battleground states.

Data Analysis

One of the big changes in campaign operations has been the collection, integration, and analysis of personal data on voters. Each party has amassed large quantities of information, which when combined with a candidate's own data and supplemented by data amassed by private political consulting firms, is used to direct messages, assess their effectiveness, and predict turnout and the level of voter support. This information, which includes past registration and voting data, present concerns, and positions on salient issues, guides the candidates and their volunteers: where to go, what to say, and when to campaign in certain areas. It directs them to most likely supporters and away from partisan opponents and politically uninterested citizens. In his first campaign, the Obama organization collected millions of email addresses, cell phone numbers, and zip codes to broaden the candidate's potential electorate. However, his digital campaigners were unable to integrate all these data into one single file. Thus, each campaign operation from fundraising to canvassing to get-out-the-vote activities used its own data bank and software, which was not a efficient operation.

Beginning in 2011, the reelection campaign began to develop programs for integrating data lists. Chaired by founders of Napster, Facebook, LinkedIn, Yelp, and Craigslist, the group solicited revenue, contacted experts, and developed analytical models for massive data analysis. A new computing program, known as Narwhal, named after an Arctic whale, combined, processed, and stored the information, and another program, known as Dashboard, matched volunteers to their communities, provided them with personal contact information, and directed their activities. Another app, Call Tool, listed phone numbers to call and scripts to use by the callers. The campaign claimed that it contacted 150 million people over the course of the campaign.[35]

Two specific population groups were targeted: Democrats who were less likely to vote and a smaller group of Independents who had not yet decided whether and for whom to vote. How to reach less likely voters, especially those in the youngest age cohort that lacked a voting history and landline phone was the principal problem. The campaign's modus operandi for doing so was to get their friends to do it on Facebook and then incorporate personal information into the campaign's database. Hillary Clinton began her 2016 presidential campaign with Obama's data file plus those of his Super PAC, Organizing for America, and the DNC. Biden broadened his targeted groups to reach Republican and Independent suburban voters who were unhappy with Trump.

Romney could not match the size or sophistication of Obama digital campaign in 2012. He had a paid staff of five hundred compared with Obama's three thousand; his data analytics team consisted of only four techies; Obama had more than fifty. Romney also had fewer friends on Facebook (12.1 million compared with Obama's 32.3 million). And to make matters worse, Romney's automated turnout system for the key battleground states failed repeatedly on election day.

As she began her campaign operation in 2014, Hillary Clinton hired specialists experienced in digitized campaigning, social media communications, and graphic designers and illustrators. Her technical staff created a complex algorithm, called Ada, to guide its resource allocation, candidate events, field operations, and political advertising. Kept under close wraps with its own internal server, it was accessible to only a few senior advisers. Hundreds of thousand campaign simulations were conducted daily, using the algorithm.[36]

Toward the end of the campaign, the model's predictions and public and private poll results began to differ, but it was only during the night when the actual results started coming in that it became clear that the assumptions on which the model was based were not on target. The voting percentages of women and minority groups were overestimated and those from rural areas underestimated. These calculations misdirected the campaign's geographic focus and its social media communications. Incorrect analytical estimates by the Clinton campaign contributed to Trump's surprising victories in Pennsylvania, Michigan, and Wisconsin.[37]

Despite Trump's initial belief that quantitative voter analytics were overrated and overpriced, his campaign turned to digital analysis to raise money, allocate resources, increase rally attendance, amplify the impact of his tweets, and design and target advertising strategies. The operation, known as "Project Alamo" and run by Brad Parscale, collected and analyzed data from Trump's nomination campaign, the Republican National Committee, and private firms, such as Cambridge Analytica, TargetPoint, and Causeway.[38] Online ads, mostly on Facebook, were sent to people who matched the psychological and political profile of Trump supporters, using that site's marketing mechanism to target and personalize the messages. The effectiveness of these ads was continually assessed with a Facebook marketing tool, "Brand Lift."[39] The Trump models proved to be more accurate in the competitive states than Clinton's. Some of the surveys on which the campaign relied measured intensity, an attribute of Trump's most ardent backers. Intensity is a predictor of turnout and voting behavior. A hidden Trump vote, not evident in the polls, was also anticipated. In the end with a smaller technical staff, Trump's digital operation maximized his vote and may have reduced Clinton's.

Brad Parscale, designated as campaign manager for 2020, said that Trump's reelection campaign relied more on direct contacts with supporters through emails and text messaging than on digital advertising. They believed the major news networks and social media platforms, such as Twitter, Facebook, and Google, were biased against them.

Both campaigns advertised heavily on social media in 2020.

Summary

Throughout much of the nineteenth century, presidential campaigns were run by the political parties on behalf of their nominees. The goal of the campaign was to energize and educate the electorate with a series of public activities. Beginning in the 1840s and accelerating in the 1880s, presidential candidates themselves became increasingly involved in the party's campaign. Starting in the 1920s, they had become active participants, using radio, television, and the internet to reach as many voters as possible.

Most presidential campaigns follow a general strategy based on the prevailing political attitudes and perceptions of the electorate, the reputations and images of the nominees and their parties, and the geography of the Electoral College. The strategy includes designing a basic appeal, addressing the salient issues, creating a leadership image, dealing with incumbency (if appropriate), and allocating campaign resources to the key battleground states.

In projecting their basic appeals, Democratic candidates emphasize their party's label and its familiar narrative as the party of the people, the party that understands the problems that most Americans face, and the party that has and will continue to design policies that give more Americans greater economic and social opportunities to achieve their dream, the American dream.

In contrast, Republicans stress the importance of individual initiatives, private ownership, and traditional family values. Since 1980, they have rallied against large, intrusive, inefficient government, claiming it creates dependency, saps energy, and discourages creativity in a free enterprise system.

Projecting an image of leadership is also critical. Candidates do so by trumpeting their own strengths and exposing their opponent's weaknesses. They emphasize those attributes that the public desires in the president, traits that are endemic to the office and resonate with the times. They articulate their leadership skills.

An established record, particularly by presidents seeking reelection, shapes much of their imagery. That record may contribute to or detract from their reelection potential. In good times, incumbents have an advantage; in bad times, they do not. When national security issues are salient, incumbents tend to benefit. Public grievances must be deeply felt and broad based to defeat a sitting president.

When allocating resources, the geography of the Electoral College must always be considered. Each party begins with a base of safe states. In the 1980s, that base was thought to be larger for the Republicans; more recently the Democrats were thought to have an advantage. In 2000 and 2004, the Electoral College was divided closely between red (Republican) and blue (Democratic) states, and there was stability in the states' voting preferences. In 2008, the Obama campaign made gains in the South and Southwest as well as in some of the traditional battleground states of the Midwest, inroads it mostly maintained in 2012 but not in 2016.

The level of competition within states is another factor that affects campaign strategy and resource allocation. Only about twenty states are perceived as truly competitive at the beginning of the general election and are usually less than eight by the end. Time, effort, and money are concentrated within the most competitive states; the rest of the country witnesses the campaign primarily in the national news and by word of mouth; they do not see the candidates in person except perhaps at a fundraiser or in an advertisement from a neighboring state.

Advances in transportation and communications have made campaigns more complex, more expensive, and more sophisticated. Strategy and tactics are now more closely geared to the technology of contemporary politics and run by campaign professionals: pollsters, media consultants, direct mailers, grassroots organizers, lawyers, accountants, data collectors and analysts, and experts of the new social media. Their inclusion in the candidate's organization has made the coordination of centralized decision-making critical. It has also produced several complementary organizations and campaigns all operating at the same time: those of the candidates, the national and state parties, and outside, nonparty groups. When an incumbent is running, the White House is also involved.

The job of campaign organizations is to produce a unified and coordinated effort with centralized strategic decision-making and a decentralized field operation. Since 2004, base mobilization has been the principal objective of both parties' presidential candidates. Large, integrated data banks are used to identify voters, script volunteers, and direct their canvassing efforts. Campaign communications are tested for impact prior to their delivery and then targeted to specific demographic, attitudinal, and economic and social interest groups. Microtargeting is deemed to be more effective than mass marketing with personal contact, the key to turning out voters. The name of the game is to persuade people to vote for a candidate based on their preexisting values, beliefs, and interests.

Exercises

1. Indicate the initial geographic strategies of the major party candidates in 2016 and 2020 and how those strategies changed over the course of the campaign. Now compare these strategies to those you believe should or will be employed in 2024. Design a resource allocation memo for the presidential candidate of your choice.

2. Assess how the candidates targeted their appeals in the most recent presidential election. What appeals did they direct toward their own partisans, especially to the principal groups within their party's electoral coalition, and how did they deal with Independents and others less interested in presidential politics?

3. How has the internet changed the operations of presidential campaigns in recent years and the people who direct those operations? Has it broadened participation and energized campaigning? To what extent has this new technology affected the democratic character of presidential elections?

4. Were you contracted, directly or indirectly, by a friend, party, or nonparty group during the current presidential campaign? If so, how? What arguments or campaign appeals did you find the most persuasive?

Selected Readings

Campaign for President: The Managers Look at 2020. Cambridge, MA. Harvard Kennedy
   School of Politics, 2022.
Conway, Kellyanne. *Here's the Deal: A Memoir.* New York, NY. Threshold Editions, 2022.
Cavari, Amnon, Richard J. Powell, and Kenneth R. Mayer, eds. *The 2016 Presidential
   Election: The Causes and Consequences of a Political Earthquake.* Lanham, MD:
   Rowman & Littlefield, 2018.
Clinton, Hillary. *What Happened.* New York, NY: Simon & Schuster, 2017.
Doherty, Brendan J. *The Rise of the President's Permanent Campaign.* Lawrence:
   University Press of Kansas, 2012.
Hersh, E. D. *Hacking the Electorate: How Campaigns Perceive Voters.* New York, NY:
   Cambridge University Press, 2015.
Issenberg, Sasha. "The Definitive Story of How President Obama Mined Vote to Win a
   Second Term." MIT Technology Review, 2012.
Plouffe, David. *The Audacity to Win.* New York, NY: Viking, 2009.
Popkin, Samuel L. *The Candidate: What It Takes to Win and Hold the White House.*
   Oxford, UK: Oxford University Press, 2012.
Sabato, Larry, Kyle Kondik, and Geoffrey Skelley, eds. *Trumped: The 2016 Election That
   Broke All the Rules.* Lanham MD: Rowman & Littlefield, 2017.
Sides, John, Michael Tesler, and Lynn Vavreck. *Identity Crisis: The 2016 Presidential
   Campaign and the Battle for the Meaning of America.* Princeton, NJ: Princeton
   University Press, 2018.
Sides, John, Chris Tausanouitch, and Lynn Vavrcck. *The Bitter End: The 2020
   Presidential Campaign and the Challenge to American Democracy,* Princeton, NJ:
   Princeton University Press, 2022.
Troy, Gil. *See How They Ran: The Changing Role of the Presidential Candidate.* New
   York, NY: Free Press, 1991.
White, Theodore H. *The Making of the President: 1960.* New York, NY: Atheneum, 1961.
———. *The Making of the President, 1964.* New York, NY: Atheneum, 1965.
———. *The Making of the President, 1968.* New York, NY: Atheneum, 1969.
———. *The Making of the President, 1972.* New York, NY: Atheneum, 1973.
———. *America in Search of Itself: The Making of the President, 1956–1980.* New York,
   NY: Harper & Row, 1982.

Notes

1. Keith Melder, *Hail to the Candidate: Presidential Campaigns from Banners to
   Broadcasts* (Washington, DC: Smithsonian Institution Press, 1992), 70–74.
2. Ibid., 87.
3. Ibid., 88.
4. Marvin R. Weisbord, *Campaigning for President* (New York, NY: Washington
   Square Press, 1966), 45.
5. Historian Gil Troy writes that Lincoln's avoidance of anything that smacked of
   political involvement was in fact a political tactic that he used throughout the
   campaign. Gil Troy, *See How They Ran: The Changing Role of the Presidential
   Candidate* (New York, NY: Free Press, 1991), 66.
6. Weisbord, *Campaigning for President,* 5.
7. Melder, *Hail to the Candidate,* 104; Weisbord, *Campaigning for President,* 125.
8. Keith Melder, "The Whistlestop: Origins of the Personal Campaign," *Campaign
   and Elections,* 7 (May/June 1986), 49.

9. Ibid.

10. William Jennings Bryan, *The First Battle* (1896; reprint, Port Washington, NY: Kennikat Press, 1971), 618.

11. Melder, *Hail to the Candidate*, 129.

12. Weisbord, *Campaigning for President*, 116.

13. Franklin Roosevelt had been disabled by polio in 1921. He wore heavy leg braces and could stand only with difficulty. Nonetheless, he made a remarkable physical and political recovery. In his campaign, he went to great lengths to hide the fact that he could not walk and could barely stand on his own. The press generally did not report on his disability. They refrained from photographing, filming, or describing him struggling to stand with braces.

14. Cabell Phillips, *The Truman Presidency* (New York, NY: Macmillan, 1966), 237.

15. Stanley Kelley, *Professional Public Relations and Political Power* (Baltimore, MD: Johns Hopkins Press, 1956), 161–62.

16. David Axelrod, *Campaign for President: The Managers Look at 2020*. Cambridge, MA. Harvard Kennedy School of Politics, 2022.

17. George W. Bush, "Acceptance Speech at the Republican National Convention" (August 3, 2000), 4.

18. Lee Atwater, architect of this strategy, noted: "When I first got into politics, I just stumbled across the fact that candidates who went into an election with negatives higher than 30 or 40 points just inevitably lost." Thomas B. Edsall, "Why Bush Accentuates the Negative," *The Washington Post* (Oct. 2, 1988), C4.

19. Lauren Gambino, "Trump: Hillary Clinton may be 'most corrupt person ever' to run for president," *The Guardian*, June 22, 2016.

20. Erika Franklin Fowler, Travis N. Ridout, and Michael M. Franz, "Political Advertising in 2016: The Presidential Election as Outlier?" *The Forum: A Journal of Applied Research on Contemporary Politics* 2016 14 (4): 445–69.

21. Ken Mehlman, *Campaign for President: The Managers Look at 2004* (Lanham, MD: Rowman & Littlefield, 2006), 102.

22. David Plouffe, *The Audacity to Win* (New York, NY: Viking, 2009), 249.

23. "Our response followed a standard formula. Insert a rebuttal to McCain's outrageous comment in Obama's next speech that day to create a back and forth, ensuring maximum coverage. Produce TV and radio ads for release by that afternoon and get them up in the states right away. Make sure all our volunteers and staff out in the states had talking points on this to drive home in their conversations with voters." Ibid. 32.

24. Sarah Simmons in *Campaign for President: The Managers Look at 2004* (Lanham, MD: Rowman & Littlefield, 2006), 84.

25. Brad Parscale, *Campaign for President: The Managers Look at 2016* (Lanham, MD: Rowman & Littlefield, 2017), 229.

26. Hillary Clinton, *What Happened* (New York, NY: Simon & Schuster, 2017), 406–407.

27. Karl A. Lamb and Paul A. Smith, *Campaign Decision Making: The Presidential Election of 1964* (Belmont, CA: Wadsworth, 1968), 59–63.

28. Mitt Romney, YouTube, September 18, 2012.

29. Zeke Miller, "Hillary Clinton Says Half of Donald Trump's Supporters Are in 'Basket of Deplorables,'" *Time*, September 10, 2016.

30. David Fahrenthold, "Trump Recorded Having Extremely Lewd Conversation About Women in 2005," *Washington Post*, October 8, 2016.

31. Lloyd Bentsen, "Transcript of the Vice Presidential Debate," *The Washington Post* (October 6, 1988), A30.

32. Molly Ball, "Obama's Edge: The Ground Game That Could Put Him Over the Top," *The Atlantic*, October 24, 2012.

33. Paul Beck, Richard Gunther, and Erik Nisbet, "The 2016 Ground Game From the Voter's Perspective," *Vox*, January 22, 2018.

34. John Sides and Lynn Vavreck, *The Gamble; Choice and Chance in the 2012 Presidential Election* (Princeton, NJ: Princeton University Press, 2013), 221–22.

35. Tim Murphy, "Inside the Obama Campaign's Hard Drive," *Mother Jones*, October 2012.

36. John Wagner, "Clinton's Data-Driven Campaign Relied Heavily on an Algorithm Named Ada. What Didn't She See?" *Washington Post*, November 9, 2016.

37. Nate Silver, "The Real Story of 2016," *Fivethirtyeight.com*, January 19, 2017.

38. Kate Kaye, "How the Trump Camp's Data Inexperience Helped Propel His Win," *Ad Age*, December 14, 2016.

39. Joel Winston, "How the Trump Campaign Built an Identity Database and Used Facebook Ads to Win the Election," *Startup Grind*, November 18, 2016.

Media Politics

Introduction

Media and politics go hand in hand. The press has served as an outlet for divergent political views from the founding of the republic. When political parties developed at the end of the eighteenth century, newspapers with partisan orientations became a primary means for disseminating the parties' policy positions and promoting their candidates.

The early press was contentious and highly adversarial but was not aimed at the masses. Written for the upper, educated class, newspapers contained essays, editorials, and letters that debated economic and political issues. It was not until the 1830s that the elitist orientation of the press began to change. Technological improvements, the growth in literacy, and the movement toward greater public involvement in the democratic process all contributed to the development of the so-called penny press, newspapers that sold for a penny and were directed at the general public.

The Mass Media and Electoral Politics: An Overview

The penny press revolutionized American journalism. Newspapers began to rely on advertising rather than subscriptions as their primary source of income. To attract advertisers, they had to reach a large number of readers. To do so, newspapers had to alter what they reported and how they reported it. Prior to the development of the penny press, news was rarely "new"; stories were often weeks old before they appeared and were rewritten or reprinted from other sources. With more newspapers aimed at the general public, a higher premium was placed on gathering news quickly and reporting it in an exciting, easy-to-read manner.

Print Media

Once newspapers became designed for the mass public, they began to help inform voting decisions for most of the electorate. The invention of the telegraph helped in this regard, making it possible for an emerging Washington press corps to communicate information to the entire country. What was considered news also changed. Events replaced ideas; human interest stories supplemented the official proceedings of government; and drama and conflict were featured. Stories of crime, sex, and violence captured the headlines and sold papers, not essays and letters on public policy. Joseph Pulitzer's *New York World* and William Randolph Hearst's *New York Journal* set the standard for this era of highly competitive "yellow journalism."[1]

Not all newspapers featured sensational news. In 1841, Horace Greeley founded the *New York Tribune*, and ten years later, Henry Raymond began *New York Times*. Both papers appealed to a more-educated audience interested in the political issues of the day. After a change in ownership, the *New York Times* became a paper of record. Operating on the principle that news is not simply entertainment but valuable public information, the *Times* adopted the motto "all the news that's fit to print." It published entire texts of important speeches and documents and detailed national and foreign news.

Toward the middle of the nineteenth century, newspapers began to shed their advocacy role in favor of more neutral reporting. The growth of news wire services, such as the Associated Press and the United Press, and of newspapers that were not tied to political parties contributed to these developments.

As candidates became more personally involved in the campaign, they too became the subject of press attention. By the beginning of the twentieth century, the focus had shifted to the nominees, so much so that at least one candidate, Alton Parker, Democratic presidential nominee for 1904, angrily criticized photographers for their unyielding efforts to take pictures of him while he was swimming in the nude in the Hudson River.[2] Despite the intrusion into their personal lives, candidates began taking advantage of the press's interest in them, using "photo opportunities" and political news coverage to project their images and extend their partisan appeal.

Radio and Television

With the advent of radio in the 1920s and television in the 1950s, news media coverage of campaigns changed once again. Radio supplemented the print media. Although it did not provide regular news coverage, radio excelled at covering special events as they were happening. The 1924 presidential election was the first to be reported on radio; the conventions, major speeches, and election returns were broadcast live that year. During the 1928 election, both presidential candidates, Herbert Hoover and Alfred E. Smith, spent campaign funds on radio advertising.

Radio lost its national news audience to television in the 1950s but remained a favorite communications medium of candidates seeking to target their messages to specific groups in specific locations and at specific times. A cheap and accessible electronic medium, radio continues to be used extensively. The amount of time that people spend commuting in their automobiles has increased the importance of radio as a vehicle for information, advocacy, and debate.

The influence of television on presidential elections was first felt in 1952. The most important news event of that presidential campaign was a speech by General Dwight Eisenhower's running mate, Richard Nixon. Accused of obtaining secret campaign funds in exchange for political favors, Nixon defended himself in a television address. He denied taking contributions for personal use, accused the Democratic administration of being soft on communism, criticized his campaign opponents, and vowed that he would never force his children to give up their dog, Checkers, who had been given to the Nixon family as a gift by some of his political supporters. The emotion of the speech, and particularly the reference to Checkers, generated a favorable public reaction, ended discussion of Nixon's campaign funds, kept him on the Republican ticket, and demonstrated the power of television for candidates in the political campaigns.

Paid television advertising by the major parties also first appeared in the 1952 presidential campaign. The major broadcast networks extended their evening news reports to half an hour in 1963, and by the end of the 1960s, television had become the principal source of election news for most Americans. Presidential campaigns in turn became made-for-television productions. Their public events were staged with television in mind. On-air interviews, talk-show participation, and even the entertainment format have become part and parcel of the modern electoral campaigns. During the 1970s into the 1980s, the evening newscasts had the largest viewing audience, at their peak exceeding seventy-five million viewers. Today, it is only about nineteen million.[3] One of the reasons for the decline has been the growth of cable news networks. Cable and satellite technologies began to acquire more subscribers and all-news formats, thereby fragmenting the number of news sources.

Not only did cable news sources proliferate, but they also led to the demise of the news cycle. In the age of newspapers, the cycle hinged on the time of day that the morning and afternoon papers had to go to press. During the era when most Americans received their news from the evening broadcast networks, coverage ended mid-afternoon, depending on whether visuals, pictures, or films were to be included. Video cameras, mobile trucks, and helicopters extended the deadlines, as did satellite technology and now cell phones and other recording devices. Cable news networks that were on 24/7 still further extended the deadlines for reporting speeches and campaign events. Banner headlines and developing stories regularly appear in the continuous news coverage.

The Internet

Although television remains the primary source of news in general and campaign news in particular, the internet has become increasingly important as both primary and secondary sources of information, especially among younger voters. In 2004, 21 percent of Americans cited the internet as their principal source; by 2008, that percentage had risen to 36, with 58 percent of voters younger than age thirty indicating that it was their major source of election information. Those percentages have continued to rise with more than 90 percent of the public indicating that going online has become a principal way to follow the campaign.[4] Besides being a relatively cheap and easy way to reach potential supporters, the internet has become the most important vehicle to identify and target younger voters who might otherwise not know as much about the campaign, receive direct mail, or be contacted personally by a campaign.

Contemporary campaigns provide up-to-date information, including the latest speeches, forthcoming events, and all their news, advertising, and documentaries on their websites. Social platforms, such as Facebook, Twitter, Instagram, and others, have been integrated into ongoing campaign communications. Internet advertising has also become standard and played a major role since the 2016 presidential election. The internet has also made the contemporary news cycle rapid and continuous. Reporters are constantly updating their stories online. Rumors spread with the speed of lighting on the Web. The two-source rule that print reporters used to verify the accuracy of information has been abandoned in the interests of speed and competitiveness.

Television viewership has declined while online use increased. Digital devices have become the most important source for news according to the Pew Research Center followed by television, radio, and print media.[5] People turn to sources that coincide with their political beliefs.

With the growth of the internet as a major news source, candidates, parties, and nonparty groups have adjusted their strategies to reach voters directly online and to pinpoint their messages to appeal to smaller groups with similar interests. Thus, messaging has become more precise, more personalized, and more narrowly targeted.

This chapter examines these developments and their impact on presidential electoral politics. The first section discusses the major news networks' coverage of campaigns. It examines how they interpret political events and how candidates react to those interpretations. The second section describes the techniques that candidates have used in recent campaigns to circumvent the national press corps, mostly online. The third section turns to presidential debates: their history, structure, staging, and impact on the electorate. Political advertising is the subject of the fourth and final section. It describes some of the most successful commercials on air and online, the increasing emphasis on negativity, and the effect of mass marketing and microtargeting on voters. It also examines the surreptitious advertising and messaging of foreign groups on the 2016 US presidential election.

Traditional News Coverage

The modus operandi of news reporting is to inform the public. But the press does so with its own professional orientation—one that affects what is covered and how it is covered.

Horse Race Journalism

Political scientist Thomas E. Patterson argues that the dominant conceptual framework for election reporting is that of a game. The candidates are the players and their moves (words, activities, and images) are seen by journalists reporting on the campaign as strategic and tactical devices to achieve their principal goal, winning the election. Even their policy positions, while evaluated in much less detail than who is ahead in the horse race, are assessed within this gaming framework; issue stands are described as calculated appeals to certain groups of voters. In short, the gaming aspect of electoral politics is the major organizing principle for the press throughout the entire election cycle.[6]

Why do the news media use the game metaphor ("the race") as its primary one? The answer is that viewing as a game heightens people's interest. Heightened interest, in turn, increases the audience size and, of course, profits because advertising revenue is based on the estimated number of people watching or hearing a particular program or reading a paper.

There is another reason for employing the game format. It lends an aura of objectivity to reporting. Rather than presenting subjective accounts of the candidates' positions and their consequences for the country, the news media can present quantitative data on public opinion and the campaign. Polls are frequently reported as the dominant election story. They are easy to report and often change (much like the standings do in organized sports). Change makes them more newsworthy.

Covering campaigns as if they were sporting events is not a new phenomenon. In 1976, Patterson found about 60 percent of television election coverage and 55 percent of newspaper coverage treated the campaign as if it were a contest between the candidates.[7] Michael J. Robinson's and Margaret Sheehan's analysis of the CBS Evening News during the 1980 election revealed that five out of six stories emphasized the competition between the candidates and their parties.[8] The focus on the game of politics has continued.

The problem with this type of journalism is that it diverts public attention from substance to strategy. Instead of examining the merits and limitations of a candidate's proposal, journalists explore the underlying political motivations for making the proposal, moving from the what to the why in the process. Such a perspective skews the information people receive; it heightens the partisan political component of elections and reduces and simplifies the substantive policy debate; it also contributes to the amount and tone of the coverage, in both cases, helping the candidate that is ahead unless that candidate's lead is declining.

In 2012, the amount of news coverage that Obama and Romney received was approximately equal until the final week of the campaign when the president, who was ahead in the polls and in the Electoral College math, got more. In 2016, Trump got more coverage than Clinton. The press perceived him as more newsworthy throughout the nomination and general election campaigns. The amount of presidential news coverage was about even in 2020.

The orientation of cable news networks and the proliferation of online news sources have contributed to the partisan spin on the coverage. Fox and other conservative news outlets provide a different ideological spin than do MSNBC, National Public Radio, and New York Times. There are dissimilarities in the descriptive content as well. Truth has become a debatable issue in election news and also in the news about government and public policy.

According to Professor Diana C. Mutz, the penchant of some news organizations to cast their reports within an ideological framework has fueled and been fueled by the partisan political divide in the United States in the last three decades. It has led to selective exposure, exposure that reinforces rather than challenges people's political attitudes.[9] Whereas partisan politics and selective exposure help clarify the issues for people with an ideological perspective, providing them with information to support their beliefs, it also makes them less open to opposing views, simplifies policy problems, reduces common ground, and generates strong emotions that impede compromise. It produces the confirmation bias that we mentioned previously.

Newsworthiness: Bad News Is "Good" News

The tone of election coverage tends to be negative. In 2012, 20 percent of the news stories on Obama were positive and 29 percent negative. Romney fared even worse. Only 15 percent of the stories on him were favorable compared with the 37 percent that were unfavorable.[10] The negativity of the press increased in 2016. Although Trump received more negative coverage (77 percent) than Clinton did (64 percent) during the general election, Clinton got the more unfavorable press during the entire election cycle.[11]

In 2020, it was more of the same. Trump received more coverage than Biden, especially during the early stages of the 2019–2020 election cycle. The tone of his coverage was also more negative, with the exception of Fox and other conservative news outlets. Biden also received considerable negative comments and references in the reporting of his candidacy.[12]

Why all the negativity? Most academic experts see it because of several factors: the news media's watchdog role, the increasing negative tone of campaigns themselves, especially political advertising, and the press's concept of newsworthiness. Conflict is more newsworthy than consensus; emotion attracts more attention than passivity or even rational discourse; and outcomes, particularly when they are unexpected, generate more interest than those that are anticipated. A fresh face winning and an experienced candidate losing are news; an experienced one winning and an unfamiliar one losing are not. Similarly, the first time a candidate states a policy position, it may be newsworthy; the second time, it is old news; the third time, it is not news at all. Candidates cannot give new speeches every time they make one during a six- to nine-month campaign.

In looking for something interesting to report, contemporary campaign journalists have often focused on verbal slips, embarrassing incidents, quotes taken out of context, inconsistent statements, and mistakes candidates make. They use tapes, videos, and recorded off-the-record comments to illustrate nonpresidential language and behavior. Such reporting encourages the candidates not to be spontaneous, not to be candid, and, above all, not to make mistakes. It also encourages speechwriters to put in sound bites and applause lines that they want the press to highlight, such as Trump's critical Clinton refrain in 2016: "lock her up."

From the candidates' perspectives, the negative tone of the news is magnified by the fact that they are not given the opportunity to tell their own stories in their own words. Their responses are edited and shortened by the major news networks. The average length of a quotation from candidates on the evening news shows in 1968 was 42.3 seconds. Since 1988, it has been less than 10 seconds. Reporters and correspondents are on camera much longer than are the candidates; they present the election to the voters more than the candidates are able to do in the news.

The orientation of the coverage has led to criticism by academics and the general public. The reporting emphasis on strident rhetoric has contributed to partisan incivility and passionate politics that characterizes the political environment in the United States today. It has also led to increasing distrust of the news media, elected officials, and government itself, public perspectives that are antithetical to a vibrant electoral democracy.

Story Lines

Frequently, the news is also fitted into a framework. According to Professor Patterson, a dominant story line emerges and much of the campaign is explained in terms of it. He enumerates four generic media scenarios: the *likely loser* (McGovern 1972, Mondale 1984, Dole 1988, and Trump 2016), the *skillful front-runner* (Reagan in 1984 and Bill Clinton in 1996), the *losing ground candidate* (Carter in 1980 and Hillary Clinton in 2016), and the opposite, *the bandwagon effect* (McGovern in the 1972 Democratic nomination, Carter in the 1976 nomination, Reagan in the 1980 general election, Trump during the 2016 GOP nomination, and Biden during the 2020 Democratic nomination after the South Carolina primary).[13]

The story line in 2000 focused on the closeness of the race, attributed in part to the weaknesses of both candidates: Gore's personal shortcomings and Bush's lack of depth on the issues. A variant on the competition theme toward the end of the campaign was the spoiler scenario for Ralph Nader. In 2004, the focus was on leadership, Bush's leadership in the war against terrorism and the war in Iraq. Four years later, the story line was the failure of that leadership and which candidate would be best able to achieve policy and political change. In 2012, it was the political divide, two competing ideologies, and the president's small but steady lead; in 2016; it was voter discontent, anger, and dissatisfaction with both candidates; and in the 2020 election, the story was about Trump's leadership and the pandemic.

Patterson's point is that the press fit the news of the campaign into the principal story rather than creating a new story from the changing campaign and unanticipated events. Naturally, the perceptions of the news media affect the electorate's understanding of what is happening.

Candidates try to create and maintain their own narrative. In this narrative, they present their goals, records, and accomplishments. The narrative is an explanation that leads to a conclusion, an argument for supporting them and opposing their opponent. Obama's narrative in 2008 was the need for change in politics and policies and his confidence that the change can be achieved ("yes, we can!" a refrain he asserted repeatedly.). Four years later, it was to continue his leadership that had improved the economic and social conditions he inherited. He also contrasted the failed Republican policies that got the country into the recession with the Democratic programs that were getting the country out of it. Romney reversed blame and credit, contending that the tepid economic growth was the consequence of too much government and too many restraints on the private sector. Trump's 2016 narrative argued that the country's fortunes and reputation had slipped badly during the eight years the Democrats controlled the White House, and he would "Make America Great Again." Clinton's theme in that election campaign was not as distinctive. She focused on Trump's unfitness for the presidency. Nor was her style as distinctive as his. Whereas Trump emphasized his skills as a strong and independent CEO, Clinton talked about togetherness and bonding. Trump continued his theme of American greatness in 2020, while Biden emphasized the need to reduce the deep partisan divide and bring the country back together again.

Often press coverage and campaign narratives conflict with one another. To reduce the interference with their narrative, campaigns try to circumvent the national press in reaching and broadening their base. One way to do this is to appear on talk-entertainment shows that offer a much less hostile environment than interviews by national reporters and network anchors. The candidates are treated better, more like celebrities than politicians, and asked easy, "softball" questions in comparison with the "hardball," gotcha journalism of the national press corps. The audiences that watch these shows are also different, consisting of people less interested and oriented toward partisan politics. Thus, they provide an opportunity for learning about them that might not have had.

A second and increasingly utilized vehicle to avoid the national news media is social media. In 2004, blogs were first used by campaigns; in 2008, YouTube and Facebook expanded viewership while Twitter conveyed information more quickly to larger numbers of people. Digital platforms have continued to expand and more people use them for personal communications and campaign information, a principal reason that campaigns, parties, and nonparty groups have turned to this media format in their campaigns.

Trump's use of Twitter in 2016 and 2020 was particularly innovative. He communicated his personal beliefs, opinions, and messages to the public. Unfiltered by the press, they were reported by the news media and reached more people than would have read them on Twitter.

Impact of the News Media

The news media remain important for priming and framing the agenda by highlighting salient issues. They inform but do so critically in their watchdog role. They question the motives of candidates, compartmentalize their speeches into sound bites, highlight any slip-ups or inconsistencies, focus on character frailties, and provide information on and critical analysis of policy stands. They also do fact checks on the statements and claims that candidates make.

In a highly polarized political environment, press negativity contributes to perceptions of news bias. In surveys taken during the last twenty-five years, the

Pew Research Center and the Gallup Poll have found growing correlations between partisan orientation and beliefs of journalistic fairness, with Republicans on a whole more critical of campaign press coverage than Democrats.

These perceptions have led the public to lose confidence in the news media. Forty years ago, most people thought that the news media got their facts right. Today, a majority believes that they do not, that the news media lack compassion, that they blur objective reporting with opinionated analysis, and that they are too negative. Confidence in the press (newspapers, television, and the online news sites) has declined sharply.

Yet even with all the negative coverage, most candidates conclude that critical coverage is still better than no coverage at all, particularly in the early phases of the nomination process, and especially for the candidates who do not begin with national reputations. At the outset of the candidates' quest for their party's nomination, news media attention conveys credibility; it is an indication that the press takes a candidate seriously. That is why candidates try their utmost to get coverage. No other recent presidential candidate has gotten as much attention for as long a period during the campaign as Donald Trump in 2016 and 2020.

Although the news tends to be concentrated and focused on certain controversial issues, events, and personal traits, the press does not speak in a single voice. The proliferation of news sources and the orientations of news networks provide some balance to election reporting, although the self-selection process by which people choose the news outlets from which they get information tends to reinforce rather than challenge their preexisting partisan and ideological orientations.

Presidential Debates

Debates constitute another important "informational" component of presidential campaigns, one in which the candidates, particularly those who are behind, find useful. They see debates as an opportunity to improve their images and damage their opponents, a potential game changer. Unlike most of their campaign rhetoric—speeches, statements, and responses to questions—debates are live and unedited, however, the formats, agreed to beforehand, limit the time for responses. Although the candidates' responses are usually prepared in advance, carefully crafted, and well-rehearsed, they sound more authentic than speeches read from a teleprompter. They also convey a more human dimension.

The news media like the debate format because it facilitates comparison. It fits into their game motif. It is a newsworthy event although not a money-maker for the news networks that carry them because advertisements are not usually permitted during the debates themselves.

The public likes the debates because they are more exciting and "real" than staged events and canned speeches. They can be dramatic. Theoretically, they conform to the rational discourse model on which electoral democracy is based. They allow the electorate to evaluate the candidates at the same time and on the same stage, providing voters with a basis for making an informed voting decision. People learn from them.

History

The first series of televised debates occurred in 1960. John Kennedy used them to counter the impression that he was too young and inexperienced. Richard Nixon, on the other hand, sought to maintain his stature as Dwight Eisenhower's knowledgeable and experienced vice president and the obvious person to succeed him in office. In the three elections that followed, Lyndon Johnson and then Nixon, both ahead in the polls, saw no advantage in debating their opponents and refused to do so. Gerald Ford, however, trailing Jimmy Carter in the polls, saw the debates as his best opportunity to come from behind and win. The Carter camp, on the other hand, saw them as a means of shoring up Democratic support. In 1980, the rationale was similar. From Reagan's perspective, it was a way to reassure the electorate about his views and his qualifications for office. For Carter, it was another chance to emphasize the differences between Reagan and himself, their parties, and their ideological orientations, issue stances, and personal attributes, including age and experience.

By 1984, presidential debates had become so much a part of the campaign that incumbents could not avoid them without making their avoidance a major campaign issue. Thus, Ronald Reagan was forced by public and press pressures to debate Walter Mondale, even though he stood to gain little and could have lost much from their face-to-face encounter. And in the 1992 election, George H. W. Bush's initial refusal to accept a plan for a series of campaign debates put forth by the Commission on Presidential Debates, a nonpartisan group that had organized the 1988 presidential and vice presidential debates, hurt him politically. Bill Clinton chided Bush for his refusal to debate. Democrats dressed as chickens appeared at his campaign rallies. President Bush finally relented, telling his handlers, "I am tired of looking like a wimp."

The principal debate issue in 1996 and again in 2000 was not whether to do so but whom to include in them. In 1992, Ross Perot and his running mate, Admiral James Stockdale, were invited to participate, and they did. In 1996, Perot and his running mate, Pat Choate, were not asked to participate. The Commission on Presidential Debates, composed of five Democrats and five Republicans, concluded that Perot's candidacy was not viable ad that he had no chance of winning the Electoral College even though his name appeared on the ballot in all fifty states and the District of Columbia. The commission based its decision on Perot's standing in the polls, about 5 percent at that time and on the judgment of a small number of political scientists and journalists who unanimously concluded that Perot not only could not win the election but also that he would not carry a single state. They were right, but their decision may have contributed to that result.

The Commission on Presidential Debates has employed similar reasoning since then in excluding third-party candidates. In doing so, it has established three criteria for inclusion in the debates in addition to the US Constitution's eligibility requirements of being a natural-born citizen, thirty-five years of age or older, and a resident of the United States for at least fourteen years. Candidates have to be on the ballot in enough states to have a chance of winning a majority of the electoral votes, be organized in a majority of the congressional districts within the state, and demonstrate a sufficient level of electoral support by receiving an average of 15 percent or more in the preelection public opinion polls (to be calculated by averaging surveys of five different polling organizations). Not surprisingly, the only candidates to meet these criteria have been the Democratic and Republican presidential standard-bearers.

The debates attract more viewers than any other single campaign event. In 2016, eight-four million people watched the first debate between Trump and Clinton; in 2020, the audience size was seventy-three million. The number of viewers decline for subsequent debates with the vice presidential candidates' debates having the smallest audience. Although presidential debates have now become part of the fabric of American presidential elections, their scheduling and format are still subject to arduous negotiation between the staffs of the major party candidates. In these negotiations, each side naturally wants to maximize its strengths. Candidates who are ahead in the polls when these negotiations are underway, usually the incumbent if running for reelection, call the shots. The Commission on Presidential Debates hosts the events.

TABLE 8.1 ★ Presidential Debates, 1960–2020

Year	Candidates	Number of Debates	Average Estimated Size of the Television Audience (in Millions)	Households Watching (%)
1960	Kennedy v. Nixon	4	77	60
1976	Carter v. Ford	4*	65	51
1980	Carter v. Reagan	1	81	59
1984	Mondale v. Reagan	3*	66	46
1988	Dukakis v. Bush	3*	66	36
1992	Bush v. Clinton v. Perot	4*	66	42
1996	Clinton v. Dole	3*	40	29
2000	Gore v. G. W. Bush	4*	40.6*	26
2004	G. W. Bush v. Kerry	4*	53.5†	36.3
2008	Obama v. McCain	4*	60.5†	37.6
2012	Obama v. Romney	4*	64.0†	44.3
2016	Clinton v. Trump	4*	74.0†	42.1
2020	Biden v. Trump	3*	56.9	37.8

*Includes one vice presidential debate.

†The average for just the three presidential debates.

Sources: Estimates of audience sizes for 1960–1992, "How Many Watched," *The New York Times* (October 6, 1996). Copyright © 1996 by the *New York Times*, reprinted by permission. Estimates for 1996, "Debate Ratings Beat Baseball," *Associated Press* (October 17, 1996). Copyright © 1996 by the Associated Press, reprinted by permission. Estimates for 2000–2020 based on ratings by Nielsen Media Research.

Preparation

Despite the appearance of spontaneity, debates are highly scripted and carefully orchestrated events. The candidates are coached and rehearsed weeks, even months, in advance. There have been a few exceptions to the extensive preparation rule, the most notable being Richard Nixon in his first debate with John Kennedy in which Nixon did not prepare as much as Kennedy.

To get ready, candidates go over briefing books that their aides prepare, view videos of their opponent, and engage in debates with stand-ins playing the role their adversary. The objective of this preparation is to anticipate the questions and provide thoughtful answers that are consistent with campaign speeches, press releases, political advertising, and the basic themes.

Trump's advisers provided him with a detailed analysis of Clinton's style based on her sixteen years of public debates in her quests for the Senate and the presidency. Included was a psychological profile of Clinton, developed by Cambridge Analytica, a political consulting group. Clinton's preparation included detailed briefing papers of Trump's rhetoric and policy positions and mock debates with her advisers who mimicked Trump's style and typical response to questions.

In addition to their concerns about substance and rhetoric, campaign media consultants also consider how candidates look, dress, speak, and interact with the questioners and with their opponents. Kennedy and Carter talked faster than Nixon and Ford to create an action-oriented image in the minds of the viewers. Both tried to demonstrate their knowledge by citing many facts and statistics in their answers. Ford and Reagan spoke in more general terms. Reagan's wit and anecdotes in 1980, Bush's manner in 1988, and Perot's down-to-earth language and self-deprecating humor in 1992 conveyed a human dimension with which viewers could identify in contrast to their opponents' less empathetic responses.

Appearance and manner during debates is also considered important. Nixon looked like he needed a shave in his 1960 debate with Kennedy. George H. W. Bush looked at his watch during his debate with Michael Dukakis, suggesting he wanted the debate to end as soon as possible. Gore waked to and towered over his opponent George W. Bush, an aggressive tactic. Four years later, Bush wore an ill-fitting suit that lumped on his back, suggesting to reporters and others that he might have a device imbedded in his clothing that was feeding him answers. Trump constantly interrupted and angrily challenged Biden in the first presidential debate in 2020. He seemed overly aggressive and at times out of control.

Challengers especially need to demonstrate their leadership credentials, their experience, their command of the issues, and their proposals for change. Incumbents need to defend their record and the progress they anticipate in the next four years. Both need to counter negative personal and partisan perceptions about themselves that have appeared in the news media and in their opponent's statements and advertising. Naturally, they also have to magnify their positive attributes. Trump did so by adhering to his unconventional and controversial rhetoric that enhanced his authenticity and perceptions of his toughness, decisiveness, and resolution. Clinton emphasized her experience, knowledge, and tenacity to appear more presidential than Trump.

FIGURE 8.1 ★ President Donald Trump and Democratic presidential candidate and former Vice President Joe Biden during the first presidential debate Tuesday, September 29, 2020, at Case Western University and Cleveland Clinic, in Cleveland, Ohio.

AP Images/Julio Cortez

Impact

The first debate usually helps challengers more than incumbents. Just getting on the same stage with the president of the United States increases their stature. They have other initial advantages. Having gone through a competitive nomination process that included numerous debates is a learning experience for them. Incumbents, on the other hand, tasked with the continuous problems of governing, may be less focused, overconfident, and, as a result, seem less prepared, particularly in their first reelection debate.

Incumbents also usually have higher performance expectations, particularly in the eyes of the news media. Moreover, with the press hyping the debate, fitting it into its horse race storyline, and evaluating it in terms of the winner and loser, the leading candidate, more likely to be the incumbent than the challenger, is disadvantaged.

The primary effect of debates is to shore up partisan support, particularly for the candidate whose electoral coalition has not coalesced as quickly. Mondale in 1984, Kerry in 2004, and Romney in 2012 gained such support from their first debate but could not extend it enough over the course of them, much less to election day.

In close races, debates can potentially make a difference. They can do so by increasing interest, clarifying issue positions, and shaping images. Theoretically, they can convince the undecided for whom to vote and counter weak partisan preferences, but they do not usually do so. There is little evidence that debates have a major influence on election results.

The principal reason that debates rarely shift public opinion on a large scale is because most voters have their minds made up or at least have their partisan predilections intact before viewing the debates. In fact, they are attracted to the debates precisely because of their partisan orientations. They see the debate through a political lens and root for their candidate. In situations in which information is contested, they tend to believe their party's nominee, not the opponent.

Campaign Advertising

Candidates are marketed much like any commercial product. Political advertising is used to gain attention, make a pitch, leave an impression, generate an emotion, and ultimately to turn out and influence the vote.

Advertising allows candidates to state their policy positions in their own words, articulate the merits of their proposals, trumpet their qualifications, and criticize their opponents. More importantly, it allows them to reach people who are less interested in electoral politics, less likely to follow the campaign on a regular basis, less knowledgeable about the candidates, and less likely to vote. It gives them information and may enhance their involvement in the election.

The trick is to make the commercials convincing. Candidate-sponsored ads are not unbiased, and the public knows it. To refine advertisements and improve the odds that they project the desired messages and images, which in turn produce the desired effects, ads are pretested before focus groups and online to gage their effectiveness. When they are not, they can do more harm than good. Michael Dukakis's ad in 1988 is a good example of a bad ad. Dukakis is seen wearing an army helmet and riding in a combat-ready tank. Although the goal of the advertisement was to demonstrate Dukakis's support for the military and for a strong national defense policy, the picture of Dukakis in the tank looked so silly and contrived that the Republicans countered with a commercial of their own in which Dukakis in the tank is featured along with information about the Democratic candidate's opposition to a long list of military programs and weapons systems.

Designing and sponsoring political commercials constitutes the principal expense of contemporary presidential campaigns, and those expenses have mushroomed in recent elections. In 2000, the total amount paid for advertising by the candidates, parties, and nonparty groups in the race for the presidency was $263 million; by 2012, it had risen to $950 million; the advertising expenditures during the 2015–2016 election cycle dipped to $845 million but rose to a whopping $1.5 billion in 2020. In the 2022 midterms, it was almost $3 billion.[14]

The increased amount spent on contemporary political commercials is a consequence of several factors: the closeness of races for president, the passion of polarized partisans and supporters, and the proliferation of party and nonparty groups.

Format and Tone

Political messaging takes many forms. Short ads, usually about thirty seconds, are interspersed with other commercials during regular television programming, while longer ones such as interviews, documentaries, and campaign rallies pre-empt scheduled programs and usually attract fewer viewers.

There are basically three types of political commercials: those that praise candidates and their accomplishments (*positive ads*), those that compare the candidates to the obvious advantage of the ad's sponsor (*contrast ads*), and those that just criticize opponent's policy preferences or personal attributes (*negative ads*). In most campaigns, candidates use all three types, more positive ads in the beginning when less is known about them and more negative ones near the end of the race.

Positive commercials point to the strengths of a candidate. For presidents seeking reelection, or even vice presidents running for the top office, one of those strengths is clearly experience in office. One of Jimmy Carter's most effective commercials in 1980 showed him in a whirl of presidential activities ending as darkness fell over the White House. A voice intoned, "The responsibility never ends. Even at the end of a long working day, there is usually another cable addressed to the chief of state from the other side of the world where the sun is shining and something is happening." As a light came on in the president's living quarters, the voice concluded, "and he's not finished yet." Incumbents use variations of the president-at-work ads with the White House as a backdrop to emphasize their work ethic, know-how, and leadership abilities. Challengers need to stress their qualifications. Their first task is to present themselves to the American people. Otherwise, their opponents will do so. They also need to contrast their skills, experience, and policy stands with their opponent's in a way that highlights their strengths and their opponent's weaknesses.

Negative ads exploit a candidate's character deficiencies, issue inconsistencies, and false leadership claims. They are not new. There has always been much negativity in presidential campaigns. George Washington was called a philanderer and a thief; Andrew Jackson was accused of marrying a prostitute; at the outset of the Civil War, Abraham Lincoln was charged with being illegitimate and Black; Theodore Roosevelt was said to be a drunkard; Herbert Hoover, a German sympathizer during World War I; and Franklin D. Roosevelt, a lecher, lunatic, and a closet Jew whose real name was Rosenfeldt.

What seems to be different today is the increasing emphasis placed on pure negativity. Data from the Wesleyan Media Project, indicate 44 percent of the ads during the presidential general election in 2004, 51 percent in 2008, 64 percent in 2012, and 54 percent in 2016 were of the attack, negative variety. In 2016, half of the ads run by the Clinton campaign in the general election were negative compared with about one-fourth of Trump's. The ads were more positive in 2020.[15]

Why all the negativity? Increased sponsorship of advertising by nonparty groups, primarily Super PACs, has contributed significantly to the critical tone of contemporary campaigns. Super PACs ads are almost all negative. Because non-party groups cannot coordinate their advertising with the candidate they support, they go negative against the candidate they oppose.

Emotive Content

Ads have emotive content. Positive ads are "feel good" ads. Designed to make people feel good, proud, or patriotic, they convey feelings of warmth, empathy, and sensitivity. President George W. Bush's reelection campaign ran such an ad in 2004. The president was pictured giving a big hug to Ashley, a little girl whose mother died in the terrorist attacks at the World Trade Center in New York City. He said, "I know that's hard. Are you all right?" Ashley replied, "He's the most powerful man in the world and all he wants to do is make sure I'm safe." Ashley's father added: "What I saw was what I want to see in the heart and in the soul of the man who sits in the highest elected office in our country."

Many times, ads are designed to enhance character. Make people feel better about the person for whom they are voting. Take this excerpt for a 2008 ad for Senator John McCain. "Shot down, bayoneted, tortured, offered early release, he said, "no." He'd sworn an oath. Home, he turned to public service. His philosophy: before party, polls, and self—America. A maverick, John McCain tackled campaign reform, military reform, spending reform . . . a man who has always put his country and her people before self, before politics. Don't hope for a better life, vote for one, McCain."

Negative ads convey unpleasant emotions: fear, repulsion, anger. The Daisy Girl and Willie Horton ads (see box 8.1.) generated fear. In the 2004 election, the Bush campaign played on the fear produced by the terrorist attacks in one ad, titled "Risk," that included pictures of terrorist attacks, frightened children, and a warning:

> After 9/11, our world changed, either we fight terrorists abroad or face them here. John Kerry and liberals in Congress have a different view. They opposed Reagan as he won the Cold War, voted against the first Gulf War, voted to slash intelligence after the first Trade Center attack, repeatedly opposed weapons vital to winning the war on terror. John Kerry and his liberal allies: are they a risk we can afford to take today?

In 2012, the Obama campaign ran an ad that showed Mitt Romney singing "America the Beautiful" with graphics that suggested he had sent jobs overseas, sought tax havens for his income, and stowed family wealth in Swiss bank accounts. After his comments that 47 percent of Americans don't pay taxes, are dependent on government, and believe that they are entitled to food, housing, and health, the Obama campaign ran an ad that simply showed the video of Romney making these remarks.

The 2016 Clinton campaign designed a strategy to highlight Trump's personal negatives. Ninety percent of her campaign's ads focused on his fitness for the presidency. In contrast, Trump's ads were more policy oriented. They distinguished his goals and positions from those of the Obama administration and, by extension, policies that would be pursued if Hillary Clinton won the election.

Some of the most outrageous ads in 2016 appeared on Facebook and were sponsored fake groups and paid for by Russians trying to influence the outcome of the US election. In 2020, the ads were more positive.

Do negative ads have an impact on voting behavior? Political consultants believe they do. They claim that they provide information, frame the debate, and motivate partisans to vote. Political scientists, however, are not so sure. Although they see activation and reinforcement of preexisting partisan beliefs as their primary effect, they also believe that negative advertising increases public cynicism, decreases feelings of efficacy, and can turn off independent and less partisan voters.

The electorate is also skeptical. People claim that they do not like the ads and do not find them helpful in making an informed voting choice, but a majority do find the presidential helpful.

Box 8.1 describes two famous examples of negative ads in presidential campaigns.

BOX 8.1 ★ Notorious Negativity

In 1964, Lyndon Johnson ran as the peace candidate. He and his Democratic supporters suggested that Republican Barry Goldwater was a trigger-happy zealot who would not hesitate to unleash nuclear weapons against a communist foe and get the country into a nuclear war. This scary scenario was captured in the "Daisy Girl" ad in which a little girl is pictured in a meadow plucking petals from

FIGURE 8.2 ★ Monique Luiz as she appears in the infamous "Daisy Ad."

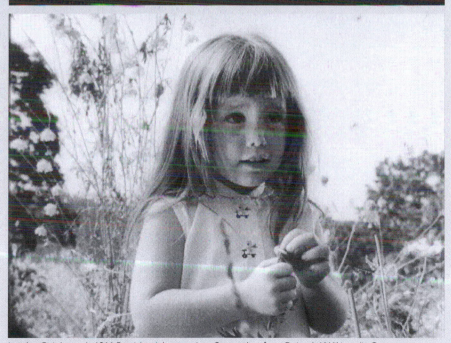

Lyndon B Johnson's 1964 Presidential campaign. Screenshot from Daisy Ad/Wikimedia Commons.

BOX 8.1 ★ Notorious Negativity *continued*

a daisy. She counts to herself softly. When she reaches nine, the picture freezes on her face, her voice fades, and a stern-sounding male voice counts down from ten. When he gets to zero there is an explosion, the little girl disappears, and a mushroom-shaped cloud covers the screen. Lyndon Johnson's voice is heard: "these are the stakes—to make a world in which all of God's children can live or go into the dark. We must either love each other, or we must die." The ad ended with an announcer saying, "Vote for President Johnson on November 3. The stakes are too high for you to stay home."

The commercial was run only once. Goldwater supporters were outraged and protested vigorously, but their protestations kept the issue alive. Parts of the ad were reshown on television newscasts. The Democrats had made the point, and the news media made it stick.

A second infamous ad, "Willie Horton," featured a mug shot of an African American prisoner who had raped a white woman while on a weekend furlough from a Massachusetts jail. Aimed at those who were fearful of crime, and especially those committed by African American males, the ad, sponsored by a PAC support-ing George H. W. Bush in 1988, was supplemented by other prisoner ads designed by the Bush campaign.

Accuracy and Truthfulness

The content of the political ads, especially negative ones, has always been con-troversial. Their hyperbole and shrill accusations, exaggeration and false claims, and their overwhelming volume have contributed to public skepticism, even numbness. Newspapers, television commentators, and opposition candidates and parties have pointed to the inaccuracies and false claims in campaigns.

Beginning in 2003, the Annenberg Public Policy Center at the University of Pennsylvania set up and continues to operate a website (factcheck.org) that monitors the accuracy of ad claims, candidate statements, and press releases. In 2007, another fact-check website, PolitiFact (politifact.org) was established by the *Tampa Bay Times* to independently monitor campaign oratory. Today many major newspapers and other media organizations do so as well.

These sites report that truthfulness in presidential campaigning has de-clined. More than half the statements of the presidential candidates in recent presidential have been misleading or partially or totally false. According to PolitiFact, 70 percent of Trump's remarks and 45 percent of Clinton's in 2016 were not true.[16] One would think and hope that these fact checks would have influenced informed judgments and evaluations of public officials, but they have not seemed to do so in elections. They are one story among many for the major news outlets, whereas ads run continuously. People see and believe what they want to believe.

Digital Communication Controversies

Foreign Interference

Starting in 2014 and extending to more recent elections, the surreptitious role of foreign agents has become an issue, one that threatens the integrity of the American electoral system. On March 19, 2016, Russian hackers sent a phishing email to John Podesta, chairman of Hillary Clinton's presidential campaign. Their objective was to gain his computer password to examine his campaign emails. They succeeded. They also were able to insert malware into the DNC and Democratic Congressional Committee's computers, stealing passwords, financial information, and the contents of thirty-three of the party's computers. They examined the stolen files and gave them to WikiLeaks, which made them publicly available on its website. The contents not only revealed Democratic strategy, the partiality of the DNC to Hillary Clinton during the nomination process, but they also fed into the issue of Mrs. Clinton "careless" use of a private server as secretary of state. The Russian interference even extended to state and local officials charged with overseeing the election and to private companies contracted to develop the software and manage the equipment for voting. Foreign agents tried to gain access to state and local computer networks, especially registration lists to gain data on thousands of voters; they also attempted to infiltrate state voting software and machinery for voting. Emails were sent to state and local election officials.

And that's not all. Russian trolls, posing as Americans, obtained personal data on individuals compiled by Facebook. They used the website's targeting mechanisms to sponsor eighty thousand posts, reaching an estimated 26 million people directly and 126 million indirectly (when recipients sent the ad to friends).[17] They set up thousands of Twitter accounts. More than 1 million people may have been in contact with these fake Russian accounts. According to a report prepared for the Senate Intelligence Committee by a US cybersecurity firm, there were also 10.4 million tweets by the Russian Internet Agency, 1,107 videos on YouTube attributed to Russian agents, and over 30 million Facebook and Instagram posts and advertisements linked to the IRA that were sent and shared on social media.[18] Focusing on divisive social issues such as race relations, immigration, gun control, and LGBTQIA-related concerns, the ads, posts, tweets, and videos were designed to arouse the emotions of people who felt strongly about these matters: abortion, immigration, and race relations. The Trump campaign was the beneficiary of these campaign activities by foreign agents, although the actual impact of the Russian communications on turnout and voting behavior in the 2016 presidential election has not and may never be determined.

Allegations of Russian influence-peddling on behalf of Trump prompted the Justice Department to appoint a Special Counsel, Robert S. Mueller, a former director of the FBI, to examine these alleged activities: collusion between Trump's campaign aides and Russian operatives, the hacking of email correspondence of the DNC and Clinton campaign officials, their release to WikiLeaks, and a host of other actions in which Russians and some Americans were engaged. The Mueller investigation also examined whether President Trump or any of his aides obstructed justice by impeding the investigation or lying about it to investigators.

Over the next two years, Mueller and his aides investigated a wide range of illegal contacts and activities during the 2016 electoral process. Based on this investigation, the Justice Department indicted thirteen Russian nationals, most of whom worked in their country's Internet Research Agency for violating US election laws. Foreigner nationals are not permitted to contribute directly or indirectly to American election campaigns.

In addition, the Special Counsel brought charges against nine US citizens associated with the Trump campaign. They were accused of crimes such as perjury, obstruction of justice, failing to register as a foreign representative, and paying off women who had liaisons with Trump to buy their silence.

Although the Special Report noted numerous contacts between Russians and Trump campaign operatives and numerous attempts by surrogates of Trump to promote the Russian-sponsored messages on social media, the report did not conclude that the Trump campaign colluded with foreign agents to aid his election. Nor did it confirm or refute the allegation that the president committed a crime in obstructing justice.

Use and Abuse of Personal Data

Russian and American citizens associated with the Trump campaign were not the only ones affected by these illegal activities. Social media companies, especially Facebook, came under congressional scrutiny for their marketing of the personal data. Obtaining information on peoples' beliefs, web activities, and interests is valuable not only in electioneering but also for public and private corporations. Internet companies that have compiled this information on their users profit from sharing it with marketeers, particularly those that advertise on their websites. Political parties, campaign organizations, and nonparty groups depend on it to enlarge their electoral coalitions. The Trump campaign relied on Facebook to compensate for its organizational weaknesses during both the primaries and general election. Cambridge Analytica, a British firm hired by Trump during the early stages of his general election campaign and by Ted Cruz during the Republican nomination process, developed psychological profiles from these data to discern which type of person might be moved by certain kinds of appeals. Both presidential campaigns and major parties used Facebook data to expand their voting lists, target their messages, and provide field staff with information that would facilitate their personal contacts.

Mark Zuckerberg, Facebook's founder, and other Facebook officials testified before Congress after the election as did executives from Google and Twitter. Members of Congress wanted to know about their marketing policies, particularly their use of personal data for profit making.

As a consequence of public and congressional criticism and revelations from investigative reporting by the *New York Times*, and to a lesser extent, other news organizations, Facebook said it would increase its verification of information posted on its platform, require advertisers to provide more documentation for their political ads, and identify and close fake foreign accounts. The group sponsoring the ad had to be American and located in the United States.

Facebook set up a "war room" to monitor these activities. New arithmetic programing tools were designed to determine fake news and false information and remove it from their site.

Cyber experts and privacy proponents, however, raised questions about Facebook's transparency in doing so. They were concerned about the thoroughness of the Web companies' analysis of these data, the fake ads and posts, and the continued marketing of private information.

The digital technology that revolutionized campaign communications, facilitated fundraising, and improved information access, all assets for a democratic electoral process, had a downside as well. Digital campaigning was warping political debate, manipulating campaign communications, compromising election integrity, and invading personal privacy for millions of American. European democracies were facing similar threats.

Summary

The mass media have a profound effect on presidential elections: on the organization, strategy, and tactics of the campaign; the distribution of resources; and directly or indirectly on the electorate's voting decisions. That is why so much of a presidential campaign is devoted to media-related activities.

First newspapers, then radio and television, and now the internet have provided the primary communication channels through which information flows to and from voters, sometime with the news media as an intermediary and sometimes not. The multiplication of major news networks on cable and websites, the increasing importance (and length) of local news shows, the entertainment/news format, and social media platforms have provided additional, and, for the most part, more favorable outlets for candidates to reach the electorate than they had when the broadcast television news networks monopolized election campaign reporting. The news cycle has evolved into one of almost instantaneous and continuous coverage from multiple, and increasingly from partisan and ideologically oriented sources.

Most of the traditional news media see and report the election as a game, fitting statements, events, and activities into various story lines. Their schema highlights drama and the contest. They devote special attention to controversy: statements, events, and anonymous leaks, many emanating from the campaigns themselves. This attention downplays in-depth discussions of policy issues. Campaign coverage also plays up the personality dimension of candidates.

Candidates naturally try to present their own narrative and maintain it in the face of unanticipated events, opponent's attacks, and critical news media coverage. They do so by planting stories, leaking their opposition research, scripting their speeches with sound bites, orchestrating events, usually minimizing spontaneity to prevent ad hoc remarks that damage their campaign's narrative. Scripting and orchestrating campaigns reduces the authenticity of the candidates and people's trust in them when they engage in "political talk."

Presidential debates also provide large-audience opportunities for candidates to reiterate appeals, look presidential, and expand and excite their partisan base.

Debates, especially, facilitate candidate comparisons that initially work to the advantage of challengers who need to present themselves as the equal of their incumbent opponents. The news media play a role here as well, covering the debates and often participating in them by asking questions and reporting the candidates' responses, the public's reaction, and their own evaluations of the winners and losers. They then integrate the debate into the ongoing storylines of the campaign.

In a close race, debates can make a difference, although they have not usually changed public opinion or reversed anticipated election outcomes. Partisans disproportionately comprise the debate audience; they tend to root for *their* candidates and believe in the information that these candidates present, not their opponents'. Bounces from the debates tend to be short-lived and fade quickly over time.

Because campaign news may disrupt or deviate from a candidate's basic themes and leadership imagery, campaigns try to reinforce their appeals through simplification, repetition, and emotion, using mass-marketing techniques and microtargeting messages to do so.

To win over undecided voters and energize supporters, political ads utilize both positive and negative arguments and graphics. Since the beginning of the twenty-first century, negative campaigning has increased. Negative ads capture press attention and are thought to mobilize the partisan base.

Voters have become increasingly leery about the claims of these ads, in part because of their obvious bias, stridency, and slickness. News organizations and nonpartisan public policy institutes also evaluate the accuracy of the ads, their hyperbole and exaggeration.

Ads have an impact; they contribute to the public knowledge, frame and clarify the debate, extend the campaign to people who might otherwise tune out, and reinforce partisan loyalties. But whether they are cost-effective, whether they change political attitudes, and how much they affect voting behavior remain contentious issues among political practitioners, political scientists, and other campaign analysts. In the last several elections, candidates have used social media platforms to circumvent the national press corps to reach the voters directly. They do so by blogging, tweeting, advertising, and videoing.

Internet technology has its strengths and weaknesses for a democratic electoral process. It benefits the candidates by facilitating the collection, integration, and analysis of data to reach more people in a more personalized manner. Digital communications have provided more information to more people, helped campaigns connect to more voters, revived grassroots politics, enticed more small donors and more volunteers, and increased interest in elections, all of which invigorates electoral democracy.

On the other hand, there is little evidence that the American electorate is more knowledgeable, big donors less important, campaigns less manipulative, and US citizens more rational and less cynical in their voting behavior. Digital communications also present partial and biased accounts of the campaign. There is more "fake news," unsubstantiated rumors, and inaccuracies. In 2016, digital communications by inauthentic groups on Facebook, Google, Twitter, and other social media, accentuated these problems and allowed noncitizens to try influence US elections, thereby undermining a fair and democratic electoral system.

Exercises

1. Follow the campaign on the news source from which you receive most of your information about the current election. Do you feel that the news coverage on this source was balanced? Was there a reporting bias? Compare your perceptions on the amount and tone of coverage with the surveys conducted by the Pew Research Center.

2. Indicate the principal narratives of the campaign as articulated by the major party candidates and by the news media. Which of these narratives did you find most compelling and why?

3. View one of the nomination or general election presidential debates and note the principal policy positions of the candidates. Which of these policies are apt to be most appealing to most people? Which of them will be the easiest to achieve and ones the most difficult? (Transcripts and videos of the debates can be found on the networks that sponsor or cover the debate, YouTube, and for the general election, the website of the Commission on Presidential Debates.)

4. Contrast the on-air and online advertisements of the presidential candidates on the basis of their messages to specific groups. These ads should also be available on the candidates' websites and on those of major research organizations that track presidential ads, such as Living Room Candidate and the Political Communication Lab at Stanford University. When the ads targeted the same groups, how did their messages differ?

5. Check the accuracy of the ads you examined on Factcheck or PolitiFact. Which of them seem to be the most accurate, the most persuasive, and the most interesting?

Selected Readings

Bartels, Larry M. "Remembering to Forget: A Note on the Duration of Campaign Advertising Effects." *Political Communication* 31, no. 4 (2014): 532–44.

Denton, Robert E., Jr. *The 2020 Presidential Campaign: A Communication Perspective.* Lanham, MD: Rowman & Littlefield, 2020.

Enli, Gunn. "Twitter as Arena for the Authentic Outsider: Exploring the Social Media Campaigns of Trump and Clinton in 2016 US Presidential Election." *European Journal of Communication* 32, no. 1 (2017): 50–61.

Farnsworth, Stephen J., and Robert Lichter. *The Nightly News Nightmare: Network Television Coverage of Presidential Elections, 1988–2008.* Lanham, MD: Rowman & Littlefield, 2010.

Fowler, Erika Franklin, Travis N. Ridout, and Michael M. Franz. "Political Advertising in 2016: The Presidential Election as Outlier?" *The Forum* 14, no. 4 (2016): 445–69.

Fridkin, Kim, Patrick J. Kenny, and Amanda Wintersleck. "Liar, Liar, Pants on Fire: How Fact-Checking Influence Citizens Reactions to Negative Advertising." *Political Communication* 42 (February 2, 2015): 127–51.

Geer, John G. *In Defense of Negativity: Attack Ads in Presidential Campaigns.* Chicago, IL: University of Chicago Press, 2006.

———. "The News Media and the Rise of Negativity in Presidential Campaigns." *PS: Political Science and Politics* 45 (July 2012): 422–27.

Gerber, Alan S., James G. Gimpel, Donald P. Green, and Daron R. Shaw. "How Large and Long-Lasting Are the Persuasive Effects of Televised Campaign Ads? Results from a Randomized Field Experiment." *American Political Science Review* 105 (2011): 135–50.

Hill, Seth, James Lo, Lynn Vavreck, and John Zaller. "How Quickly We Forget: The Duration of Persuasion Effects From Mass Communication." *Political Communication* 30, no. 4 (2013): 521–47.

Huber, Gregory, and Kevin Arceneaux. "Identifying the Persuasive Effects of Presidential Advertising." *American Journal of Political Science* 51 (October 2007): 957–77.

Jamieson, Kathleen Hall, ed. *Electing the President 2012: The Insiders' View*. Philadelphia: University of Pennsylvania Press, 2013.

Kenski, Kate, Bruce W. Hardy, and Kathleen Hall Jamieson. *The Obama Victory: How Media, Money, and Message Shaped the 2008 Election*. Oxford, UK: Oxford University Press, 2010.

Mattes, Kyle, and David P. Redlawsk. *The Positive Case for Negative Campaigning*. Chicago, IL: University of Chicago Press, 2014.

Mutz, Diana C. "How the Mass Media Divide Us." In Pietro S. Niola and David W. Brady, eds., *Red and Blue Nation? Characteristics and Causes of America's Polarized Politics* (pp. 223–62). Washington, DC: Brookings/Hoover, 2006.

Patterson, Thomas E. "News Coverage of the 2016 General Election: How the Press Failed the Voters," Shorenstein Center on Media, Politics and Public Policy in conjunction with Media Tenor, December 2016.

———. *Out of Order*. New York, NY: Knopf, 1993.

West, Darrell M. *Air Wars: Television Advertising and Social Media in Election Campaigns, 1952–2016*, 7th ed. Washington, DC: Sage/CQ Press, 2018.

Notes

1. The term "yellow journalism" comes from the comic strip "The Yellow Kid," which first appeared in Joseph Pulitzer's *New York World* in 1896. The kid, whose nightshirt was colored yellow in the paper, was an instant hit in the black-and-white newspapers of the day and sparked a bidding war for the comic strip between Pulitzer and William Randolph Hearst. Although the strip's popularity lasted only a few years, the competition between these two media titans continued for decades.

2. David Stebenne, "Media Coverage of American Presidential Elections: An Historical Perspective," in Martha Fitzsimon, ed., *The Finish Line: Covering the Campaign's Final Days* (New York, NY: Freedom Forum Media Studies Center, 1993), 83.

3. "State of the News Media 2016: Network News Fact Sheet," Pew Research Center, January 13, 2021.

4. Ibid.

5. Ibid.

6. Thomas E. Patterson, *Out of Order* (New York, NY: Knopf, 1993), 53–133.

7. Thomas E. Patterson, "Television and Election Strategy," in Gerald Benjamin, ed., *The Communications Revolution in Politics* (New York, NY: Academy of Political Science, 1982), 30.

8. Michael J. Robinson and Margaret A. Sheehan, *Over the Wire and on TV: CBS and UPI in Campaign '80* (New York, NY: Russell Sage Foundation, 1983), 148.

9. Diana C. Mutz, "How the Mass Media Divide Us," in Pietro S. Nivola and David W. Brady, eds., *Red and Blue Nation? Characteristics and Causes of America's Polarized Politics* (Washington, DC: Brookings/Hoover, 2006), 224–40.

10. Thomas E. Patterson, "A Tale of Two Elections: CBS and Fox News' Portrayal of the 2020 Presidential Campaign," Shorenstein Center on Media, Politics, and Public Policy, Harvard University, December 17, 2020.

11. Thomas Patterson, "News Coverage of the 2016 General Election: How the Press Failed the Voters." Shorenstein Center on Media, Politics and Public Policy, December 2016.

12. Patterson, "A Tale of Two Elections."

13. Patterson, *Out of Order.*

14. Wesleyan Media Project.

15. "4.3 million Ads with Spending Nearing $3 Billion," Wesleyan Media Project, November 3, 2022.

16. PolitiFact.com.

17. Report into the Investigation of Russian Interference in the 2016 Presidential Election Department of Justice, March 2019.

18. Ibid.

The Election

Its Meaning and Consequences

Understanding Presidential Elections

9   Chapter
★ ★ ★ ★ ★

Introduction

Predicting and assessing the results of the election is a favorite American pastime in which politicians, journalists, academics, and the politically engaged public participate. Presidential campaigns are newsworthy, both informative and entertaining. Forecasting election outcomes, monitoring and analyzing public opinion, and anticipating the effect of the election on governance and public policy is fair game, consistent not only with democratic debate but also with commentary that accompanies sporting events.

Predictions and assessments of the vote are based on elaborate equations, predicated on past elections, current surveys and economic data, and the wisdom of those who study elections: political scientists, historians, and communication scholars, politicians and media consultants, and of course, reporters and other political pundits. Their analyses provide important information to candidates running for office and to those who have been elected.

For campaign staff, surveys of public opinion indicate the issues that can be effectively raised and those that should be avoided, which audiences should be targeted, and what messages should be communicated to them, including the words and expressions that are apt to produce the most desired effect. For public officials, analyses of voter preferences, opinions, and attitudes provide an interpretation of the vote, indicate the range and depth of concerns on the key issues, and signal the amount of support and opposition newly elected presidents are likely to receive when they begin their term in office.

This chapter discusses the presidential vote from these perspectives. We first anticipate the vote by examining the environment and public opinion as the election approaches. There are many ways to assess the electoral environment. The first part of this section looks at how political scientists have tried to do so, the models they have used, and the success that they have had in predicting the popular vote. The focus then shifts to the electorate itself. Here we look at snapshots of public opinion over the course of the election campaign. This part of the chapter discusses polls. It describes their methodologies and evaluates their predictive success. We then examine the news media's election night forecasts and analyses based on the large exit poll that is conducted as voters leave the precincts in which they have cast ballots and from surveys of those who engaged in early voting.

The second section of the chapter turns to an explanation of the vote. After discussing the results of exit polls, it reports on the American National Election Studies (ANES), which have been conducted since 1952 by researchers at the University of Michigan and, since 2005, in conjunction with researchers at Stanford University. These studies, which interview voters before and after the election, provide data that scholars have used to analyze elections, determine demographic and attitudinal trends, and the impact of the campaign itself on people's vote. The principal findings of these analyses are summarized for each presidential election beginning in 1952.

The final section of the chapter turns to the relationship between campaigning and governing, between issue debates and public policy making, and between candidate evaluations and presidential style. How do campaign promises shape the new agenda and leadership expectations impact on performance evaluations? Does the projected or perceived image of the candidates affect the tone of the presidency or the actions of the president once in office? Can the winning electoral coalition be converted into one for governing the country?

Predicting Presidential Elections

Political scientists have had a long-running debate about how much campaigns really matter. Do they dictate, influence, or have relatively little impact on the outcome of the election?

There are several schools of thought. One of them argues that campaigns usually do not matter all that much and that the environment in which elections occur shapes the electorate's judgment and augurs the outcome of the vote; another suggests that it is the preexisting political views that matter; a third alternative is that campaigns can be decisive, particularly when the electorate is closely divided. These contending points of view are not necessarily inconsistent with one another, but they do reflect differences in the perceptions of what the most important influences on voting are, the economic, social, and political environment; political attitudes, salient issues, the personalities of the candidates; or the conduct of the campaign itself.

Forecasting Models

Those in the environment-conditions-the-outcome school have constructed formal models by which they forecast the popular vote. They identify critical variables that have influenced past elections; assess them within the current economic, social, and political climate; quantify them for the purpose of analysis; and then place them in an equation intended to predict the percentage of the two-party vote that the candidates will receive. They test the model based on how successfully it would have predicted past presidential elections.

The components of most models include economic and political variables. Because economic performance is a major criterion by which the electorate evaluates the party in power and its candidates for office, especially if the incumbent is running for reelection, almost all the election models contain current measures of the economy; some modelers also try to anticipate how the economy will perform in the year of the election and how the public thinks it will perform. To accomplish this task, they use indicators such as the gross domestic product (GDP), rate of economic growth, level of unemployment, number of new jobs created since the previous election, rate of inflation, wage growth, consumer confidence, and forecasts about the country's economic future. Most political analyses that use economic variables to forecast the likely result believe that the second quarter of the election year, April–June, is the key period when people formulate their judgments on the economy and begin to shape their perceptions of the candidates.[1] Conditions change, however, so the closer to election that they factor these variables into their model, the more accurate their models are apt to be.

Forecasters face another problem. The actual state of the economy and public perceptions of it may differ. The economic conditions that the press highlights, the diverse effect of the economy on different people in different areas at different times, and partisan views that shape how many people evaluate the economy can exacerbate the gap between public perceptions and economic analysis, although it is possible to anticipate what public perceptions of the economy may be.[2] To capture these campaign-related variables, the modelers frequently have to incorporate polling data into their equations during the election cycle.

A second set of variables concerns the political environment: the partisan disposition of the electorate, the public's approval of the current president, and the length of time that president's party has been in control of the White House. Of these factors, partisanship is the most important influence on voting, so important that it has lessened the independent impact of nonpolitical factors on the outcome of the election. Many of these nonpolitical factors are evaluated through a partisan lens. The fact that the parties have been at or near parity for almost four decades, however, has made the popular vote in presidential elections since 2000, with the exception of 2008, very close. The margin of victory has not exceeded 4 percent in national elections, although competitiveness between the major parties within many of the states vary a lot more.

Until recently, the division between the red (Republican) and blue (Democratic) states has remained remarkably steady. Only three states switched their presidential vote from 2000 to 2004 and two from 2008 to 2012. In 2016, however, six states moved from blue to red and one state (Maine) divided its electoral vote, while in 2020 the same states switched back to Democratic. Changing demographics, the increase of minorities in the electorate, the movement of people from rural to urban areas and from the interior of the country to the coasts, and resistance to social changes and the uneven recovery from the recessions and economic downturns help explain the shifts.

Another factor that may affect the political environment is incumbency. Incumbents, whose party has just won the White House, usually get reelected; only Jimmy Carter, George H. W. Bush, and Donald Trump failed to do so since 1980.

After retaining control of the White House, however, for a period of eight to twelve years, the "time-for-a-change" variable kicks in. Grievances mount and public discontent is directed toward the party in power and its candidates. Challengers face another disadvantage if they have to go through a competitive nomination process to become their party's standard-bearer. As we have previously mentioned, competitive primaries and caucuses can damage images of the winners, decrease their financial resources, and deepen the divide within a party, hurdles that must be overcome to win the general election. In recent times, the influence of party activists on nomination process has forced candidates to take more extreme policy positions that may adversely affect them in the general election.

The third set of factors is election specific. Events that occur during the campaign, such as the financial crisis of 2008, Hurricane Sandy in 2012, and the COVID-19 pandemic of 2020 can affect voters' opinions of the candidates. The campaign itself may also be a factor: disproportionate resources, more effective outreach, controversial statements or actions, and any personal health problems of the candidates, real or rumored, may influence the outcome, particularly if the country is closely divided politically or the economy is uneven and its future trajectory unclear.

To identify which of these variables is likely to be most important, and in what combination with one another, forecasters turn to history. They calculate the relationship of these factors to past election outcomes. In doing so, they assume that factors that best predicted the vote in the past will continue to do so in the future. There are several problems with this assumption, however, changing conditions, opinions, even beliefs. Take the views on gender orientation, for example, or the longer-term, psychological and economic consequences of recessions and pandemics.

The longer the time period from the date of the forecast to the vote of the public can also affect the accuracy of prediction. If the forecast is made early, if the variables that are analyzed are based on data from previous years or months before the election, if the impact of the campaign itself is not considered—either because one group of economic or political factors is so dominant or because the modelers assume that the major party campaigns will cancel each other out—then forecasts may be inaccurate because models are incomplete or the assumptions on which they were based are incorrect. With all these difficulties, why do political scientists forecast election outcomes long before they occur? One reason is that they believe environments matter, in some cases more than campaigns themselves, that most people make retrospective judgments that shape their political outlook and their voting behavior, and that these judgments tend to be predictable. They assume that when an accumulation of factors point to one direction, the die has been cast.

How accurate have the forecasters been? In 2000, well before the election, all the modelers predicted a Gore victory over Bush with Gore receiving 52.8 percent to 60.3 percent of the popular vote. They did so on the basis of a booming economy, the absence of a national security threat, the US status as a super power, and President Bill Clinton's high job approval ratings. Gore actually received 48.4 percent of the total vote and 50.2 percent of the two-party vote.[3]

In 2004, the modelers did better. They all forecast that Bush would win the popular vote, receiving anywhere from 49.9 percent to 57.6 percent of the two-party vote. The average forecast was 53.8 percent; Bush actually received 50.7 percent of the total vote and 51.2 percent of the two-party vote.[4]

The outcome of the 2008 presidential election was not hard to predict, particularly after the financial crisis of mid-September of that year. But even before that crisis, a Democratic victory seemed probable with economic growth declining; an unpopular, two-term Republican in the White House, and a war in progress that a majority of Americans had come to believe was a mistake. Most of the political science forecasters predicted a Barack Obama victory by an average of 52 percent of the two-party vote.[5] He won 52.9 percent of the total popular vote and 53.7 percent of the two-party vote.

In 2012, the forecasters were divided. Of the thirteen who published their predictions before the election, eight said Obama would win and five indicated that Romney would. Their estimates ranged from 53.8 percent for Obama to 53.1 percent for Romney. The average forecast of the two-party vote was 50.4 percent for Obama. He actually won 52 percent of that vote and 51.1 percent of all the votes cast.[6]

Forecasters also disagreed in 2016. Six of eleven predicted a Clinton popular vote victory; two forecast a Trump win; the other three said that the election would be very close; and it was. Clinton received 51.1 percent of the two-party vote and Trump 48.9 percent. Seven of the modelers were within 1 percent of the actual vote; two were within 0.1 percent. But remember, they were forecasting the popular vote, and Trump won the Electoral College vote.[7]

In 2020, they more accurately predicted Biden's victory. Of the seven modelers that made specific presidential predictions, six calculated that Biden would win and only one believed Trump would do so.[8] The percentages that they calculated for each of the candidates varied.

Public Opinion Polls

If campaigns matter and if opinions change, then forecasters and analysts need to follow the polls. So do journalists that rely on them to describe the race, anticipate the outcome, and explain the opinions and behavior of the voters, the whys of the campaign. Polls also are thought to contribute to the objectivity of reporting.

Sometimes proprietary polls paid for by the campaigns are given to the press to try to affect media coverage. Obviously, candidates want the most favorable data released. Nate Silver, chief polling analyst for fivethirtyeight.com, contends that these internal polls tend to be less accurate not only because of their selective release of information but also because pollsters hired by the campaign do not want to provide bad news that undermines the morale of fellow campaigners and could result in fewer polls being authorized and, thus, less business for them.[9]

There are hundreds of public opinion surveys at the state and national levels. Real Clear Politics, an online political news organization, lists preelection presidential polls on a daily basis. It also aggregates them over time.

Preelection polls are reported by the news media and may affect the tone of campaign coverage. They could affect the impact of how many people volunteer for the campaign and turn out to vote, particularly if the polls indicate that the race is not close. They also may affect the public's perception of the candidates that might influence the answers people give to survey researchers. In this sense, polls can be self-fulfilling and also provide an inaccurate prediction of actual voting behavior (see box 9.1). In chapter 8, it was noted that there has been some speculation that Trump supporters in certain communities were less likely to reveal to pollsters that they would vote for Trump than were Biden supporters in 2012 and 2020.

Election-Night Predictions

Forecasts continue right to the end, until all the votes are tabulated. The final projections and vote analyses are presented by the major television broadcast and cable news networks during the night of the election as well as the following day.

BOX 9.1 ★ A Brief History of Polling Glitches, 1932–2020

Although the number of polls has mushroomed in recent years, polling itself is not a new phenomenon. There have been nationwide assessments of public opinion since 1916. The largest and most comprehensive of the early surveys were the straw polls conducted by the *Literary Digest*, a popular monthly magazine. The *Literary Digest* mailed millions of ballots and questionnaires to people who appeared on lists of automobile owners and in telephone directories. In 1924, 1928, and 1932, the poll correctly predicted the winner of the presidential election. In 1936, it did not: A huge Alfred Landon victory was forecast, and a huge Franklin Roosevelt victory resulted.

What went wrong? The *Literary Digest* mailed ten million questionnaires over the course of the campaign and received two million back. As the ballots were returned, they were tabulated. This procedure, which provided a running count, blurred shifts in public opinion that may have been occurring during the campaign. But that was not its only problem. The principal difficulty with the survey was that the sample of people who responded to the survey was not representative of average Americans at that time. Automobile owners and telephone subscribers who were contacted were simply not typical voters. Most people did not own cars or have telephones in 1936. This distinction mattered more in 1936 during the Great Depression than it had in previous years because there was a deep socioeconomic cleavage within the electorate. The *Literary Digest* sample did not reflect this cleavage; thus, its results were wrong. Although the *Literary Digest* was tabulating its two million responses and predicting that Landon would be the next president, a number of other pollsters were conducting more scientific surveys and correctly forecasting Roosevelt's reelection. The polls of George Gallup, Elmo Roper, and Archibald Crossley differed from *Literary Digest*'s in two major ways: They were

BOX 9.1 ★ A Brief History of Polling Glitches, 1932–2020 *continued*

considerably smaller, and most importantly, their samples were more representative of the population as a whole.

Literary Digest went out of business, but the scientific methodology of the successful pollsters continued and improved. In 1940, Gallup predicted Roosevelt would receive 52 percent of the vote; he actually received 55 percent. In 1944, Gallup forecast a 51.5 percent Roosevelt vote, very close to his actual 53.2 percent. Other pollsters also made predictions that closely approximated the outcome of the popular vote. Consequently, public confidence in election polling began to grow. The confidence was short-lived, however. In 1948, all major pollsters forecast a victory by Republican Thomas E. Dewey. Their errors resulted from poor sampling techniques, from the premature termination of polling two weeks before election day, and from incorrect assumptions about how the undecided would vote. The results of the 1948 election once again cast doubt on the accuracy of public opinion polls. Truman's victory also reemphasized the fact that surveys reflect opinion at the time they are taken, not necessarily days or weeks later.

Beginning in 1952, national election surveys became more accurate. The method of selecting people to be interviewed and to determining whether or not they would likely vote was refined. The results of the polls were weighted on the basis of the demographics of the population. Rolling polls were also instituted. In this type of polls, a percentage of the sample, usually one-third, changes with each new analysis and often on daily. These surveys now continue right up to election day, enabling them to mirror shifts in public sentiment during the last weeks of the campaign. The polling profession requires organizations that conduct polls to indicate the number of respondents, the sampling error, and the level of confidence that the results are within the margin of error.

Nonetheless, there have still been glitches. In 1980, the magnitude of Reagan's win was substantially underestimated; in 1992 and 1996, Clinton's margin of victory was overestimated. In 2012, Obama's was underestimated by every major national pollster in its final preelection poll. Two major survey organizations, Rasmussen Reports and the Gallup Poll, had Romney ahead in their final poll.

In 2016, all the major polls but two, indicated a victory for Hillary Clinton. Why did the polls fail to predict the winner? Actually, they did predict the popular vote winner. In fact, they were more accurate than in 2012. Most of the national polls anticipated a 3 percent Clinton popular vote victory in 2016; she actually won by about 2 percent (well within the margin of error in these polls.

What happened? The American Association of Public Opinion Researchers (AAPOR) created a task force of specialists to find out. Their report emphasized several major problem areas that may have skewed poll predictions, particularly the smaller and less frequently conducted state polls: The state polls did not capture voting shifts in the week before the election. There were many more undecided voters on election day in 2016 (12.5 percent) than there were in the three previous presidential elections. In those elections, only about 4 percent of the electorate did not know how they would vote. According to the report by the AAPOR, "[A]bout 13 percent of voters in Wisconsin, Florida, and Pennsylvania decided on their presidential choice in the final week."[10] These voters disproportionately voted for Trump.

> **BOX 9.1 ★** A Brief History of Polling Glitches, 1932–2020 *continued*
>
> The polls underestimated the turnout of Trump voters and overestimated the turnout of Clinton's, particularly in the Midwest. They may have done so because their likely voter questions were too general. Are you registered to vote? Did you vote in last election? Do you plan to vote in the forthcoming presidential election? The one pollster who correctly predicted a Trump victory asked respondents to assess their likelihood of their voting on a 0–10 scale.[11]
>
> The samples the polls used, particularly those with fewer respondents, overweighed educated voters who tend to respond to public opinion surveys at a higher rate than do people with less formal education. Less educated voters disproportionately supported Trump. Moreover, the estimates of likely voters were based on the previous presidential election; In doing so, the polls anticipated an African American vote similar to the one four years earlier; they also underestimated the vote of people with less education. Besides, Trump voters were less likely to admit that they would vote for him (the Shy Trump effect) than Clinton voters were to say that they would vote for her.

In the early polls, personal interviews were held in people's homes, a method that put respondents at ease. Establishing a personal relationship with the people being interviewed was thought to contribute to the truthfulness of their responses. But home interviewing was slow and costly for polling organizations. During the 1980s, telephone interviews replaced personal visits; random-digit dialing was used to reach both listed and unlisted numbers to create a random sample.

A random sample is necessary to determine the odds of the sample being representative of the population being surveyed. Every poll, which is based on a random selection of respondents, has a sampling error that varies with the size of the poll. Most of the major national surveys' sampling errors range from ±2 to 3.5 percent. That variation is the extent to which the polling results may differ from that of the entire population studied. The larger the sampling error the less accurate the polls are apt to be. How confident are pollsters that their findings

TABLE 9.1 ★ Accuracy of Final Major Preelection Polls in 2020

Poll	Size of Poll	Biden	Trump	Others
270 to Win	—	50.6%	43.2%	2.4%
IBD/TIPP	1,080	49	46	5
Redfield & Wilton	8,765	53	41	6
RMG Research	1,200	51	44	5
Quinnipiac	1,516	50	39	11
Yahoo/YouGov	1,360	53	43	4

All polls were released on November 2, 2020, the day before the election.

Source: 270 to Win (*270towin.com*)

are within the calculated error range? The answer is usually 95 percent, if their sample is truly random.

Achieving random selection has become more difficult today for several reasons. When survey researchers began to use telephones to conduct interviews, they automated dialing, eventually turning to computers to determine and call the random numbers. Telemarketers also began to use automated dialing. As a consequence, the number of phone calls people received rose exponentially, especially during the evening hours when they returned home from work. Complaints about being constantly disturbed by callers, particularly telemarketers, led Congress to enact legislation that allowed people to place their phone numbers on the Federal Communication Commission's "Do-Not-Call List." Survey researchers, nonprofit organizations, bill collection agencies, and companies with whom a person had done business were exempted from these call prohibitions. The exceptions, however, encouraged telemarketers to pretend they were doing research and conducting a survey to gain information and use it for marketing purposes. As the calls persisted, the "pick-up" rate dropped, and the "hang up" rate increased. The number of uncompleted surveys rose significantly. If the survey was not completed by the respondent, it could not be used in the analysis. According to a study by the Pew Research Center, 36 percent of the people called completed the interview in 1997, 28 percent in 2000, 21 percent in 2009, and 9 percent in 2012 and 2016.[12] By 2018, it fell to 6 percent, and the Pew Research Center announced it would transition mainly to online polling.[13]

Polls are also made available by major news networks which conduct their own polls. In reporting the results, the news media have three principal objectives: to report the actual vote, forecast the winners ahead of the actual vote tabulation, and analyze the results. They want to do so quickly and accurately.

Beginning in the 1960s, the major networks and news services established a consortium, the News Election Service (NES), to pool their resources in reporting the vote count. Thousands of reporters were assigned to precincts and county election boards around the country to relay the presidential, congressional, and gubernatorial votes as soon as they were tallied by local and state officials.

If all the news media wanted to do was simply report the actual vote, this type of information would have sufficed. But they also wanted to analyze the vote and explain its meaning. Thus, they needed to know who voted for whom and why. Right after people actually cast their ballots would be the best time to find out their explanations for the candidate for whom they voted, hence, the development of exit polls.

Exit Polls

The first exit poll was conducted for CBS News in 1968, and other news networks followed. But this type of polling is expensive and requires large numbers of people who have to be trained for one day's work. It also requires sophisticated computer programming as well as considerable historical data on state voting precincts and their trends. To save money, the major news organizations formed a consortium to collect the data, project the winners, and explain the outcomes.

Initially, the participating organizations made their own election calls on the basis of the data they were receiving. The obsession to be first resulted in several incorrect projections. After a failed attempt to overhaul their combined election day polling operations, the networks contracted with an outside firm, Edison Research, to do it for them.

Here's how Edison Research's exit polling works. Many precincts across the country are randomly selected and telephone interviews conducted to capture the preferences of early voters. Random selection of polling locations is made within states in such a way that principal geographic units, cities, suburbs, and rural areas, the size of precincts, and past voting records within these precincts are all considered. Several thousand representatives of the polling organization administer the poll to voters who are chosen in a systematic way (for example, every third, fourth, or fifth person) as they leave the voting booths. Voters are asked to complete a short questionnaire of thirty to forty items that is designed to elicit information on their voting choices, political attitudes, and evaluations of the candidates, as well as their own demographic characteristics and attitudinal orientations. Several times over the course of the day, the completed questionnaires are collected, tabulated, and their results sent to a central computer bank where they are analyzed using various statistical measures.

A variety of models are used to compare the returns from the precinct to those of past elections and to returns from other parts of the state. The sequence of the votes, the order in which they are received, is also considered in the analysis. Then, after most or all of the voting in a state has been completed, the findings of the exit poll are made public by the news media paying for the polling data. Over the course of the evening, the networks adjust the exit poll results to reflect the actual vote as it is tabulated.

The exit poll is usually accurate. Because it is conducted over the course of the day, there may be a little bias that would underrepresent or overrepresent certain types of voters who cast their ballots at different times. By the end of the day, however, this bias should be eliminated.

Only voters are sampled and in large numbers thereby reducing the error to much less than that of the national surveys conducted before the election. In addition, the exit poll provides a sample of sufficient size to enable analysts to discern the attitudes, opinions, and choices of subgroups within the electorate. (See table 9.2 for the 2020 exit poll.)

Beginning in 2018, another survey system was used by the Associated Press and Fox News. Called Vote Cast, it consisted of phone and online surveys of a random sample of registered voters, a survey of the National Opinion Research Center's probability-based sample of registered voters, and an online survey in which voters could participate. Both types of surveys have produced similar predictions and results.

Early projections of the winner on election night based on exit polling have generated considerable criticism, primarily on the grounds that they discourage turnout and affect voting in states in which the polls are still open. This controversy was heightened in 1980. When the early returns and polls conducted for the networks and major newspapers all indicated a Reagan landslide, the broadcast news networks projected his victory early in the evening while voting was still occurring on the West Coast and in Hawaii.

At 9:30 p.m. Eastern Standard Time (EST), President Jimmy Carter appeared before his supporters and conceded defeat. Almost immediately, Carter's early announcement incurred angry protests, particularly from defeated West Coast Democrats, who alleged that the president's remarks discouraged many Democrats from voting. It is difficult to substantiate their claim, however. There was a small decline in turnout in the four states bordering on the Pacific Ocean and Hawaii. The minimal effect of the election reporting on the outcome of the election seems to be related to the fact that relatively few people watch the broadcasts and then vote. Most people vote first and watch the returns later in the evening. Perhaps this pattern of voting and then watching or listening to the returns explains why George H. W. Bush's projected victory on the networks in 1988 before the polls closed on the West Coast did little to change the results in three out of four Pacific states (Washington, Oregon, and Hawaii) that voted for Michael Dukakis.

Nonetheless, sensitivity to the criticism that early returns affect turnout and voting behavior in states still voting led the networks to agree prior to the 1992 election not to project winners in any state until its polls had closed. In states with different time zones, most of its polls have to close before winners would be projected. The networks amended their pledge to make a national prediction in 1996 even as people were voting on the West Coast. Promptly at 9 p.m. EST, they forecast a Clinton victory. In anticipation of this early forecast, Republicans criticized the practice of "calling" the election before the polls had closed and warned of possible legislation to prevent it from happening in the future. No such legislation has been enacted, however.

Another early prediction controversy in which speed and accuracy collided occurred in 2000. At 7:50 p.m. EST on election night, the television broadcast networks forecast a victory for Al Gore in Florida on the basis of exit polls even though residents in the central time zone, living in the Florida Panhandle, were still voting. The announcement elated Democrats. However, as the evening wore on, a discrepancy became evident between the actual returns and the exit poll results. Based on this discrepancy, CNN retracted its prediction of a Gore victory. The other networks quickly followed suit. At 2:16 a.m. EST, Fox News declared Bush the winner on the basis of tabulated returns. Again, the other networks quickly followed. Hearing the news, Vice President Gore called Governor George W. Bush to concede the election and was on his way to make a public announcement to his supporters. Before he did so, however, he learned from his staff that the election was still too close to call. Gore then telephoned Bush again and retracted his concession while the networks retracted their prediction of a Bush victory. In the end, the closeness of the Florida vote, combined with the voiding of thousands of improperly punched ballots, precluded a valid exit poll prediction. The vote took weeks of court battles and county recounts to determine the winner.

The release of the first batch of exit polling data in 2004 at 12:59 p.m. on election day showed Kerry with a small but statistically insignificant lead. By midafternoon, however, his lead had jumped to 3 percent, a percentage that was statistically significant. Democrats were gleeful; Republicans were puzzled. A subsequent analysis of the polling data found that in the morning, Democrats, especially women, were more willing to complete the survey than were men, thereby skewing the results in Kerry's favor. His lead, however, diminished as the day wore on. The completed poll confirmed Bush's popular and Electoral College wins.

There have been no major exit poll controversies since then, although in 2020 some Republicans had difficulty believing the accuracy of Fox's early prediction, based on exit polling, that Biden had won Arizona. Biden's national victory was predicted by most major news organization by 11:25 p.m., EST.

In addition to predicting the results, the television networks and major news organizations also provide an instant analysis of results on election night and the days after. This analysis, based primarily on exit poll data, relates voting decisions to the issue positions, ideological perspectives, and partisan preferences of the electorate. Patterns among demographic groups, issue stands, and electoral perceptions and choices are noted and used to explain why people voted for particular candidates and parties.

Although the exit poll provides a portrait of the electorate, it does not provide an explanation of how the campaign has affected the vote. To understand changes in public attitudes and opinions during the campaign, it is necessary to survey people over the course of the election cycle, asking them similar questions to discern shifts in their perceptions, opinions, and potential voting behavior. The nationwide polls conducted by major commercial polling organizations do so but not usually with the same respondents.

Since 1948, ANES has conducted surveys with many of the same people before and after the election. They have utilized an interview–reinterview model to collect data on issue preferences, political attitudes, and voting decisions. These data have been utilized by political scientists and others to explain why the American electorate voted as it did. The Census Bureau's "Current Population Studies" also examines data it collects on self-reported registration and voting.

Models of Voting Behavior

There are two basic theoretical models that electoral scholars have proposed: the prospective, which emphasizes the issues and looks to the future, and the retrospective, which evaluates the candidates and their parties on the basis of their past behavior.

Prospective Voting

In the prospective voting model, voters compare their beliefs and policy preferences with those enunciated by the parties and their nominees. They determine which party and which candidates espouse positions that are closer to their own and would more likely pursue them if elected. In other words, voters make a judgment on the prospects of obtaining future policies they desire based on the current positions of the candidates and their parties, the policies they promote, and the promises that they make.

To engage in prospective decision-making, voters must have discernible beliefs and opinions of their own, enough information to differentiate the candidates' beliefs and opinions from one another, and finally, must be able to make a judgment about which party and candidate's views are more consistent with their own beliefs on which the issues they deem most important.

If people were only concerned with a single issue, the choice might be easy. But alas there are usually multiple issues upon which the candidates and parties take stands. To simplify the task for voters, the issues are frequently bundled together by the parties and their nominees and given an ideological label. Since the 1980s, voters have no difficulty discerning the Democratic Party as more liberal and the Republican Party as more conservative. The issues have changed, but the ideological orientation of the parties has not. In fact, that orientation has become clearer. Thus, people who think of themselves as conservative and would like government to pursue more conservative policies tend to vote Republican, and people who identify themselves as liberal tend to vote Democratic. Exit poll data indicate a high correlation between ideological preferences and voting behavior.

Not everyone has strong ideological convictions, however. There are many people who think of themselves as moderate, a plurality of people according to the most recent polls. In fact, today, most people see elected officials of both parties as more extreme in their beliefs than they themselves are. People who do not have strong ideological inclinations or whose views fall between the positions of the major party candidates need to consider other factors in deciding how to vote. But what choice do they actually have if the major party's candidates present such diverse policy stands? Professor Morris Fiorina and his colleagues argue that they have little, that elected partisan leaders have sorted the options in such a way that forces moderate voters to support ideologically extreme candidates.[14]

Retrospective Voting

Another way to make a voting decision is to evaluate current economic, social, and political conditions and determine which party is primarily responsible for them. People who determine how they are going to vote in this manner are making a retrospective judgment. History serves as a prologue for the future. Unlike the prospective voters who compare their policy preferences with those of the candidates running for office, retrospective voters make decisions for whom to vote on the basis of which party is in power, what partisans of that party have achieved, and whether they believe the policy outcomes have produced favorable or unfavorable conditions.

If the economy is strong, society harmonious, and the nation secure and at peace, people assume that their leaders, particularly the president, must be doing a good job. If conditions are not good, then the president gets much of the blame. Thus, the key question that voters ask themselves when making a retrospective evaluation is, "Am I and my country better off now than I was before the party now in power and its presidential and vice presidential candidates won control of the White House?"

In 2012, Romney asked voters to make a retrospective judgment on President Obama and his inability to turn the economy around quickly enough. Obama admitted that more needed to be done even though the economic trajectory was going in the right direction. He asked voters to make a prospective judgment on which policies, his or the ones that Romney proposed, were most likely to help more Americans in the future.

Trump criticized Democratic policies initiated by Obama and supported by Clinton in 2016 while promising to address the grievances of disaffected Americans by exercising a more forceful style of presidential leadership. With a large and vocal portion of the electorate demanding change, Clinton's problem was how to demonstrate that her experience in the public sector and knowledge of government would make her more qualified to refine, improve, and implement Democratic policies. At the same time, she had to project an image of newness, freshness, and strength. Trump's appeal was prospective and Clinton's for the most part, retrospective.

In 2020, Trump articulated much the same message as he had four years earlier, "Make America Great," and he projected much the same strong leadership image. In contrast, Biden noted the problems in America, which he blamed on Trump's policies and actions as president, particularly his initial downplaying of the COVID-19 virus, the economic downturn that resulted from it, and the decline of America's reputation abroad. He urged unity at home and internationalism abroad. Biden was more empathetic, less strident, and more humane, for the middle class and not the upper class (figure 9.1).

FIGURE 9.1 ★ Vice President-elect Kamala Harris holds hands with President-elect Joe Biden and her husband Doug Emhoff as they celebrate in Wilmington, Delaware, after their election win.

AP Images/Andrew Harnik

Regardless of the prospective–retrospective orientation, partisanship remains the critical variable on electoral behavior and the judgments people make in arriving at their voting decisions. In the retrospective model, partisanship, reinforced by ideology, functions as a summary judgment of how the parties and the candidates have done and as a basis for anticipating how they will do in the future. Partisans who make a retrospective evaluation are more apt to rate presidents of their party more favorably before, during, and after the election. They also tend to see themselves as closer to the positions of their candidate and party.

Explaining Presidential Election Results

Although partisanship is a stabilizing force, the candidates and the issues vary from election to election. These variations affect voting decisions and the election outcomes, particularly during periods of partisan parity, periods that have characterized the American political climate since the mid-1980s. The next section briefly discusses the interaction of partisan support, candidate imagery, and salient issues from the election of 1952 to the present.

1952-1956: The Impact of Personality

In 1952, the Democrats were the majority party, but the Republicans won the presidential election and gained control of both houses of Congress. The issues of that election—the fear of communism at home and abroad, the presence of corruption in high levels of government, and the US involvement in the Korean War—benefited the GOP, as did the popularity of its presidential candidate, former General, Dwight D. Eisenhower. These short-term factors offset the Democrats' longer-term, partisan advantage among the electorate and resulted in a Republican victory.

The Republicans lost their congressional majority two years later, but the president remained popular. Personality trumped partisanship in the presidential vote in 1956, but the Democrats maintained their advantage within the body politick.

1960-1972: The Increasing Importance of Issues

Beginning in 1960, the policy issues of the campaign seemed to play a more important role in the election's outcome than they had since the New Deal realignment. In general, noneconomic issues contributed to the defection of Democrats from their party's presidential candidates in 1960, 1968, and 1972 and to defections by Republicans and southern Democrats in 1964.

John Kennedy's Catholicism was a primary concern to many voters in 1960 and helps explain the closeness of the presidential election. Despite the Democrats' dominance within the electorate, Kennedy received only 115,000 more votes than Richard Nixon, 0.3 percent more of the total popular vote. Kennedy's Catholicism cost him votes in the heavily Protestant South. Outside the South, Kennedy actually picked up Democratic votes because of the massive support he received from Catholics and the concentration of this religious group in the cities in the large industrial states with the most electoral votes. Although Kennedy barely won in 1960, Lyndon Johnson won by a landslide four years later.

Short-term factors contributed to the magnitude of the Johnson victory. Barry Goldwater was perceived as a minority candidate within a minority party, ideologically to the right of most Republicans. Moreover, he did not enjoy as favorable public image as Johnson did. Policy attitudes also favored the Democrats, even in foreign affairs. Goldwater's militant anticommunism scared many voters. They saw Johnson as the peace candidate.

Two groups of voters began to change their voting preferences and eventually their partisan orientations in the mid-1960s. White southern Democrats, opposed to their party's civil rights initiatives, cast a majority of their votes for Goldwater, and moderate, northern Republicans, those who disagreed with their nominee's conservative policy positions, voted for Johnson. For the first time since the New Deal era, five states in the solid Democratic South (plus Goldwater's home state of Arizona) voted Republican, auguring the major regional realignment in the elections that followed. In addition to civil rights, a new set of foreign policy issues also split the Democrats in 1968.

The Vietnam War and the unrest and protests it generated on college campuses increased Democratic defections as that party's share of the vote declined by 19 percent. The Republican vote, however, increased by only 4 percent. The third-party candidacy of George Wallace accounted for much of the difference. Wallace's popular support was issue based. Although he did not have much personal appeal, his policy positions did, particularly among white southerners, young new voters, and some blue-collar workers. Had Wallace not run, the Republican presidential vote undoubtedly would have been larger because former vice president, Richard Nixon, was the second choice of most Wallace voters. The results of the 1968 presidential election thus deviated from the partisan alignment of the electorate. A significant number of voters had grievances against the Democratic Party and against Lyndon Johnson's prosecution of the Vietnam War. That party's candidate, vice president, Hubert H. Humphrey, suffered accordingly. A decline in the intensity of partisanship and a growth in the number of Independents contributed to issue voting during this period. Had it not been for the Democrats' partisan advantage and the overwhelming African American vote that the Johnson-Humphrey ticket received, the presidential election would not have been nearly as close.

The trend away from partisan voting for the majority party's presidential candidate continued in 1972. With a nominee who was ideologically and personally unpopular, the Democrats suffered their worst presidential defeat since 1920. Richard Nixon enjoyed a better public image than George McGovern. Nixon was seen as the stronger of the two presidential candidates. These perceptions, positive for Nixon and negative for McGovern, contributed to Nixon's large victory in the 1972 election. More of the electorate saw the Republican standard-bearer as closer to their policy positions than the Democratic candidate who was perceived as liberal on all issues and ideologically to the left of his party. Democrats defected in considerable numbers; Republicans stayed with their nominee. The Democrats retained control of Congress, however.

1976-1996: The Evaluation of Performance

Issue differences narrowed in 1976. Neither Gerald Ford nor Jimmy Carter emphasized the social and cultural concerns that played a large role in previous presidential contests. Both focused their attention on trust in government and on domestic economic matters. In the wake of the break in of the DNC's offices at the Watergate building complex, Nixon's coverup of the crime, and a recession that occurred during the Ford presidency, it is not surprising that these issues worked to the Democrats' advantage. Carter was also helped by a slightly more favorable personal assessment than Ford. The latter's association with the Nixon administration, reinforced by his pardon of the former president, his difficult struggle to win his own party's nomination against Ronald Reagan, and his seeming inability to find a solution to the country's economic woes adversely affected his personal image, although being the current president probably helped him more than it hurt him. With sociocultural issues muted and the Vietnam War over, economic concerns divided the electorate along partisan lines. This division put the candidate with the most partisan support back in the driver's seat. Carter won primarily because he was a Democrat and secondarily because he was a southerner. He received the electoral votes of every southern state except Virginia. In an otherwise divided Electoral College, this southern support proved to be decisive.

When Carter sought reelection four years later, being a Democrat, an incumbent, and a southerner was not sufficient to win. Poor performance ratings overcame the advantage that incumbency normally brings to a first-term president. In 1976, Carter was judged on the basis of his potential for office, and he beat Ford. In 1980, Carter was judged on the basis of his performance in office, and he lost badly to Ronald Reagan. Economic conditions—high inflation, large-scale unemployment, and the decreasing competitiveness and productivity of American industry—worked to the advantage of the party out of power.

In addition, dissatisfaction with the conduct of foreign affairs culminating in frustration over the Soviet Union's invasion of Afghanistan, and especially in the failure of the United States to obtain the release of American hostages held in Iran, contributed to Carter's defeat and to changing public attitudes toward defense spending and foreign affairs. By 1980, most Americans supported increased military expenditures, a position with which Reagan was closely identified, combined with a less conciliatory, tougher, international posture. The voters made a negative retrospective evaluation of Carter's presidency, and he lost. His opponent appeared to offer greater potential for leadership.

Four years later, voters rewarded President Reagan for a job well done with a huge victory. It is interesting to note that ideology did not work to Reagan's advantage in either 1980 or 1984. External conditions in the country influenced the electorate's judgment more than Reagan's conservative ideology did. A resurgent economy, strengthened military, and renewed feelings of national pride brought the president broad support. Although voters agreed more with Walter Mondale, his Democratic opponent, on many specific domestic policy positions, they viewed

Reagan's leadership skills more highly. It was a retrospective vote. The electorate supported Reagan primarily for his performance in office. In other words, they voted for him in 1984 just as they had voted against Carter four years earlier.

The trend of retrospective voting continued in 1988 with the election of Republican vice president, George H. W. Bush. Bush won because the electorate evaluated the Reagan administration positively, associated Bush with that administration, and concluded that he, not Michael Dukakis, would be better able and more likely to maintain the good times people associated with the so called "Reagan Revolution." That Bush was not as favorably evaluated as Reagan had been in the previous election partially accounts for his narrower victory. From a partisan perspective, the electorate was almost evenly divided, but it had also become more conservative.

In 1992, with the economy in recession, budget and trade deficits rising, and layoffs of white-collar managers and blue-collar workers dominating the news, Bush was placed on the defensive. His performance in office was evaluated negatively. Although the president was credited with a successful foreign policy, especially the reversal of Iraq's invasion of Kuwait, the lower salience of foreign policy issues in 1992 undercut the president's achievements within that policy realm and even served to highlight his inattention to domestic matters. The economy was the principal issue and Clinton its principal beneficiary. With slightly more Democrats in the electorate than Republicans, Clinton received the votes of three out of four Democrats. For the first time since 1964, Republican defections actually exceeded those of Democrats. Turnout, that traditionally advantages the Republicans, was neutralized in 1992 with Democratic voters turning out at a higher rate than Republicans. Still, Clinton's partisan advantage could have been offset by a lopsided vote of Independents against him, but they divided their support among the three candidates (the third being H. Ross Perot), giving Clinton a plurality of their vote (38 percent) with Perot and Bush splitting the rest.

By 1996, domestic concerns were still dominant, but the economy was stronger, crime had decreased, and the nation remained at peace—all conditions that favored the incumbent. Despite misgivings about some aspects of the president's personal character and behavior, voters saw him as more caring, more in touch with the times, and more visionary than his Republican opponent, Robert Dole, and they responded accordingly, reelecting the Democratic president but also the Republican congressional majority.

2000-2012: Partisanship, Ideology, and Incumbency

Although the 2000 election could have been another referendum on the Clinton presidency (as many perceive the 1988 election was on the Reagan presidency), it was not. Vice President Al Gore sought to distance himself from the scandals of the Clinton years; he emphasized the policy differences between himself and Governor George W. Bush rather than contrasted the economic, social, and international conditions at the end of 2000 with those of 1992, the last time the Republicans controlled the White House. Encouraging voters to make more of a prospective choice than a retrospective judgment turned out to be a poor strategic decision for the vice president. Gore's proportion of the Democratic vote dropped below Clinton's. By severing his ties with the Clinton administration, Gore hurt his own candidacy. He won the popular vote but not the Electoral College vote.

Although third-party candidates Ralph Nader and Pat Buchanan attracted much less attention and support than Perot, the closeness of the 2000 election enhanced their influence, especially Nader's. Had Nader not been on the Florida ballot, Gore would have probably won that state and thereby the Electoral College. In the exit polls, 70 percent of those who said that they voted for Nader indicated that they would still have voted had he not run. Of this group, Gore was preferred over Bush by a margin of two to one.

The election of 2004 extended and reinforced most of the cleavages within the body politick that had been evident since the late 1980s; the major parties were at parity and deeply divided by ideology. President George W. Bush was viewed as a highly polarizing figure: Republicans overwhelmingly supported him, and Democrats overwhelmingly disapproved of his presidency. The electoral strategies of the presidential candidates changed with both parties trying to maximize their base partisan vote. The ability of the president to focus public attention on the terrorism issue combined with perceptions of his strong leadership following the attacks on September 11, 2001, worked to Bush's advantage. It motivated Republicans in the key battleground states; in addition, Republican partisans were slightly more loyal to their party's nominees than were Democrats to theirs. Nonetheless, the popular vote was close and the red state–blue state division persisted. Only three states—Iowa, New Hampshire, and New Mexico—switched colors between 2000 and 2004.

After the election, the Bush administration ran into trouble. The president's domestic initiative to privatize Social Security failed; his administration's response to Hurricane Katrina was late and inadequate; public opinion turned against the war in Iraq; and the economy was faltering and the budget deficit was rising. There was a major financial crisis in mid-September 2008. The president's approval ratings dropped dramatically. On election day, 72 percent of the population disapproved of the job Bush was doing.

Beginning in 2006 and continuing through 2008, a majority of Americans believed that the Democrats would do better than the Republicans in keeping the country prosperous. Democratic partisans increased by 3 percent during this period; the Republican base declined, while a larger proportion of the population identified themselves as Independents. All these factors helped the Democrats. The grassroots support Barack Obama was able to muster, the large war chest he had raised, and the more disciplined, thematic campaign he mounted led to his large electoral victory. Obama won 52.9 percent of the popular vote and 67.8 percent of the electoral vote

Although the 2008 election was described as historic because Obama identified himself as an African American and was the first person of color to be elected president, trends evident in past elections persisted. Partisan and ideological voting patterns remained, so did the gender gap with the voting differences between men and women. The secular-sectarian divide continued as did the distinctive voting patterns of different age groups.

There was one major change, however. The composition of the electoral majority shifted from red to blue. The only competitive battleground state that Obama lost was Missouri. He won Colorado, Indiana, North Carolina, and Virginia in addition to Ohio and Florida.

In 2008, the electorate made a retrospective judgment. More than three out of four voters thought that the country was "seriously off on the wrong track" and most blamed the Bush administration for the unsatisfactory conditions. People wanted change; they saw Obama as the candidate most likely to achieve it.

There was some prospective voting. The electorate was closer to McCain than Obama on many issues; however, the high level of dissatisfaction and the deteriorating economy proved to be more important than policy preferences. Those preferences, however, were to become a problem for Obama when he pursued his government-oriented domestic agenda.

The economic recession and its aftermath plagued the Obama administration throughout the next four years. The Democrats controlled both Houses of Congress by large margins in 2009–2010 and succeeded in enacting a $787 billion stimulus package of government spending including grants to states. They extended unemployment insurance, provided mortgage relief, enhanced credit card accountability, and enacted the Affordable Care Act, the Dodd-Frank regulations on the financial community, and a host of other measures. The impact of all of this legislation on the economy and society, however, was slow and uneven. Unemployment stayed over 8 percent throughout most of the election cycle; job growth was tepid and wages stagnant as the gap between rich and poor increased. Most people's evaluation of the economy remained fair or poor with a majority believing that the country was still on the wrong track.

Although the president remained personally popular, his policies did not. With the Republicans gaining seats in the Senate and a majority in the House in the 2010 midterm elections, cooperation between the Congress and the White House decreased, and the president's legislative agenda stalled. Each party blamed the other for the impasse.

During the 2012 election campaign, voters perceived President Obama to be more empathetic, competent, and honest than his GOP opponent, Mitt Romney. Romney's much quoted reference to the 47 percent of Americans that didn't pay taxes and were dependent on government welfare programs reinforced the Democrats stereotype of him as a candidate of and for the rich, more interested in business profits than people's jobs. Only on the issue of economic leadership did Romney lead Obama but only slightly.

On most other policy issues, voters evaluated Obama more highly. In short, voters looked to the future rather than cast a referendum on the first Obama years. The president won but lost a few of the states that he had turned from red to blue in the previous election: North Carolina, Indiana, and one congressional district in Nebraska.

2016 and 2020: The Disgruntled Electorate

Despite Donald Trump's surprising victory in the 2016 presidential election and Biden's less surprising win in 2020, many of the demographic and attitudinal trends evident in recent presidential elections persisted. The political parties remained at rough parity with one another and partisanship continued to be the most consistent predictor of voting behavior. Ideology also continued to reinforce partisanship. One difference in 2016 from the three presidential elections that proceeded it, however, was the proportion of the electorate, primarily Independents, who remained undecided as election day neared, a higher percentage than usual. Since both major parties and their candidate organizations continued to pursue their base-mobilizing strategies, the large number of people undecided at or near the time for voting, provided a variable that influenced the election outcome. Independents broke for Trump in the final days of the campaign.

The gender gap persisted and grew even larger in 2020. Trump had been accused of sexual improprieties throughout much of the 2016 campaign. A 2005 tape in which he boosted of his sexually oriented advances toward women reinforced the public's belief that Trump had many sexual liaisons throughout his adult life. Trump denied these allegations. According to the exit polls there was a 22 percent difference in the way men and women voted in 2016. That difference increased to 23 percent in the 2020 election.

Racial and ethnic voting trends also continued although the decline in African American turnout in 2016 hurt Clinton and other Democrats, especially in cities of the key industrial, competitive states; in 2020, the turnout of people of color returned to their previous levels of Democratic support. The preference of white men for the Republican presidential candidate continued in both elections.

The sectarian-secular divide remained. People that engage themselves more regularly in religious activities continued to be more likely to vote Republican and those who participate in them less frequently or not at all tended to vote Democratic. The decline in religious affiliation among the Americans has helped the Democrats. Protestants, particularly white, "born-again Christians" stayed strongly Republican, Catholics remained divided, but tilted toward Trump; minority religious groups, with the exception of Mormons, leaned toward the Democrats. Income differentials were much less apparent, although lower-income voters were still more likely to vote Democratic and those in the highest income bracket Republican. Younger voters (younger than age 30) continued to be heavily Democratic while older voters (older than sixty-five) Republican. The higher turnout of older citizens has helped the GOP. It is somewhat ironic that Democratic programs such as Social Security, Medicare, and Obamacare have contributed to the increase in age expectancy in the United States that has, in the short run, benefited the Republicans more than the Democrats.

Education and geography are other factors that differentiated voters in 2016 and 2020. During most of the New Deal–Great Society period, people with less education, lower incomes, and fewer high-earning job opportunities supported Democratic candidates, while those with more education and income tended to support the Republicans. This pattern began to change in the twenty-first century when the most educated group of voters, people with postgraduate degrees, became more Democratic. An educational divide clearly emerged in 2016 and continued in 2020. Voters with less education and presumably fewer opportunities for economic advancement in an increasing technological society backed Trump whose campaign theme coincided with their beliefs that life had been better for them in the past than in the present. They yearned for the good old days with more manufacturing jobs, a more vibrant middle class, a more patriarchal society, and one that was more homogeneous in race, religious beliefs, and ancestry. Trump's appeal to "Make America Great Again" resonated with this group of voters in 2016 but less so in 2020. The retrospective judgment had turned negative. Biden's popular vote victory by more than seven million votes indicated that more people thought four more years of Trump did not bode well for America.

Trump did best in rural areas and in 2016 in the suburbs. Democratic support was highest in urban metropolitan areas. (See tables 9.2 and 9.3 for the results of the 2020 Edison Research's exit poll and telephone interviews.)

The President's Imprecise Mandate

It is not unusual for the meaning of the election to be ambiguous. The reasons that people vote for presidents vary. Some do so because of their party affiliation, some because of issue stands, and some because of their assessment of the candidates' potential and their past performance. For most people, a combination of factors contributes to their voting decision. That combination makes it difficult to discern exactly what the electorate means, desires, or envisions by its vote.

The president is rarely given a clear mandate for governing. For a mandate to exist, the presidential candidates must take discernible and different policy positions, and the electorate must vote for them primarily because of these positions. Moreover, the results of the election must be consistent. If there is a discrepancy between the popular and the electoral vote, or if one party wins the White House and another wins the Congress, it is difficult for a president to claim an electoral mandate.

Few elections meet the criteria for a mandate. Presidential candidates usually take a range of policy stands, sometimes waffle on a few highly divisive and emotionally charged issues, may differ from their party and its other candidates for national office in their priorities and even on some of their issue stands, and rarely have coattails long enough to sweep congressional candidates into office. In fact, the presidential candidates tend to run behind the congressional candidates of their own party in those candidates' legislative districts.

Mandates may not exist, but that has not prevented most presidents from claiming them. They do so mainly for political reasons. Winning a large popular and electoral vote and gaining control of Congress creates opportunities that most newly elected presidents want to seize.

Professor Patricia H. Conley argues that the elections of 1952, 1964, and 1980 encouraged the winners to claim a policy mandate. Eisenhower's campaign promise to go to Korea himself, Johnson's proposed domestic policy initiatives, and Reagan's rejection of Democratic liberalism provided the electorate with a clear choice of which policy direction it preferred. The winners' sizable victories were interpreted as mandates for these presidents to pursue their policy goals and the legislation designed to achieve them.[15]

The election of 2008 might also be seen as a mandate, a mandate for change. President George W. Bush was extremely unpopular; a majority of

TABLE 9.2 ★ Portrait of the 2020 American Electorate (in Percentages)			
	Biden	Trump	Others
Popular Vote in 2020	51.3%	46.9	(1.8)
Gender			
Female	57	42	
Male	45	53	
Age			
18–24	65	31	
25–29	54	43	
30–39	51	46	
40–49	54	44	
50–64	47	52	
65 and older	47	52	
Race and Ethnicity			
White	41	58	
Black	87	12	
Hispanic	65	32	
Asian	61	34	
Others	55	41	
Labor Union Household			
	56	40	
Income			
Less than $30,000	54	46	
$30,000 to $49,999	56	43	
$50,000 to $99,999	57	42	
$100,000 to 199,999	41	58	
$200,000 or higher	44	44	

(continued)

TABLE 9.2 ★ Portrait of the 2020 American Electorate (in Percentages) *continued*

	Biden	Trump	Others
Family's Financial Situation is			
Better Today	26	72	
Same Today	77	20	
Worse Today	65	34	
Party			
Republican	6	94	
Independent	54	41	
Democrat	94	5	
Ideology			
Liberal	89	10	
Moderate	64	34	
Conservative	14	85	

Source: CNN: "Report of the Exit Poll Conducted by Edison Research of 15,590 People."

TABLE 9. 3 ★ Candidate Qualities and Important Issues in 2020

	Percentage of the Electorate	Trump	Biden
Most Important Candidate Qualities			
Can Unify the Country	24	19	75
Is a Strong Leader	72	33	28
Cares about People (Me)	50	21	49
Has Good Judgment	26	24	68
Most Important Issues			
Economy	83	25	17
Racial Inequality	7	20	92
COVID-19 Virus	15	17	81
Crime and Safety	71	11	27
Health Care Policy	37	11	62

Source: CNN: "Report of the Exit Poll Conducted by Edison Research of 15,590 People."

Americans opposed the war in Iraq; and both presidential candidates promised to transform policies and politics. Obama and his fellow Democrats had designed a legislative package of economic and social reforms even before assuming office and succeeded in getting many of them enacted into law within the administration's first two years.

Obama's legislative policy successes, however, failed to produce the discernible economic, social, and political changes he desired and the public expected before the first midterm election during his presidency. With Republicans becoming even more critical, presidential job approval declining, and support for his health care initiative waning, Democrats lost control of the House of Representatives, seats in the Senate, and defeats in many state elections in 2010. Obama's window of opportunity had closed very quickly as had Clinton's in 1994 and Bush's in 2006. With the exception of a bill to lower federal income taxes and reform the criminal justice system, Trump's never seemed to materialize. He had to use his executive powers to achieve his policy goals.

Even if they occur, mandates are short-lived. In an era of party unity and parity, mandates take on a partisan coloration with success tied to relatively quick, tangible results that address the most important issues of the election.

Much of a president's governing problems stem from the campaign itself; candidates become their own worst enemy if elected. They make more promises than they can deliver and may not establish their priorities clearly. Nor do they usually discuss the costs of their proposals, the trade-offs that may be necessary to achieve them, much less how long it will take for the policy to have an effect on conditions perceived as unsatisfactory.

But candidates do try to redeem many of their campaign goals. They do so because they believe in them, need to maintain their personal and partisan credibility, want to be reelected, and desire a legacy. Of the 533 promises Obama made in his two presidential campaigns, the website, politifact.com reported he had achieved 48 percent of them, compromised on 27 percent, and failed on 25 percent.[16] Donald Trump made 101 specific campaign promises in 2016. By the end of his second year, politifact.com calculated that he had redeemed 17 percent of them, compromised on 11 percent, had 28 percent in the works, and 36 percent were stalled or broken. After two years and three months in office, politifact.com assessed that Biden had kept 25 percent of his campaign promises, compromised on 5 percent of them, failed on 1 percent, with 32 percent stalled, and 35 percent still in the works.[17]

Campaign Expectations and Presidential Performance

There is another problem. Presidential campaigns encourage party nominees to project an image of strong leadership. If they do not do so, they fear that they will not be elected. Kennedy promised to get the country moving, Johnson to continue the New Frontier–Great Society programs, Nixon to "bring us together," and George H. W. Bush to maintain the Reagan policies but do so in "a kinder and gentler" way. In 1992, Clinton pledged policy change in a moderate direction and an end to gridlock between Congress and the presidency; in 1996, he promised to build a bridge to the twenty-first century. In 2000, George W. Bush promised to defuse the strident partisan political climate in Washington, and in 2004, to "do whatever it takes" to win the war on terror. Barack Obama promised to change policy and politics in his 2008 campaign and continue his efforts to promote greater opportunities and improve conditions for middle-class Americans in 2012. Donald Trump's campaign theme, "Make America Great Again," advocated policies that addressed the issues that divided and disaffected many Americans. Biden said during the 2020 election that he would control the pandemic, revitalize the economy, and unify the country. He also promised to be truthful, honest, and candid with the American people.

Presidential promises shapes performance expectations. In the 1976 election, Jimmy Carter heightened these expectations by his constant reference to the strong, decisive leadership he intended to exercise as president. His decline in popularity stemmed in large part from his failure to lead as he espoused. After George W. Bush, reelected in large part because voters saw him as a stronger leader than his Democratic opponent, did not exercise such leadership in the aftermath of Hurricane Katrina, and because of the extended military and political occupations in Iraq and Afghanistan, his job approval suffered significantly. Barack Obama was thinking of the expectations and the short time he would have to achieve them in his 2008 election-eve victory speech:

> The road ahead will be long, our climb will be steep. We may not get there in one year or even one term, but America—I have never been more hopeful than I am tonight that we will get there.[18]

Trump blamed the news media, Democrats, and the Mueller investigation for diverting attention and support for his policy agenda although his constant, angry tweets had much the same effect. Biden blamed his partisan political opponents and the news media but not until his second year in office. Doing so before that time would have jeopardized his bipartisan strategy and damaged his "good guy" image.

All new administrations and, to some extent, most reelected ones, face diverse and often contradictory demands. By their rhetoric, candidates encourage voters to see what they want to see and believe what they want to believe. Disillusionment naturally sets in once a president begins to make decisions and beneficial results do not quickly follow from them. Political scientist John E. Mueller has referred to the disappointment that people may experience with a president as "the coalitions of minorities variable."[19] In explaining declines in popularity, Mueller notes that presidents' decisions inevitably alienate parts of the coalition that elected them. This alienation usually produces a drop in the presidents' popularity unless they achieve a major goal, confront a crisis, or look good in comparison with their political adversaries.

Not only does the selection process inflate performance expectations and create a set of diverse policy objectives, but it may also decrease the president's power to achieve them. Presidential candidates begin their quest for office largely on their own. They essentially designate themselves to run. They create their own organizations, choose professionals to run them, mount their own campaigns, and make their own promises.

The coalitions that presidential candidates must assemble to win the election are composed of people with a variety of interests. Those interests are represented by groups that play a large role in both the electoral and governing processes. They contribute and spend money, communicate with their members and sympathizers, and try to turn out the vote. But they do so with strings attached. They encourage candidates to take policy positions they favor and, if elected, to pursue policies they advocate. They maintain their access to decision makers. Critics argue that interest group leaders "buy" their access with their political contributions and their group's electoral activities, although they spend more money lobbying than electioneering. Presidents who deviate from their campaign agenda do so at the risk of alienating these groups.

The anti-Washington, antigovernment mood of the electorate, evident since the 1980s, has given outsiders, who are less experienced in national politics and may as a result be less knowledgeable about the demands of the office when they first assume it, an electoral advantage but governing disadvantage. Carter in 1976, Clinton in 1992, Obama in 2008, and Trump in 2016 made much of the fact that they did not owe their nomination to the power brokers within their own party, but neither did most other elected national officials owe their election to these presidents.

Even experienced candidates have difficulty, however. As we have noted, campaigns encourage presidential candidates to promise new programs and project an image of strong leadership. Normally, candidates indicate what they will do if elected but rarely do they add the caveat, if Congress is willing to do so, if the bureaucracy follows my lead, or if the courts deem it constitutional.

The coattails that tied party partisans to the winning presidential candidate have weakened. Members of Congress may choose to follow the president's lead or choose not to do so; either way, it is their electoral constituency and its perception of the president that will decide their fate and not the president's national popularity. The bureaucracy has gotten larger and more complex and the most experienced people who work there are civil servants with job security but limited political influence. The composition of the federal judiciary, when presidents first assume office, has been shaped by the partisanship and ideological orientation of their predecessor.

In short, there is a disconnect between the election and governing and between campaign promises and leadership images of winning candidates and achieving them in the presidency. The growth of autonomous state and congressional electoral systems, the proliferation of well-organized, well-funded, and well-led interest groups, the decentralization of power that the US Constitution prescribes, and divided partisan control of government much of the time has forced presidents to act more on their own; it has forced them to utilize their executive powers to redeem their campaign promises, establish and maintain their credibility, and demonstrate their leadership skills. The exercise of these powers has been and probably will be continually challenged by their policy and political opponents in the courts.

How can newly elected presidents overcome this leadership dilemma and hit the ground running? After the election, much depends on their successful transition to the presidency.

Transitioning into Office

The 2020 transition was particularly arduous. President Trump did not comply with the requirements of the Presidential Transition Act (1963) until three weeks after election day. He did not designate a transition coordinator, set up White House and agency transition teams, and report to the Senate and House committees overseeing the administration of government, and do so several months before the election as required by the law. Nor did he allow the head of the General Services Administration to provide space, equipment, and funds to the newly elected president, vice president, and their staffs to facilitate their preparation for governing. In 2020, Congress appropriated $9.9 million for transition funding.

President Trump continued to contest the results of the Electoral College vote. He claimed that fraudulent voting, partisan machine programing, and other illegal activities skewed the count and produced false results. He simply refused to acknowledge defeat. At first, president-elect Biden tried to ignore Trump's misleading claims about the election and his administration's obstruction of the transition, but as time passed, Biden subsequently approved his advisors' recommendation to launch a public communications campaign to inform the country about the dangers of a new administration taking office without the information it needed on the critical issues, without intelligence briefings, and without knowledge of the problems the government faced in dealing with the pandemic. Nor could the president-elect begin the process of obtaining security clearances for his nominees, much less protect his transition staff's internal communication network from hackers and malware by those who wanted to embarrass, derail, or profit from the political upheaval that followed the 2020 presidential election.

The Biden effort to pressure the Trump administration to abide by the letter and spirit of the law worked. Trump finally relented. In a Saturday evening tweet on November 21, 2020, almost three weeks after election day, he indicated that he would not prevent government officials from meeting with Biden's representatives and briefing them on pending issues. Two days later, Emily Murphy, General Services Administrator, formally acknowledged Biden as president-elect, thereby permitting the Trump-Biden transition to proceed.

Still, some of Trump's political appointees were slow to comply. Top officials in the Department of Defense, Office of Management and Budget, Environmental Protection Agency, and the Voice of America postponed their meetings with the president-elect's transition teams; some did so until the beginning of the new calendar year, forcing the postponement of classified briefings, which had to be held in secure government facilities. Some written requests for information from Biden's transition staff also went unanswered. The failure of the Office of Management and Budget to provide financial data on government operations and private-sector contracts further hampered Biden transition team's efforts.

Moreover, when sessions between civil servants and transition teams did occur, many of Trump's political appointees insisted on attending, thereby politicizing the information that Biden's representatives received.

There were other problems that Biden encountered prior to his inauguration. After the election, the Trump administration tried to reclassify numerous agency positions from political to nonpolitical to allow the "burrowing-in" of Trump's operatives into the more permanent civil service system. This practice was not unique to Trump; Obama and his predecessors did so as well. Biden's desire to get his own team in place was further aggravated by the Trump administration's refusal to identify most of the converted career positions to which political appointees had been placed, forcing Biden's transition teams to do so on their own. They also had to evaluate the qualifications of officials placed in these positions to make sure that Trump's appointees did not violate the rules of merit-based hiring and promotions.

The appointment process itself proved to be another, continuing problem. Trump filled the 705 top executive branch positions much more slowly than his predecessors. By the end of his second year in office, only 460 people had been confirmed for major political positions in the executive branch.[20] Cabinet and White House staff turnover was extensive.[21] Biden did not fare much better. By the end of his second year in office, only 469 of the top government positions that required confirmation had been filled.[22]

Summary

Americans are fascinated by presidential elections. They want to know who will win, why the successful candidate has won, and what the election portends for the next four years. Their fascination stems from four interrelated factors: elections are dramatic, decisive, participatory, and affect leadership in government and public policy for the country.

Using past elections as a guide, political scientists have tried to construct models to anticipate how the electorate will react to economic, political, and social conditions prior to the election. Their models provide formulas for calculating the percentage of the popular vote the winning candidate is likely to receive on the basis of a combination of quantifiable economic and political variables. Although these forecasters have been reasonably accurate in predicting the popular vote, they did overestimate size Gore's vote in 2000 and Bush's in 2004, underestimated Obama's win in 2012, and did not anticipate Trump's Electoral College victory in 2016. Four years later, they predicted Biden's win correctly.

To discern how election campaigns affect the electorate and to anticipate the probable outcome of the vote, researchers constantly monitor public opinion. They do so by analyzing data from national and state opinion polls. The key is to identify likely voters. The electorate is not the public; it is only a portion of it. In 2016, most of the polls were reasonably accurate in predicting the popular vote within their margin of error but not in predicting the Electoral College outcome. In 2020, they underestimated Trump's vote but predicted the winner of the popular and Electoral College vote.

Usually, polls are also an important instrument for campaigning. They provide information on what to emphasize and whom to target with specific policy and personal appeals. They also provide data, especially the large national exit poll and the ANES, to help explain the meaning of the election, the issues that were most salient, and the public's policy expectations for the government.

The personality of the candidates, the issues of the campaign, and, most importantly, the partisanship of the electorate influence turnout and voting behavior. Singularly and together, these factors, as seen through the prism of partisanship, explain the election outcome. Since the mid-1980s, the electorate has been at or near partisan parity. However, demographic population shifts, the unequal impact of the economy on portions of the electorate, and multicultural tensions are difficult to measure precisely, particularly on a statewide basis. State polls of voters are not usually as large or as timely as the national polls that are conducted throughout the campaign.

The election results affect the operation of government: its personnel, its policies, its public support, and often its news coverage. Campaigning for the presidency frequently results in a leadership problem in office. Multiple campaign promises create high expectation; the projection of leadership imagery clashes with a governing system that divides power and a polarized political environment. These problems tend to reduce public confidence in the new president unless the major problems that the campaign addressed improve quickly or an unexpected crisis creates short-term unity in support of presidential leadership.

Exercises

1. Look at polls over the course of the election, and explain opinion shifts on the basis of events in the campaign or in the country as a whole. You can obtain the polling data on the websites of Real Clear Politics or from the Polling Report. Another excellent site is fivethirtyeight.com.

2. Determine how the results of several national polls at different points in the election cycle compare with one another. If the polls show different results for the same period, try to ascertain which groups were being sampled (the general public, registered voters, or most likely voters), whether the same questions were being asked, how many people were surveyed, and the extent to which the results were within the margin of the sampling error.

3. After the election has concluded, access the large exit poll that will appear on the websites of most major news networks. In your analysis, note how major demographic groups voted, what the primary issues were, how important partisanship and ideology seemed to be, and the feelings voters expressed about the candidates and their parties. Are the trends, evident in past elections, continuing, or do you see changes in the voting patterns of the American electorate and the composition of the winning Electoral College vote?

4. On the basis of the results of the presidential election, write a memo for the winning candidate explaining the meaning of the election, the policy agenda that should be pursued, and the president's chances for achieving it, given the outcome of the congressional elections and the current partisanship and political climate of the country.

Selected Readings

Abramowitz, Alan I., and Steve Webster. "The Rise of Negative Partisanship and the Nationalization of the U.S. Elections in the 21st Century." *Electoral Studies* 41 (2016): 12–22.

Aldrich, John H, Jamie Carson, Brad T. Gomez, and Jennifer L. Merolla. *Change and Continuity in the 2020 Elections*. Lanham, MD: Roman and Littlefield, 2022.

Campbell, James, ed. "Politics Symposium: Forecasting the 2016 American National Elections." *PS: Political Science and Politics* 49 (2016): 649–90.

Clinton, Hillary. *What Happened*. New York, NY: Simon & Schuster, 2017.

Conley, Patricia Heidotting. *Presidential Mandates: How Elections Shape the National Agenda*. Chicago, IL: University of Chicago Press, 2001.

Dahl, Robert A. "Myth of the Presidential Mandate." *Political Science Quarterly* 105 (Fall 1990): 355–72.

Dassohneville, Ruth, and Tien, Charles. "Forecasting the 2020 US Elections." *PS: Political Science and Politics* 54, no. 1 (2021): 47–51.

Denton, Robert E. Jr., ed. *Political Campaign Communication: Principles and Practices*. Lanham, MD: Roman & Littlefield, 2022.

Fiorina, Morris. *Retrospective Voting in American National Elections*. New Haven, CT: Yale University Press, 1981.

"Forecasting the 2020 US Elections." *PS: Political Science and Politics* 58 , no. 1.

Jacobs, Nicholas, and Caesar, James W. "The 2016 Presidential Election by the Numbers and in Historical Perspective." *The Forum: A Journal of Applied Research on Contemporary Politics* 14 (2016): 361–85.

Sabato, Larry J, Kyle Kondik, and Geoffrey Skelley, eds. *Trumped: The 2016 US Presidential Election That Broke All the Rules*. Lanham, MD: Rowman & Littlefield, 2017.

Notes

1. James E. Campbell, "Forecasting the 2016 American National Elections, *PS: Political Science and Politics* 49 (September 2016): 649–90.

2. Michael S. Lewis-Beck and Charles Tien, "Proxy Models and Nowcasting: U.S. Presidential Elections in the Future," *Presidential Studies Quarterly* 44 (September 2012): 541.

3. Some critics attributed the incorrect estimates of the 2000 final popular vote to ideological bias. They see political scientists as liberal-leaning and Democrats—hence more favorable to Gore than Bush. Others, however, contended that the 2000 election was unique, or at least different from previous elections. Personal digressions may also have been a factor that none of the models included. Perhaps the economy didn't help the Democrats as much as in the past because the prosperity had lasted too long and people had become complacent.

   For a discussion and synopsis of the 2004 model forecasts, see Alan I. Abramowitz, James E. Campbell, Robert S. Erikson, Thomas M. Holbrook, Michael S. Lewis-Beck, Helmut Norpoth, Charles Tien, and Christopher Wiezien, "Forecasting the 2004 Presidential Election," *PS: Political Science and Politics* 37 (October 2004): 733–67.

5. James E. Campbell, ed., "Symposium: Forecasting the 2008 National Elections," *PS: Political Science and Politics* 41 (October 2008): 679–707.

6. James E. Campbell, ed., "Symposium: Forecasting the 2012 American National Elections," *PS: Political Science and Politics* 45 (October 2012): 591–668.

7. Larry Sabato, "How Accurate Were the Political Science Forecasts of the 2016 Presidential Election?" *Larry Sabato's Crystal Ball*, November 21, 2016.
8. Nate Silver, "When Internal Polls Mislead, a Whole Campaign May Be to Blame," *New York Times*, December 1, 2012.
9. "Forecasting the 2020 US Elections," *PS: Political Science and Politics* 58 no. 1.
10. "An Evaluation of 2016 Election Polls in the U.S.," American Association of Public Opinion Research, 2017.
11. David Shook, "How One Pollster Saw Trump's Win Coming," *Bloomberg Businessweek*, November 11, 2016.
12. "Assessing the Representativeness of Public Opinion Surveys," Pew Research Center, May 15, 2012.
13. Cliff Zukin, "What's the Matter With Polling," *New York Times*, June 20, 2015. Courtney Kennedy and Claudia Dean, "What Our Transition to Online Polling Means for Decades of Phone Survey Trends," Pew Research Center, February 27, 2019.
14. Morris P. Fiorina, *Retrospective Voting in American National* Elections (New Haven, CT: Yale University Press, 1981).
15. Conley, Patricia Heidotting, *Presidential Mandates: How Elections Shape the National Agenda* (Chicago, IL: University of Chicago Press, 2001).
16. "Tracking Obama's Promises," politifact.com.
17. "Tracking Trump's and Biden's Promises," politifact.com.
18. Barack Obama, "Victory Speech," *Huffington Post*, November 4, 2008.
19. John E. Mueller, *War, Presidents, and Public Opinion* (New York, NY: Wiley, 1973), 205–208, 247–49.
20. "Political Appointee Tracker," *Washington Post*.
21. Kathryn Dunn Tenpas, "And Then There Were Ten: With 85% Turnover across President Trump's A Team, Who Remains?" Brookings Institution, April 13, 2020.
22. "Political Appointee Tracker," *Washington Post*.

Reforming the Electoral System

10

Introduction

The American political system has evolved significantly since the second half of the twentieth century. Party rules, campaign finance laws, news media coverage, and campaign communications are now very different from what they were before the 1950s. The composition of the electorate has changed as well, with the expansion of suffrage to all citizens eighteen years of age or older and the continuing modification of legal procedures for registering and for voting. Some of these procedures have made it easier to vote such as simplifying registration, obtaining absentee ballots, and early voting, and some have made it harder, such as requiring a government-issued photo identification to vote, shortening the period in which votes can be cast, and using antiquated equipment in some precincts that lengthen the lines and the time required to cast ballots.

Campaigning for president has changed as new communication technologies have enabled the parties and their nominees to measure public opinion more precisely, focus resources in the most competitive states, and target and personalize appeals to specific groups of potential voters in the electorate. But digital communications have also facilitated the use of private data obtained from social media platforms; fake advertising from illegal, foreign sources, hacking into proprietary data and releasing those data publicly; and attempts to change and subvert state registration lists, electors, and even computer programs that tabulate the votes.

On a whole, have these changes been beneficial or harmful? Have they improved the democratic character of the political system? Have they made the elections more efficient, more representative, and more legitimate in the eyes of voters? These questions have elicited a continuing, and sometimes spirited, debate, but no public consensus.

Critics allege that the electoral process is too long, too costly, too burdensome, too error prone, and too easily subject to discretionary decisions by state election officials and to manipulation by the parties, candidates, and wealthy outside groups and individuals. They claim that it wears down candidates and numbs voters and that it results in too many personal accusations and too little substantive policy discussion, too much name-calling and "sound bite" rhetoric, and too little real debate on the issues. They have said that many qualified people are discouraged from running for office; much of the electorate is uninformed, uninterested, and uninvolved; and a sizable proportion of the citizenry still do not vote in most elections. Finally, the Electoral College system results in campaigns in which candidates concentrate their efforts in a handful of states that decrease in number over the course of the campaign. Thus, the one national election which is held in the United States is *not* conducted nationally.

Other criticisms are that the system benefits the rich and powerful; encourages factionalism; weakens the party's control over the campaign of its presidential and vice presidential candidates; overemphasizes personality and underemphasizes policy; encourages deceptive claims, exaggerations, and false allegations; and is unduly influenced by news organizations motivated more by their audience size and economic gain and oriented more by ideology and partisanship than public service. As a consequence, trust in the news media has declined, and the distinction between truth and falsity has become blurred.

In contrast, proponents of contemporary elections argue that the political system is seen as more legitimate and operates more democratically than it did in the past. There are relatively few disputed elections; people abide by the results; and the number of people voting has increased. Candidates, even lesser-known ones, now have an opportunity to run for the presidency and in the process demonstrate their competence, endurance, motivation, and leadership skills. The major parties remain important as vehicles through which the system operates and by which governing is accomplished. Those who defend the electoral system believe voters do receive as much information as they desire and enough to make informed and reasoned judgments. Most voters believe that as well according to recent postelection surveys conducted by the Pew Research Center.[1] Although political advertising provides the electorate with information and perhaps motivation, few admit that ads influence their vote. Box 10.1 summarizes the pros and cons of the Electoral College.

The old adage "where you stand affects what you see" is applicable to the debate about electoral reform. No political process is completely neutral. There are always winners and losers. To a large extent, the advantages that some enjoy are made possible by the disadvantages that others suffer. Rationalizations aside, much of the debate about the system—about equity, representation, and responsiveness—revolves around a practical, political question: Who gains and who loses?

In the light of this question as well as claims by Donald Trump that the 2016 and 2020 elections were rigged, that noncitizens voted, and investigations that revealed foreign influence, primarily from Russians, in the 2016 and 2020 campaigns, the system should also be judged based on how such changes would affect the operation of the electoral system, the agenda and composition of government, and the public policies made by elected officials.

This chapter discusses some of these proposals and the effect they could have on the road to the White House. The chapter is organized into two sections: The

BOX 10.1 ★ Pros and Cons of the Electoral College

Pros
- The Electoral College reflects and even exaggerates the popular vote in its aggregation of the vote most of the time, giving the president a larger mandate for governing.
- The Electoral College is consistent with the US federal system of representation and government.
- The Electoral College enhances the influence of large minority communities in battleground states.
- The Electoral College buttresses the two-party political system.

Cons
- The outcome of the Electoral College vote can result in the election of a candidate who did not receive the most popular votes.
- Individual electors can deviate from their pledges and vote for other candidates who are listed or not listed on the ballot.
- The Electoral College depresses voter turnout in noncompetitive states.
- Independent and third-party candidates are greatly disadvantaged and have never won a presidential election.

first deals with the more recent developments and proposed modifications of party rules, campaign finance inequities, and the adequacy of the traditional news media coverage and digital communications in providing the electorate voters with enough information to make an informed judgment when voting, and the second part of the chapter examines the long-term, democratic issues of citizen participation, representation, and equity in the electoral process. Throughout this discussion, basic dilemmas central to a democratic electoral process are addressed.

Improving the Nomination Process

Of all the changes that have recently occurred, the reforms in the nomination process, particularly the selection of delegates and the calendar for selecting them, have engendered the most controversy and resulted in the most persistent fine-tuning. Designed to encourage grassroots participation and broaden the base of partisan representation, these reforms have also extended the nominating period, increased the costs of the campaign, and made the quest for early money more critical. They have also generated candidate-based organizations, weakened the influence of some state and local party leaders, converted conventions into coronations, and loosened the ties between the parties and their nominees. All these consequences have made governing more difficult.

Since 1968, when the Democrats began to rewrite their rules for delegate selection, the parties have suffered from unintended repercussions of their rule changes. Each succeeding presidential election cycle has seen reforms to the reforms, modifications that have attempted to reconcile expanded participation and more equitable representation with the traditional need for party unity, victory in the general election, and if successful, the pursuit of a partisan agenda in government. Although less reform-conscious than the Democrats, the Republicans have also tried to steer a middle course between greater rank-and-file involvement and fairer representation of the party's supporters on one hand and the maintenance of successful electoral and governing coalitions on the other.

How to balance these often-competing goals has been a critical concern. Those who desire greater public participation have lauded the trend toward having more primaries and a larger percentage of convention delegates elected in them. Believing that the reforms have opened up the process and made it more democratic, participatory advocates favor the continued selection of delegates based on the proportion of the popular vote that they or the candidate to whom they are pledged receives. In contrast, those who believe that greater control by state and national party leaders is more desirable argue that the reforms have gone too far and that extended nomination campaigns have fractionalized the parties and disadvantaged their standard-bearers in their general election campaigns. These critics of the nomination process would prefer fewer primaries, a smaller percentage of delegates selected in them, more unpledged delegates and party leaders participating in the nominating conventions, and a larger role for state and national party organizations during the entire presidential campaign.

Who Should Choose the Nominees?

Party rules have consistently sought to limit participation in primary elections to registered or self-declared partisans, although such restrictions are difficult to enforce. The participation of Independents and crossover voting by the partisans of the other party, which some states allow, has remained a contentious issue and a strategic choice that candidates for the nomination must consider. Do they direct their appeals to Independents, as did John McCain and Barack Obama in 2008 and Bernie Sanders in 2016 and 2020 when running for the nomination, or do they appeal primarily to their own party partisans, as Hillary Clinton did in 2008 and 2016 and most Republican candidates did in 2012 to 2020?

From the party's perspective, the issue of allowing nonpartisans to participate dilutes the influence of party regulars and creates the possibility of selecting a nominee who does not best reflect the interests, needs, or ideological views of most of the party's rank and file. A special fear is that adherents of the other party will cross over to vote for the weaker opposition candidate to enhance their own nominee's chances for victory in the general election.

On the other hand, from the perspective of the citizenry, a primary closed to all but registered partisans preclude much of the population from participating and reduces the incentive for nonparticipants to become informed and involved during the nomination process. Moreover, it allows party elites, interest group leaders, and big donors to extend their influence over the campaign and its outcome; it also permits partisan activists, who tend to have the strongest ideological convictions, to exercise disproportionate influence on the policy positions of the candidates and if those candidates are successful, on their actions in office. The bottom line, however, is that the states determine the dates, procedures, and eligibility of voters, putting the burden on the party to challenge or penalize them.

How Should the Votes for Candidates or the Delegates Who Support Them Be Allocated?

Another rules issue concerns the allocation of the votes in primaries. Since 1992, the Democrats have used a straight proportional voting system that allocates pledged delegates according to the percentage of the popular vote they or the candidate to whom they are committed receives. The Republicans permitted the states to decide on the method of allocation, which could be proportional or winner-take-all within districts or on an at-large basis. In 2012, however, the GOP modified its rules to require states that schedule their contests before a certain date in the calendar, mid-March, to select convention delegates on the basis of a proportional vote. After that date, states can decide on their own allocation formulas.

Proportional voting more closely reflects the view of a state's primary electorate, but it also could have the effect of extending the nomination period, delaying a consensus on the eventual nominee, costing more money, and making it more difficult for a candidate to start slowly and then gain sufficient delegates to catch up. A good example would be Bernie Sanders in 2016. The longer a party is divided by a competitive nomination process, the weaker its candidates are likely to be in the general election, or so the thinking has been within the national leadership of both major parties. The reduction in the number of unpledged "super" delegates by the Democrats and the prohibition of their voting on the first convention ballot makes a potentially undemocratic result less likely.

Should the Nomination Process Be Shortened or Changed in Other Ways?

Some people have urged that the period during which presidential nominations occur be condensed. Professor Thomas E. Patterson has argued that an extended nomination "disrupts the policy process, discourages the candidacies of responsible officeholders, and wears out the voters."[2] It also diverts public attention from issues of government to campaign-related controversies and does so for many months, even years, before the general election campaign officially begins. A long election cycle generates more negative news about the candidates, souring voters on the choices they have on primary day and creates image problems for the successful nominees in the general election.[3] On the other hand, it gives lesser-known candidates a better chance to demonstrate their qualifications, provides more time for voters to evaluate them, and generates greater interest in the forthcoming election.

Several proposals have been made for addressing the issue of excessively long campaigns. Some have even been introduced in the form of legislation in Congress, but none have been successful. Parties could limit the period during which caucuses and primaries can be scheduled to two or three months but that limit would not prevent potential candidates from meeting with party and inter-est group leaders, donors, potential volunteers and supporters, and, of course, the news media before then. Although both major parties have provided incentives for states to hold their nomination contests later in the spring and sanctions for holding them before the official calendar begins, they have not reduced the front-loading of the process very much.

Front-loading creates inequities. It gives greater influence to those states that hold their caucuses and primaries earlier than the others. To the extent that vot-ers in these early states are not representative of the party's rank and file, much less the electorate as a whole, they can generate momentum for a candidate who may not be the first or most acceptable choice for the party and may, as a conse-quence, be disadvantaged in the general election. Front-loading also helps well-known and well-financed candidates and hurts long shots that must raise more money more quickly and must also enter more early contests to demonstrate their electoral viability. It forces them to make strategic choices of where and how to spend limited resources. In short, a compressed calendar reduces the likelihood that a non-front-runner can win the party's nomination.

From the perspective of a democratic political system, perhaps the most negative aspect of front-loaded campaigns is that the decisive stage of the nomi-nation process occurs before most people are paying attention to presidential electoral politics. By the time the party's electorate tunes in during and after the first contests are held, the field has already thinned out. Moreover, there is little incentive for the public to stay attentive or even turn out to vote in later contests once the nominee has been effectively determined.[4]

Which states should begin the nomination cycle became an issue in 2022 when President Biden proposed a new schedule for the states that vote before the official calendar opens. To enhance diversity and reflect the Democrats elec-toral constituency, the president suggested that South Carolina go first, followed by New Hampshire and Nevada, then Georgia, and finally Michigan. The DNC approved these changes in 2023. The Republicans had already decided to keep their 2024 "go-first" states as they had in the previous nomination cycle in 2020.

Because the states themselves decide when they will hold elections for nomi-nations, would states controlled by the Republican adhere to these Democratic changes? What could and would the national parties do to states that violate their nomination calendar? These questions remained unanswered as the 2024 nomi-nation process got underway.

Should Regional Primaries or a National Primary Be Required?

The nomination process could be regionalized, with states in different regions of the country required to hold their caucuses and primaries on the same day. Since the 1980s, there have been voluntary agreements among states in some regions to do so. The argument for regional primaries is that they would be more equitable for the states, providing more focus for the candidates, and, ultimately, more benefits for the region. To make it fair for all regions, over the years, the regions would have to be rotated in nomination scheduling.

Regional primaries would force candidates to address regional concerns and appeal to regional interests. A nomination that extended to the four major regions of the country would probably ensure that the winning candidate had broader-based geographic support, the kind of support that is necessary to win in the Electoral College. But regionalization is not without its critics, who fear that it would exacerbate sectional rivalries, encourage local or area candidates, and produce more candidate organizations to rival those of the state and national parties. Moreover, like straight proportional voting, a regional primary system could impede the emergence of a consensus national candidate, thereby extending the process to the convention and increasing, not decreasing, burdens on the nominees in the general election. In addition, regional primaries help the best-organized and best-financed candidates in the region and require more resources be devoted to the mass media markets in those areas.

Imposing a regional system on all the states would be difficult; it would infringe on their authority, granted in the US Constitution, to conduct elections for federal officials. It would also impose enforcement problems for the parties if some states refuse to hold their nomination contests when the rest of their region does. Finally, it would undermine the Republican Party's tradition of letting the states determine their own nomination mechanism and schedule within the framework of party rules.

Another alternative, and the most radical one, would be to hold a national primary on the same day for both major parties. The general public favors such a proposal,[5] but Congress has been cool to the idea.

Most proposals for a national primary call for it to be held in the late spring or early summer, followed by party conventions. Candidates who want to enter their party's primary would be required to obtain a certain number of signatures. Any aspirant who won a majority of their party's vote would automatically receive its nomination. In some plans, a plurality would be sufficient, provided it was at least 40 percent of the total vote. In the event that no one received 40 percent, a runoff election could be held several weeks later between the top two finishers, or the national nominating convention could choose from among the top two or three candidates. In any event, nominating conventions would continue to be held to select the vice presidential candidates, to decide on the platforms, and to determine party rules.

A national primary would be consistent with the "one-person, one-vote" principle that guides most aspects of the US electoral system and a democratic selection process. All registered voters would have an equal vote in the selection.[6] No longer would those people in the states that held the early caucuses and primaries exercise more influence.

It is also likely that a national primary would stimulate turnout. It would give more people more incentive to get involved, to work for the candidates, and to vote. A national primary would probably result in an outcome more representative of the party's electorate than is currently the case.

A single primary election for each party would accelerate a nationalizing trend. Issues that affect the entire country would be the primary focus of attention, forcing candidates to address the problems they would most likely debate in the general election and initially confront as president.

Well-regarded, well-funded, newsworthy candidates would benefit initially from a national primary, especially an incumbent running for renomination. But a national primary would also undoubtedly discourage challengers who lacked national reputations. No longer could an early victory catapult a relatively unknown aspirant into the position of serious contender. In fact, lesser-known candidates, such as George McGovern, Jimmy Carter, Michael Dukakis, and even Bill Clinton in 1992, might find it extremely difficult to raise money, build an organization, and mount a national campaign. Barack Obama would certainly had a harder time beating Hillary Rodham Clinton in 2008 without his victory in Iowa.

From the standpoint of the major parties, a national primary might further weaken the ability of party leaders to influence the selection of the nominees. Moreover, a post-primary convention could not be expected to tie the nominee to the party, although it might tie the party to the nominee, at least through the general election and longer, if that nominee were victorious and maintained popularity as president.

Whether a national primary winner would produce the party's strongest candidate is also open to question. With a large field of contenders, those with the most devoted or ideological supporters might do best. On the other hand, candidates who do not arouse the passions of the diehards, but who are more acceptable to the party's mainstream, might not do as well. Everybody's second choice might not even finish second, unless systems of approval voting or cumulative voting were used.[7]

Finally, a national primary would in effect produce two presidential elections every four years. Could public attention be maintained throughout the entire election cycle? Could sufficient money be raised? If so, by which candidates—those who are personally wealthy or have reputation and position to attract such support? Could the candidates' grassroots organizations handle such a task, not once but twice? These questions have tempered widespread support within the parties for a national primary despite the general appeal of the idea to the public.

Several political scientists have proposed a combination of rotating small-state primaries followed by a national primary.[8] Their plan calls for randomly selecting about one dozen small states and allowing them to hold their contests—caucuses or primaries—in which candidates would compete. Later in the spring or early summer, a national primary would be held in which voters in all states would be able to participate.[9] The parties could limit the number of candidates based on their success in the small-state contests or allow anyone to enter. If no one received a majority, a runoff election could be held or the national nominating convention could decide among the top candidates.

The architects of this plan believe that partisans of both the small and large states would benefit. The small states would essentially narrow down the field, and people in all the states could then decide on the nominee. This idea, however, reverses the logic of delegates at the Constitutional Convention in 1787 who thought that the large states, with the most electoral votes, would choose the top candidates, but in all likelihood, no one, other than George Washington, would have the required Electoral College majority. Thus, the House of Representatives, voting by states, would select the president and the vice president.

The merits of combining a state vote and a national vote are that it might contribute to a more representative selection process in which partisans in both small and large states would exercise more equal influence over the selection of the nominee than occurs in the current system. But would the small states that go early agree to a selection lottery? Would the large states be willing to allow the small states to participate twice? Would a combined process save money or be more expensive? Would it extend or shorten the nomination process? Would it favor front-runners or provide greater opportunities for non-front-runners than currently exist? Would it make for a more enlightened public choice? Would people who register as Independents be able to vote in a national primary or would that vary, as it currently does, from state to state? It is doubtful that Congress would enact such a proposal at this time.

Regulating Campaign Finance

Closely related to the delegate selection process are the laws governing campaign finance. These laws were first enacted in the 1970s in reaction to the secret and sometimes large illegal bequests to candidates, the disparity in contributions and spending among the candidates and parties, and the spiraling costs of modern campaigns. The federal finance laws were designed to improve accountability and transparency, reduce spending, subsidize nominations, and provide funding for the general election. Some of these objectives have been partially achieved; others have not, but unintended and what many consider to be undesirable consequences have also resulted from the laws and Supreme Court decisions on them.

Although the laws have taken campaign finance out of the back rooms and put much of it into the public spotlight, they have also created a nightmare of compliance procedures and reporting requirements for the candidates, parties, and outside groups. Detailed records of practically all contributions and expenditures of the presidential campaign organizations must now be kept and periodically reported to the Federal Election Commission. Accountants and attorneys, specializing in election law, are now as necessary as pollsters, image makers, mass marketers, grassroots organizers, and experts in digital technologies.

Campaign costs have risen dramatically. Can they be controlled? The public thinks they should be. Most people believe that money adversely affects politics, discourages good candidates from running, and gives some groups disproportionate influence on election outcomes, government decisions, and public policy.[10] They want change; they want campaign finance reform.[11]

Yet there has been little public support for the government to pay for elections. The Federal Election Campaign Act, enacted in the 1970s, has effectively been rendered inoperable by the limitations it places on candidates who accept public funds. Unless Congress raises those limits, provides matching grants earlier in the nomination process, allows candidates to supplement their public funds with private contributions, and increases the amount of taxpayer money in the Treasury Department's election fund, the law is dead and only fringe candidates will take advantage of it. What else can Congress do in the light of the Supreme Court's *Citizen United* decision that has opened the doors to unlimited contributions to nonparty groups and to unlimited election expenditures by corporations, labor unions, and candidate-oriented Super PACs. Even nonpartisan, nonprofit (501c) groups can spend up to half their budget on electioneering, and many of them can keep their donors anonymous.

The answer thus far has been very little. In 2010, Democrats were unsuccessful in restricting election expenditures of large government contractors and increasing disclosure requirements. In 2019, Democrats that won control of the House in the 2018 midterm elections, passed a bill that included campaign finance reforms, but the measure was opposed by Republicans in the Senate and President Trump. Similarly, in 2021, the House passed the For the People Act, but the bill was defeated in the Senate by a filibuster. Had it been enacted into law, the legislation would have increased matching grants from 2 to 1 to 6 to 1, limited foreign lobbying, and required all PACs to name their donors.

But there is some good news for campaign finance reformers. The proportion of the population that contributes to candidates running for office has increased, helped largely through internet solicitation fueled by the increased intensity of polarized politics. Candidate organizations continue to benefit from lower advertising rates that are charged to nonparty groups.

Campaign resources buy recognition and contribute to strategic plans and operational costs, but they do not guarantee favorable election results. The presidential candidates who had the most money spent on their behalf lost in 2012 and 2016 but won in 2020. The congressional candidates with the largest war chests win most of the time.

Informing the Electorate

For voters to make an enlightened judgment, they must have sufficient and accurate information about the candidates and parties, their policy positions, and campaign promises. They also must have some knowledge about the candidates' experience and the parties' record while governing. Past performance is a criterion for anticipating future behavior.

Is the amount and type of information available in contemporary campaigns sufficient for people to make an informed judgment when voting? As we previously noted, most voters continue to answer "yes" to this question, but political scientists and other students of election behavior are not so sure. Almost everyone agrees that the more information people have about the candidates, issues, and parties, the better able they will be to cast an enlightened vote. But how much information is necessary and desirable? And what type of information does the electorate currently receive from the candidates, news media, and other groups?

Changes in communication technologies have made more information available and accessible but sometimes much less reliable, particularly when sources of the information and the objectives of the communicators are not known. Nor do surveys reveal that the public is more knowledgeable about electoral politics today than in the past.[12] Selective exposure to a partisan news media combined with personalized and microtargeted appeals from campaigns, parties, and outside groups provide voters with a barrage of tailored knowledge of the issues and candidates. Yes, there is learning, but it supports more than it challenges existing views.

Massive advertising directed toward the competitive states echoes and exaggerates campaign themes. Campaigns absorb and channel favorable communications and dispute information with which they disagree. Although there are more fact checks reported on a variety of news websites as well as by public interest institutions, these checks do not receive the amount of attention that the original statement or claim received. Moreover, competing truths, such as alternative facts or accusations of fake news, undercut informed debate.

What can be done to enhance the quantity and quality of information about the election that the public receives? Would providing candidates with free time on the news media to respond to allegations made by their opponents help? Some claim that it would, but getting or requiring news media organizations to give free time to all candidates would be difficult, given news media networks own costs, their First Amendment rights, and their needs as profit-making corporations.

Traditional News Coverage

Is campaign news coverage satisfactory? Critics say "no," pointing to news media bias and spin and to the emphasis on the horse race, campaign strategy, and personal behavior at the expense of a more substantive discussion of policy issues.

To augment public knowledge, scholars have suggested that the major news networks and wire services assign special correspondents to cover the policy issues of the campaign, much as they assign people to report on its color, drama, and personal aspects. Others have suggested that the press place greater emphasis on campaign coverage, that they continue to assess the accuracy of the statements and advertising claims of the candidates, and that they indicate the potential costs and benefits and feasibility of the policy proposals that the candidates offer.

In addition to criticizing press coverage of the campaign, academics and others have called into question the amount and accuracy of election reporting. Other than requiring fairness, preventing obscenity, and ensuring that public service commitments are met, there is little the government can do to regulate the news media without impinging on the First Amendment that protects freedom of the press.[13] The news media can choose which elections and candidates to cover, what kind and how much coverage to provide them, how to interpret the results of primaries and caucuses, and even predict who will win before the election is concluded. These choices, however, tend to be exercised by the news networks with their audience preferences in mind. Not only do corporations that own media affiliates engage in constant private polling to discern the interests of their viewers, listeners, and readers, but people also "vote" every day when they turn on a particular program on radio, television, or stream it or buy a particular newspaper or magazine.

There is much that candidates can do, however, to affect the coverage they and their opponents receive. If their words are unreported or not reported correctly, or if their ideas are misinterpreted or their motives suspected, they can seek other media formats more sympathetic to their interests. The niche press, read primarily by partisan and ideological supporters, balances, sometimes even refutes, the major networks interpretation, and its factual reporting.

Secondly, campaigns now regularly leak opposition research to the press. As investigative capacities of major news organizations have declined for financial reasons, reporters have become increasingly dependent on campaigns for obtaining new and potentially damaging information that appeals to their audience. Favorable news leaked in this matter is expected and, therefore, considered less newsworthy than unfavorable stories that reveal new, personal, and controversial information. Another media-related issue is the election night predictions based on exit polling data that the major news networks air before all voting has completed. Beginning in 1984, the networks promised not to forecast the results in any state until a majority of its polls had closed, although they violated that promise in reporting the exit poll results and projecting the winner in Florida in 2000. Are election night forecasts really a problem? Congress and some candidates, particularly the losers, think it is, but political scientists do not. Their studies have found that the early forecasts may depress turnout in states in which the polls are still open, but there is little evidence that these predictions affect overall results of the vote.[14]

What about election night reporting? Americans are glued to their television sets on election night. They want to know who won and why. The national news networks with their anchors and well-known reporters provide a running account replete with victory and concession speeches by the candidates, remarks by campaign aides, and commentary by political experts. They provide detailed exit poll data but little in-depth analysis. Exit poll data are often reported, usually more to predict outcomes than to understand who voted for whom and why.

In addition to a demographic analysis, the public would benefit from a more sophisticated understanding of what public perceptions were at the time of the election, the policy preferences of the newly elected public officials, the new administration's legislative and executive priorities, the compatibility of the people who were elected with one another and with those who remain in the government, and the likelihood of the newly elected or reelected president and Congress being able to form a governing coalition along partisan, issue, or ideological lines. But whether reporters, weary of the campaign and eager to end election stories, are in a position to provide such information is one question and whether the electorate is willing to absorb it is another. After a two-year election cycle, both reporters and the public want to move on.

Digital Communications

Direct communication among candidates, parties, and outside groups has mushroomed. Campaigns now regularly use social media to amplify, mitigate, or even circumvent much of the traditional election coverage by the major news networks.

One of the major advantages of direct communication between the campaigns and the public is that there are no intermediaries that can shade the tone and alter the content of the communication. It can be targeted and personalized to relatively small audiences with similar interests in specific battleground states. It is cheap, continuous, and expansive. It can energize supporters at relatively low cost. But it also can exploit divisive issues and divert attention from problems that government needs to address, warp political debate, and introduce and magnify factual inaccuracies and unconfirmed news stories.

More importantly, digital messaging can be invasive, inflammatory, and unethical. It frequently lacks transparency, distorts campaign dialogue, and can dupe recipients, all which detracts from informed debate and undercuts the democratic character of the electoral process.

Take the Russian advertising in the 2016 and 2020 presidential elections. US elections should be the province of its own citizenry. That belief is why foreign contributions and activities are prohibited during elections, the presidential transition, and preparations for the inauguration of the president. It is also why transparency is necessary for a democracy.

In response to the foreign hacking and the targeting of groups on their websites, Facebook, Instagram, Google, and other social media platforms have increased their identification and scrutiny of election and issue-based ads, limited the amount of personal data that are available to political and nonpolitical groups, and require advertisers to label their ads, identify themselves, and be located in the United States, although privacy advocates believe that they have not done enough.

In September 2018, President Trump issued an executive order that authorized additional penalties for countries, individuals, and groups that interfere with US elections. Members of Congress objected to the order on the grounds that it was insufficient and gave too much discretion to the president.

Most Americans want the winner of the popular vote to be elected president. There are two major democratic issues that currently mar the road to the White House. One relates to the gap between the electorate and the citizenry, a gap caused by nonvoting; the second concerns the failure to apply the principle of equity to all American voters.

Increasing Voter Participation

Nonvoting is a problem because the results of the election may deviate from the wishes of the general population. The outcome may even be unrepresentative of the opinions and wishes of the electorate. Elected officials tend to be most responsive to the people who voted for them than to their entire constituencies and in a federal system to the country as a whole.

The American Political Science Association's task force on inequality and democracy contends that nonvoting impedes responsible government.[15] In 1996, for the first time since 1920, more than half of those eligible chose not to vote in the presidential election; in 2016, about 40 percent of the eligible citizenry and 45 percent of the voting-age population did not do so; in 2020, the proportion of nonvoters declined to 33 percent for eligible voters and to 38 percent for the voting-age population.[16]

Low turnout in a free and open electoral system has been a source of embarrassment to the United States and concern to its political leaders for several reasons. It weakens their credibility when promoting democracy abroad if it is practiced so lackadaisically at home. Moreover, the demographic differences between voters and nonvoters—those in the electorate tend to be more educated with higher incomes than the general population—increase the influence gap between the advantaged and disadvantaged. People with more education and higher incomes regularly exercise more influence over the outcome of elections, the agenda of government, and its public policy decisions. Disparities in political participation reinforce and even widen the division between the "haves" and "have-nots." The income gap between the rich and poor has increased.

If nonvoting is considered a problem in a democratic electoral process, then what can and should be done about it?

Ease Registration Requirements

The national government and some of the states have been trying to make it easier for people to register to vote. The Help America Vote Act (HAVA) in 2002 provided money to computerize and consolidate state voter registration lists, made voting more accessible to the disabled and to non-English-speakers, and permitted provisional voting when a person's eligibility to vote is challenged by election officials. The law also created the US Election Assistance Commission (EAC) to oversee its implementation. Thus far, the law has helped improve the accuracy of registration lists, provided money for new voting machines, and reduced the number of incidences of voter intimidation and fraudulent voting.

More can be done to facilitate registration, such as automatic registration. Many states have also enfranchised former felons after they have served their sentences.

After his reelection, President Obama appointed a Bipartisan Voting Commission to examine problems of voter access and to improve the administration of elections, though no legislation followed from the commission's recommendations. President Trump established a Commission on Election Integrity after claiming massive voter fraud in the 2016 presidential election. Little, if any evidence, supported the president's accusation. The commission asked states to provide personal information from their voting lists, but many refused to do so. After seven months and much partisan rancor, the commission was disbanded.

Nonetheless, even without substantial data of fraudulent voting practices, a number of states have enacted voter identification requirements to prevent noncitizens and others, not properly registered, from voting. Democrats contend that these measures disproportionately affect minorities who are less likely to have the needed ID credentials, such as a driver's license or passport. The Supreme Court, however, has upheld the right of states to require voter IDs.

Make Voting Easier

Some states have extended the period for voting up to twenty-one days prior to election day. Others have enacted a "no-fault" absentee ballot system for residents who find it difficult or inconvenient to get to the polls. A few states now permit voting by mail. In 2020, more than two-thirds of the electorate voted before election day.[17]

Extending the voting period and balloting by mail are not without their dangers, however. Fear of fraud if the ballots get into the wrong hands is one concern. Voting without all pertinent information is another. People who vote early do so without knowing what may be revealed or happen later in the campaign after they cast their ballots.

Another proposal is to make election day a national holiday or move it to Veterans Day, which comes later in the month of November. Presumably, either change would prevent work-related activities from interfering with voting as much as they currently do. Many countries follow the practice of holding their elections on a holiday or on Sunday.

But critics argue that an additional national holiday would cost employers millions of dollars; veteran organizations would probably object to having politics obscure the intended purpose of the holiday—to honor those who served and sacrificed for their country. Workers in certain service sectors, religious groups, and leisure advocates might also oppose voting on Sunday.

Conduct Civic Education Campaigns

Educating people on the merits of participating and the responsibilities of citizenry might also generate greater involvement and a higher turnout. If the public better understood what difference it makes who wins, if they had greater confidence that elected officials would keep their promises, and if people believed that government would address salient issues satisfactorily, then more of them might vote.

Professor Heather Gerken, an elections expert at Yale Law School, has suggested that turnout could be increased if states and local governments measure how democratic their elections systems actually are by using an index based on the proportion of eligible voters who are registered and vote and the accuracy of the vote count itself. She is counting on the competitive spirit of state and local governments to increase their electoral democracy.[18] Gerken's proposal would not require national legislation, although it might require additional funding to collect the data necessary for the local and state indexes.

But invigorating the electoral environment and encouraging more people to vote are not easy tasks. It is difficult to convince people who are not interested in politics and do not see what difference it makes to them who wins to educate themselves on the candidates and issues, to participate in campaigns, and turn out to vote.

Another proposal is for party and nonparty groups to devote more resources to get-out-the-vote activities. They have done so in the battleground states, but in less competitive states, they have not put in as great an effort. Nonetheless, by maximizing their base partisan vote and appealing to new voters as well as to Independents, recent winners enlarge their electorate. The problem is that doing so also enlarges the political divide and gives party activists and interest group leaders more influence. It also tends to elect candidates who may be more partisan and ideological and less prone to compromise. In such an environment, shifts in party control of government are also apt to be more disruptive and produce more changes in public policy.

Require All Citizens to Vote

The most radical proposal would be to enact a law that requires citizens to vote and penalizes those who do not do so. Several countries require this obligation of citizenry. Naturally, their turnout is very high.

One obvious problem with forcing people to vote is the compulsion itself. Some people may be physically or mentally incapable of voting. Others may not care, have little interest, and have very limited political knowledge. They might not even know the names of the candidates. Would the selection of the best-qualified person be enhanced by the participation of uninformed, uninterested, and uncaring voters? Might demagogy be encouraged by slicker and more sophisticated advertising designed and targeted to a dumbed-down electorate? Would government be more responsive and more popular, or would it be more prone to what British philosopher John Stuart Mill referred to as "the tyranny of the majority?" Finally, is it democratic to force people to vote? If the right to vote is an essential component of a democratic society, then what about the right not to vote? Should that right be protected as well?

In short, the turnout issue is a difficult one to resolve. There are costs and benefits in enlarging the electorate as well as in the ways that this enlargement can be achieved. Greater participation would probably produce a more representative election outcome but not necessarily a more informed or enlightened one. It would reduce the bias that now exists between the voters and nonvoters, but it might also result in a more contentious political environment that spills over into the operation of government. It would probably produce a more representative government but not necessarily a more efficient one nor one capable of making better public policy decisions.

Changing the Way Presidents Are Elected

The Electoral College does not encourage turnout in the noncompetitive states, nor do noncompetitive, single-member districts for members of Congress. Replacing the Electoral College with a direct popular vote and either making single-member districts more competitive or converting them into multimember districts in which congressional candidates would be chosen on the basis of the proportion of the vote that they or their party received would increase turnout.

The Electoral College system for selecting the president has been criticized as undemocratic. In 2000 and 2016, the winner in the Electoral College did not have the most popular votes.

Most Americans want to change the methods by which the president is elected. Recent public opinion polls show a majority support for abolishing the system with a direct popular vote.[19] People not only object to how the winner is determined but also object to the fact that the only national election in the United States is actually conducted in only a few states in which less than one-third of the population lives.

The campaign's concentration on the competitive states not only excludes most Americans from seeing the presidential candidates up close or even in television and social media advertising but also skews the campaign away from the issues in the noncompetitive states, discourages people in those states from voting, creates the false impression that the results of the election represent a countrywide judgment, and correspondingly does not give the winner a true national mandate.

Modify the Electoral College

Over the years, there have been numerous proposals to alter the presidential voting system. The first was introduced in Congress in 1797. Since then, there have been more than five hundred others. In urging changes, critics of the Electoral College have pointed to its archaic design, electoral biases, geographic unevenness, and five times to its undemocratic results.

Eliminating the individual electors who cast ballots would be the simplest to do but would probably not affect the outcome of the Electoral College vote. There have been relatively few faithless electors and none of them have changed the winner in the Electoral College.

A more substantive change would be to alter the way most states chose their electors on a winner-take-all basis. If the winner of a state's popular vote gets all the electoral votes, the impact of the dominant party is increased, and those of other parties are decreased. It discourages them from mounting a strong campaign effort. It adversely impacts on turnout.

One way to rectify this problem would be to select electors based on proportional voting. A party that wins a certain percentage of the popular vote would receive the same proportion of the state's electoral vote. Such a plan has been introduced on a number of occasions in Congress; in 2004, it appeared as an initiative on the Colorado ballot but was rejected. It would have decreased the state's influence in the Electoral College. A proportional voting initiative only makes sense for individual states only if *all* of them adopt such a system.

Proportional state voting for president would have a number of major consequences if adopted on a nationwide basis. It would decrease the influence of the most competitive states and increase the relative importance of the less competitive ones. It would also make most elections much closer, thereby reducing the claim of a mandate by the winner. George H. W. Bush would have defeated Michael Dukakis by only 43.1 electoral votes in 1988, Jimmy Carter would have defeated Gerald Ford by only 11.7 in 1976, and Richard Nixon would have won by only 6.1 in 1968. The election of 2000 would have been even closer, with Bush winning by less than 1 electoral vote. Had this plan been in effect in 1960, Richard Nixon would probably have defeated John Kennedy by 266.1–265.6. It would not have changed the results in 2020 (see table 10.1).

A third suggestion is to institute a district voting system such as Maine and Nebraska have done. In these states, the winner in each congressional district gains a single electoral vote and the overall state winner gains two. On a national level, such a change should make the Electoral College more reflective of the partisan division of the newly elected Congress rather than of the popular division of the national electorate, perhaps improving legislative–executive relations. It would also provide more geographic balance, reflecting the federal system, which the Constitution created, more closely in the presidential vote. The less competitive states would gain in influence under such an arrangement, and the larger more competitive ones would lose. Third parties, especially those that are regionally based, might also be aided to the extent that they were capable of winning specific legislative districts. Had a district system been in place in 1960, Richard Nixon would have beaten John Kennedy; in 2012, Mitt Romney would have won (see table 10.1).

Abolish the Electoral College

Of all the plans to alter or replace the Electoral College, the direct popular vote has received the most attention and public support. Designed to eliminate the Electoral College entirely, a direct vote would elect the popular vote winner. In most direct election plans, the winner would need to receive a minimum of 40 percent of the popular vote; otherwise Congress would determine the winner from among the top two candidates or a runoff election would be held between them.[20] In others, 50 percent would be necessary to win on the first round of popular voting.

A direct vote would better reflect the application of the "one person, one vote" rule of democratic elections. Although the large competitive states would lose some of their electoral clout by the elimination of the winner-take-all system, competition within the states might be improved and turnout increased. A direct election would force the candidates to campaign in population centers, appeal more to urban and suburban voters, and would give them more justification than most have had when they claim a national mandate.

If the American public is so supportive of a direct, popular vote, then why has it not occurred, especially in the light of nonplurality winners in two of the last five presidential elections? The answer is twofold; there are potential problems that a direct popular vote might exacerbate; and the current beneficiaries of the present system would lose influence and, therefore, object to the change.

A direct popular vote would nationalize state election outcomes such as the dispute that occurred in Florida in 2000 or the allegations of fraud in 2016 and 2020. Recounts all over the country might be necessary to determine the winner in a very close election, such as Kennedy's victory over Nixon in 1960. A direct vote might also encourage third parties and independent candidates to run to prevent any candidate from receiving the required percentage to win. They could acquire leverage in the bargaining that followed before a congressional or a runoff election. Imagine Perot's influence in a Bush–Clinton vote in 1992 or Nader's in a Gore–Bush contest in 2000.

There is still another difficulty with a contingency election. It could reverse the order in which the candidates originally finished, undermining the ability of the eventual winner to govern successfully. A second national election would tax donors, try the patience of the electorate, and could shorten an already short transition period. There is considerable political opposition to a direct popular vote from the parties, states, and groups that benefit from the current Electoral College system. Republicans are opposed to it because the demographic trends in the country currently favor the Democrats. The only Republican to win a popular majority since 1988 has been President George W. Bush who received 50.7 percent of the vote in 2004.

Smaller, less-populated states would also lose influence as candidates would concentrate their campaigns in the most populous areas of the country, mostly in and around the cities on the East and West coasts. People who live in rural communities might be neglected. Others fear racial, ethnic, and religious minorities could also be adversely affected by the plurality rule principle.

A national election would cost more and last longer. Amending the Constitution is also difficult to achieve; it requires a super majority, two-thirds of the Congress and three-fourths of the states. Given the political opposition by many Republicans and others, a constitutional change to modify or eliminate the Electoral College in today's political environment seems unlikely.

Proponents of the change, however, have devised a way to circumvent a constitutional amendment. They propose an interstate compact in which states would agree to join together to pass identical laws that award all of their electoral votes to the presidential candidate who won the most popular votes in the country regardless of how their state voted. The compact would not take effect, however, until it was agreed to by enough states to constitute a majority of the Electoral College. Thus far, fifteen states and the District of Columbia, all controlled by the Democrats, with a total of 195 electoral votes, have formally agreed to join such a compact, however, a majority of Americans do not favor such a change without a formal constitutional amendment. Table 10.1 shows how the presidential vote would have looked under the current Electoral College system and three plans to modify or abolish it.

TABLE 10.1 ★ Voting for President, 1956–2020: Methods for Aggregating the Votes

	Electoral College	Proportional Plan	District Plan	Direct Election (Percentage of total votes)
1956				
Eisenhower	457	296.7	411	57.4
Stevenson	73	227.2	120	42.0
Others	1	7.1	0	0.6
1960				
Nixon	219	266.1	278	49.5
Kennedy	303	265.6	245	49.8
Others (Byrd)	15	5.3	14	0.7
1964				
Goldwater	52	213.6	72	38.5
Johnson	486	320.0	466	61.0
Others	0	3.9	0	0.5
1968				
Nixon	301	231.5	289	43.2
Humphrey	191	225.4	192	42.7
Wallace	46	78.8	57	13.5
Others	0	2.3	0	0.6
1972				
Nixon	520	330.3	474	60.7
McGovern	17	197.5	64	37.5
Others	1	10.0	0	1.8
1976				
Ford	240	258.0	269	48.0
Carter	297	269.7	26	50.1
Others	1	10.2	0	1.9
1980				
Reagan	489	272.9	396	50.7

TABLE 10.1 ★ Voting for President, 1956–2020: Methods for Aggregating the Votes *continued*

	Electoral College	Proportional Plan	District Plan	Direct Election (Percentage of total votes)
Carter	49	220.9	142	41.0
Anderson	0	35.3	0	6.6
Others	0	8.9	0	1.7
1984				
Reagan	525	317.6	468	58.8
Mondale	13	216.6	70	40.6
Others	0	3.8	0	0.4
1988				
Bush	426	287.8	379	53.4
Dukakis	111	244.7	159	45.6
Others	1	5.5	0	1.0
1992				
Bush	168	203.3	214	37.5
Clinton	370	231.6	324	43.0
Perot	0	101.8	0	18.9
Others	0	1.3	0	0.6
1996				
Clinton	379	262.0	345	49.2
Dole	159	219.9	193	40.7
Perot	0	48.8	0	8.4
Others	0	7.3	0	1.7
2000				
Gore	266*	259.9†	250	48.4
Bush	271	260.3	288	47.9
Nader/ Others	0	17	0	2.7

(continued)

TABLE 10.1 ★ Voting for President, 1956–2020: Methods for Aggregating the Votes *continued*

	Electoral College	Proportional Plan	District Plan	Direct Election (Percentage of total votes)
2004				
Kerry	251‡	258.3	221	48.3
Bush	286	275.2	317	50.7
Nader	0	4.5	0	1.0
2008				
Obama	365	283.4	296	52.9
McCain	173	246.9	242	45.7
Others	0	8.5	0	0.4
2012				
Obama	332	271.2	264	51.06
Romney	206	257.9	274	47.21
Others	0	8.8	0	2.73
2016				
Trump	304	267	290	45.9
Clinton	277	265	248	48.3
Others	7^	6	0	6.8
2020				
Trump	232	266	261	49.6
Biden	306	272	277	51.3
Others	0	0	0	0.1

*One Democratic elector in the District of Columbia cast a blank electoral vote to protest the district's absence of voting representation in Congress.

†If the vote were divided just between the two major candidates in 2000, the electoral vote would have been 268.77 for Gore and 269.23 for Bush.

‡A Minnesota elector mistakenly voted for Edwards for president and Kerry for vice president.

^Seven electors (two Republicans and five Democrats) did not cast for votes for their party's nominee, but wrote in the names of others.

Source: Data from 1952 to 1980 were supplied to the author by Joseph B. Gorman of the Congressional Research Service, Library of Congress. Calculations from 1984 to 2016 were obtained from the Federal Election Commission. Data on proportional and district aggregation of the vote in 2020 comes from National Popular Vote and the Federal Election Commission.

How members of Congress are chosen indirectly impacts the presidential elections and the exercise of presidential power. It affects the operation of government and the enactment of public policy.

The impact on the presidential election results primarily from partisan voting patterns and the turnout of voters. In the nineteenth and twentieth centuries, some presidents were said to have coattails. Their electoral victory helped members of their party win election to Congress. Since 1980, these coattails have been shortened or even reversed. Most candidates for Congress now do better than their party's presidential candidate in their own electoral districts.

Reverse coattails reduce presidential influence. Presidents have less leverage on members of their own party; ideological polarization has also diminished presidential influence on opposition party members. Dysfunctional presidential–congressional relations, the rule not the exception since the 1990s, when partisan control of government is divided, has weakened presidents' political power and incentivized their greater exercise of executive authority. The balance of power within the political system has suffered as a consequence.

The current system of electing members of Congress by a winner-take-all vote within their legislative district contributes to the problem. The fact that most states in the Electoral College are not competitive nor are many of their legislative districts not only reduces turnout but also reduces the incentive for members of Congress from these districts to follow the president's lead.

Making the congressional districts more competitive, however, reduces the clout of the dominant party within the state. It probably would increase congressional turnover. States that benefit from the seniority of their members in Congress would suffer.

A second option would be to adopt a proportional voting system in which multiple candidates run for Congress and the winners determined by the proportion of the popular vote they or their party receives. Proportional voting would encourage turnout by those in the minority. It would weaken the majority's hold on power.

The Constitution does not prescribe winner-take-all voting. The Fourteenth Amendment as interpreted by the Supreme Court does require that legislative districts be equal in population and nondiscriminatory in design. Proportional voting has been required by the Democratic Party in its presidential nomination process since 1972 and in the first weeks of the Republicans' nomination calendar since 2012.

Even though a proportional voting system would promote fairer representation within a legislative district and, perhaps, the country as a whole, it could also weaken the major party's ability to govern at a national level and result in less political stability. Presidents might behave more like prime ministers.

Summary

There have been continuities and changes in the way we select a president. The continuities link the system to its constitutional roots and its republican past. The changes on the whole have made the system more democratic.

The nomination process has been affected more than the general election. Significant modifications have occurred in the rules for choosing delegates, the laws and judicial decisions regarding them, and the ways candidates communicate with voters.

Supporters of the parties' rules changes contend that they have taken the nomination out of the back rooms and into the public arena, provided more opportunities for more candidates to compete, and given rank-and-file partisans a greater voice in choosing their party's nominees. Critics allege that the party rules still favor nationally recognized candidates, allow activists within the party to exercise more influence, and do not encourage participation in the states that hold their contests later in the year, especially those that hold them after the nominee has been effectively determined.

Campaign finance reforms system have also produced mixed results. Many of the unequal consequences of private funding remain. Even though the size of individual and group contributions to federal candidates and parties is still limited, those limits have undercut the public funding option for most presidential candidates. Today independent spending, protected by the Supreme Court's interpretation of the First Amendment, has expanded, helped by the Court's *Citizens United* decision; nonparty groups have proliferated, and large donations to them and to the major parties have increased. Small donations, a product of online solicitation, have also increased.

The public's ability to make an informed judgment has also been called into question by the amount and quality of the communications received from the candidates, the parties, and outside groups and from coverage by the news media. First radio, then television, and finally digital correspondence have become game changers in designing, targeting, and personalizing information to select groups. Although the sources of information have increased, their partisan and ideological orientation has facilitated a confirmation bias by which the public chooses the information it wants to believe. Inaccurate, incomplete, and one-sided information distorts an enlightened campaign debate.

Political commercials have become increasingly negative and emotionally charged. The traditional news media seem more concerned with reporting the race, strategies of the candidates, and their personal and professional behavior than with educating the public on the issues, the way candidates would deal with them if elected, and the short- and long-term consequences of their policies on the country.

The democratic character of elections is also affected by who votes and how the votes are aggregated. The expansion of suffrage has made the process more democratic, but the failure of a substantial portion of American citizen to vote has been a source of embarrassment and dismay to a nation that lauds and promotes its democratic character. Foreign attempts to affect US elections have also undermined America's electoral democracy. The election of two nonplurality candidates in the last six presidential elections has diminished support for the Electoral College. A majority of the public favors a direct popular vote, but beneficiaries of the current system oppose eliminating it. Surprisingly, the election results in 2000 and 2016 did not even generate a major debate in Congress or the country as a whole nor has the single-member, district system and winner-take-all voting for members of Congress. With no outcry for reform and members of Congress benefiting from the current arrangement, there is little legislative incentive to change it.

The only new legislation to be applicable to the current system for choosing the president is the Electoral Count Act, enacted in 2022, which reaffirms the procedures for certifying the Electoral College vote, thereby preventing in the future the type of changes that Trump and his supporters wanted to achieve on January 6, 2020.

Exercises

1. From the perspective of American democracy, explain what you consider to be the major problem facing the presidential electoral system today. Then describe whether (and, if so, how) liberal, moderate, and conservative groups as well as the Democratic, Republican, and minor parties see the issue you have identified and indicate any solutions they have proposed to fix it. Which of their proposals do you think is best and why? If you do not think any of their proposals will be effective, then propose one of your own.

2. Why has the Electoral College system not been modified or abolished? Examine its benefits and limitations and its winners and losers.

3. Do you think the interstate compact to elect the popular vote winner of the presidential election in the Electoral College is a good idea? Is it constitutional? Could it be successfully implemented without a constitutional amendment?

4. From the perspective of the presidential candidates, what is the most odious feature of the current presidential electoral system? Under the existing law, advise the candidates how to deal with this problem when running for president.

Selected Readings

Achen, Christopher H., and Larry M. Bartels. *Democracy for Realists: Why Elections Do Not Produce Representative Government.* Princeton, NJ: Princeton University Press, 2017.

Bennett, Robert W. *Taming the Electoral College.* Stanford, CA: Stanford University Press, 2006.

Bugh, Gary, ed. *Electoral College Reform: Challenges and Possibilities.* New York, NY: Routledge, 2016.

Desilver, Drew. "U.S. Trails Most Developed Countries in Turnout." Pew Research Center, May 22, 2018.

Dionne, E. J., and Miles Rapoport. *100% Democracy: The Case for Universal Voting.* Washington, DC: Brookings Institution, 2022.

Edwards, George C., III. *Why the Electoral College Is Bad for America,* 3rd ed. New Haven, CT: Yale University Press, 2019.

Gerken, Heather K. *The Democracy Index: Why Our Election System Is Failing and How to Fix It.* Princeton, NJ: Princeton University Press, 2009.

Koza, John R., et al. *Every Vote Equal: A State-Based Plan for Electing the President by National Popular Vote.* Los Altos, CA: National Popular Vote Press, 2013.

Neale, Thomas H. "The Electoral College: How It Works in Contemporary Presidential Elections." *Congressional Research Service, Library of Congress,* October 22, 2012,

Panagopoulos, Costas. "Are Caucuses Bad for Democracy?" *Political Science Quarterly* 125 (Fall 2010): 425–42.

Panagopoulos, Costas, and Aaron C. Weinschenk. *A Citizen's Guide to U.S. Elections: Empowering Democracy*. New York: NY: Routledge, 2016.

Rose, Tara, *Why We Need the Electoral College:* Washington DC: Regnery, 2017.

Rove, Karl. "The Lovely but Unloved Electoral College." *Wall Street Journal*, April 10, 2019.

Tarr, G. Allen. "Five Common Misperceptions about the Electoral College." *The Atlantic*, November 29, 2019.

Tolbert, Caroline J., and Peverill Squire, eds. "Reforming the Presidential Nomination Process." *PS: Political Science and Politics* 42 (January 2009): 27–79.

Tolbert, Caroline J., Amanda Keller, and Todd Donovan. "A Modified National Primary: State Losers and Support for Changing the Presidential Nominating Process." *Political Science Quarterly* 125 (Fall 2010): 393–424.

Wayne, Stephen J. *Is This Any Way to Run a Democratic Election?* 7th ed. New York, NY: Routledge, 2020.

Wegman, Jesse, *The Case for Abolishing the Electoral College*, New York, NY: St. Martin's Press, 2020.

West, Darrell M. "It's Time to Abolish the Electoral College." Brookings Institution, October 2019.

Notes

1. "Low Marks for the 2012 Election," *Pew Research Center for the People and the Press*, November 15, 2012. "Low Marks for Major Players in 2016 Election—Including the Winner," *Pew Research Center*, November 21, 2016.
2. Thomas E. Patterson, *Out of Order* (New York, NY: Knopf, 1993), 210.
3. Ibid.
4. Add to this problem the fact that front-loading presidential caucuses and primaries so early also may separate them from the nomination contests of other party candidates within the state, thereby reducing the link between the party's presidential standard-bearer and other nominees seeking elective office.
5. Jeffrey M. Jones, "Americans in Favor of National Referenda on Key Issues: Majority Also Backs Shorter Presidential Campaigns and National Primary," *Gallup Poll*, July 10, 2013; Peter Moore, "Majority Support for a National Primary Day," *YouGov*, March 5, 2015.
6. They would not have an equal voice, however, because of the disparities in resources among the candidates and their supporters.
7. Approval voting allows the electorate to vote to approve or disapprove each candidate who is running. The candidate with the most approval votes is elected. In a system of cumulative voting, candidates are rank-ordered, and the ranks may be averaged to determine the winner. Approval or cumulative voting systems, however, complicate the election, confuse the electorate, and lead some to question the validity of the results, undercutting the legitimacy of the electoral process.
8. Caroline J. Tolbert, Amanda Keller, and Todd Donovan, "A Modified National Primary: State Losers and Support for Changing the Presidential Nominating Process," *Political Science Quarterly* 125 (Fall 2010): 393–424.
9. Ibid., 421. The small states that held preprimary contests could allocate half their delegates to their early election and half to the national primary or they could allocate all of them to either election.

10. "Americans' Views on Money in Politics," *New York Times*, June 2, 2015. Drew Desilver and Patrick Van Kessel, "As More Money Flows into Campaigns, Americans Worry About Its Influence," *Pew Research Center*, December 7, 2015.

11. "Most Americans Want to Limit Campaign Spending, Say Big Donors Have Greater Political Influence," *Pew Research Center*, May 8, 2018.

12. "Public Knowledge of Current Affairs Little Changed by News and Information Revolutions: What Americans Know: 1989–2007," *Pew Research Center for the People and the Press*, April 15, 2007; "What the Public Knows in Pictures, Words, Maps and Graphs," *Pew Research Center*, April 28, 2015.

13. In 2018, President Trump proposed changing US libel laws, which currently require proof of malicious intent in addition to the falsity of the communication for a public official to gain a conviction of libel against a newspaper, magazine, or other publication.

14. Raymond Wolfinger and Peter Linquiti, "Turning Out and Turning In," *Public Opinion*, February/March 1981, 57–59.

15. APSA Task Force on Inequality and American Democracy, "American Democracy in an Age of Rising Inequality," *Perspectives on Politics* 2 (December 2004): 647–90.

16. Michael M. McDonald, *The United States Elections Project*.

17. Ibid.

18. Heather K. Gerken, *The Democracy Index: Why Our Election System Is Failing and How to Fix It* (Princeton, NJ: Princeton University Press, 2009).

19. "Polls Show More than 70% Support for a Nationwide Vote for President," National Popular Vote; Steven Shepard, "Poll: Voters Prefer Popular Vote over Electoral College," *Politico*, March 27, 2019; Jeffrey M. Jones, "Americans Split on Proposals for Popular Vote," Gallup Poll, May 14, 2019; Bradley Jones, "Majority of Americans Continue to Favor Moving away from the Electoral College," *Pew Research Center*, January 27, 2021; "Public Opinion on the Vote: 2020 Election Poll Results," *New York Times*, November 19, 2020; Rebecca Salzer and Jocelyn Kiley, "Majority of Americans Continue to Favor Moving away from Electoral College," *Pew Research Center*, August 5, 2022.

20. Abraham Lincoln was the only plurality president who failed to attain the 40 percent figure. He received 39.82 percent in 1860, although he probably would have received more had his name been on the ballot in nine southern states.

Index